Principles of CASE Tool Integration

Principles of CASE Tool Integration

Alan W. Brown
David J. Carney
Edwin J. Morris
Dennis B. Smith
Paul F. Zarrella

Software Engineering Institute

New York   Oxford
OXFORD UNIVERSITY PRESS
1994

Oxford University Press

Oxford New York
Athens Auckland Bangkok Bombay
Calcutta Cape Town Dar es Salaam Delhi
Florence Hong Kong Istanbul Karachi
Kuala Lumpur Madras Madrid Melbourne
Mexico City Nairobi Paris Singapore
Taipei Tokyo Toronto

and associated companies in
Berlin Ibadan

Copyright © 1994 by Oxford University Press, Inc.

Published by Oxford University Press, Inc.,
200 Madison Avenue, New York, New York 10016

Oxford is a registered trademark of Oxford University Press

All rights reserved. No part of this publication may be reproduced,
stored in a retrieval system, or transmitted, in any form or by any means,
electronic, mechanical, photocopying, recording, or otherwise,
without the prior permission of Oxford University Press.

Library of Congress Cataloging-in-Publication Data
Principles of CASE tool integration / Alan W. Brown ... [et al.].
  p. cm. Includes bibliographical references and index.
ISBN 0-19-509478-6
1. Computer-aided software engineering.
I. Brown, Alan W., 1962–
QA76.758.P755 1994 005.1—dc20 94-19151

9 8 7 6 5 4 3 2 1
Printed in the United States of America
on acid-free paper

Contents

Preface   *3*

Part I: *The Problem of Integration in a CASE Environment*   *9*

CHAPTER 1   Introduction   11
    1.1   Introduction   11
    1.2   What Is CASE?   12
    1.3   What Is a CASE Tool?   13
    1.4   What Is a CASE Environment?   15
    1.5   Expectations About CASE and the Need for Tool Integration   17
    1.6   A Hypothetical Example of the Problems of CASE Tool Integration   18
    1.7   Summary   24

CHAPTER 2 Previous Approaches to Understanding CASE Tool Integration — 27

- 2.1 Introduction — 27
- 2.2 Conceptual Models of Integration — 28
- 2.3 Evolution of Integrated CASE Environment Architectures — 36
- 2.4 Summary — 45

CHAPTER 3 Toward a Better Understanding of Integration — 47

- 3.1 Introduction — 47
- 3.2 A New Conceptual Model of Integration — 48
- 3.3 Integration as a Design Activity — 51
- 3.4 Realizing a Federated CASE Environment — 52
- 3.5 Summary — 55

Part II: Service, Mechanism, and Process Level Integration — 57

CHAPTER 4 A Service-Based Model of a CASE Environment — 59

- 4.1 Introduction — 59
- 4.2 Overview of the PSE Reference Model — 61
- 4.3 Description of Reference Model Services — 64
- 4.4 Uses of the Reference Model — 69
- 4.5 Summary — 72

CHAPTER 5 Properties and Types of Integration Mechanisms — 73

- 5.1 Introduction — 73
- 5.2 Properties of Integration — 74
- 5.3 The Relationship Between Data and Control Integration — 76
- 5.4 Presentation Integration — 78
- 5.5 Summary — 80

CHAPTER 6 Data Integration Mechanisms — 83

- 6.1 Introduction — 83
- 6.2 Key Issues for Data Integration — 84

6.3	Data Persistence	84
6.4	Semantic Mechanisms for Data Integration	89
6.5	Other Factors for Data Integration	92
6.6	Examples of Actual Integration Mechanisms	94
6.7	Summary	105

CHAPTER 7 Control Integration Mechanisms — 107

7.1	Introduction	107
7.2	Integration in a CASE Environment	108
7.3	The Message Passing Approach	110
7.4	Examples of the Message Passing Approach	113
7.5	Discussion	124
7.6	Summary	131

CHAPTER 8 The Role of Process in Integrated CASE Environments — 133

8.1	Introduction	133
8.2	Understanding the Nature of Process Integration	134
8.3	Process Integration and CASE Tools and Environments	138
8.4	Examples of Process and CASE Tool Interactions	142
8.5	Summary	147

Part III: Practical Experiences with CASE Integration 149

CHAPTER 9 Experiments in Environment Integration — 151

9.1	Introduction	151
9.2	The Integration Experiments	153
9.3	Summary	174

CHAPTER 10 Replacing the Message Service in a CASE Integration Framework — 177

10.1	Introduction	177
10.2	Background	179
10.3	Getting Started	181

10.4 Adding the ToolTalk Interface	183
10.5 Running the Experiment Scenario	186
10.6 Replacing ToolTalk in the Emulation Framework	187
10.7 Lessons Learned	188
10.8 Summary	189

CHAPTER 11 Integration of CASE Tools with CM Systems: Lessons Learned — 193

11.1 Introduction	193
11.2 Key Concepts Related to CM and CASE Tool Integration	195
11.3 CASE Tool Integration Scenarios Involving CM	202
11.4 Summary	212

Part IV: A Review of the Current State of CASE Tool Integration — *215*

CHAPTER 12 CASE Environments in Practice — 217

12.1 Introduction	217
12.2 Background of the Studies	218
12.3 Observations	219
12.4 An Example of a Transitional CASE Environment	233
12.5 CASE Environment Progress over the Past Decade	235
12.6 Summary	236

CHAPTER 13 Summary and Conclusions — 239

13.1 Introduction	239
13.2 Major Themes Discussed	240
13.3 How Will Progress Be Made?	243
13.4 Final Thoughts	245

References — *247*

APPENDIX A	*Sample Descriptions of CASE Integration Efforts*	*255*
APPENDIX B	*List of Figures*	*263*
APPENDIX C	*List of Tables*	*267*
Index		*269*

Principles of CASE
Tool Integration

Preface

Background

There is currently a great deal of activity within the software engineering community in efforts to provide automated support for many aspects of the software development process. The diverse tools, systems, and environments that have resulted have the basic aim of supporting (or automating) some part of the software development process with the expectation that the process will be more predictable, less expensive, easier to manage, or produce higher quality products.

While many successes have been made in individual areas, perhaps the greatest remaining challenge is to *integrate* these successes to produce an effective environment that supports the complete software development life cycle. While numerous terms have been coined, we call the components *computer-aided software engineering (CASE) tools*, and the collections of CASE tools *CASE environments*. There are many reasons why the individual successes of CASE tools have not been reflected in the success of CASE environments. Perhaps the underlying reason is that *amalgamation is not equivalent to integration*. The difficulty that arises is in precisely stating (both in terms of quality and quantity) why integration and amalgamation are different, and how integration can best be achieved. Factors to be taken into account include:

- *Scale.* Size and complexity of CASE environments bring with them their own problems in terms of management, control, and consistency. Whenever collections of CASE tools are assembled to form a CASE environment, additional services will be required to manage and support that environment.
- *Lack of maturity.* Much of the technology that is being used in CASE environments is immature. As a result, a sufficient body of relevant knowledge and expertise has yet to be built that describes which components are most appropriate, how those components should be interconnected, and how the subsequent environments can be evolved in a controlled way.
- *Diversity.* A wide range of requirements must be addressed that come from many different classes and roles of potential CASE environment users (e.g., developers, managers, and tool builders), many types of possible application domains (e.g., data processing, real-time, and financial services), and many different structures and maturity levels of organizations that may wish to use a CASE environment (e.g., size, resources, and work habits).
- *Technology base.* A CASE environment attempts to tie together a collection of different technological bases into a consistent system. A CASE environment can be seen as an extended operating system, a complex database application, a very high-level programming language, a diverse collection of user interface systems, or a combination of these. The problems found in each of these technologies are often reflected, and even magnified, when the technologies are combined within a CASE environment.

When integration requirements are combined with other CASE environment requirements, the problems are only increased. For example, it is easy to see conflicts between the need for openness, tailorability, and extensibility of a CASE environment on the one hand, and the need for consistency and predictability on the other. These trade-offs must be evaluated within the context of integration of the CASE tools that form the environment.

Not unexpectedly, the result is a wide collection of views on what integration means in a CASE environment, on how effective integration can currently be achieved, and on what is important to achieve better integrated CASE environments in the future. Perhaps the best that can be said is that *all* these views of integration are meaningful and necessary to gain a deeper understanding of the problems. Appreciating the range and complexity of the problems is essential to potential purchasers of CASE tools and environments, tool builders writing tools to work within a CASE environment, and researchers examining some aspect of CASE environment technology.

The Domain of Investigation

Most of the work discussed in this book was carried out in a relatively narrow domain of software engineering. Specifically, our observations are based on the class of CASE tools and environments that are typically used for the development and support of engineering applications in large government agencies (e.g., the U.S. Department of Defense) and industrial engineering companies (e.g., aerospace, electronics, and telecommunications companies). The applications being developed and maintained by those companies tend to be large (i.e., in the millions of lines of source code range), involve real-time control issues, and in execution are often embedded in complex hardware systems (e.g., flight control software in an aircraft, or process control of an electronics appliance).

As a result, many of the example CASE tools and environments cited in this book were developed under government contracts, or are products whose primary target audience is government or large engineering organizations. While the implications of this are that many of the lessons we discuss in this book concerning integration technology are most directly relevant to people working in those organizations, it is our belief that the concepts, methods, and techniques are much more broadly applicable. In particular, from our knowledge of related domains, we believe that many of our observations are equally applicable to the many CASE tools and environments that are specifically targeted at automated support for development and maintenance of commercial applications in areas such as banking, health care, and insurance.

Aims of the Book

Based on this background, we have the following aims in writing this book:

- to assemble existing knowledge on the topic of integration in a CASE environment,
- to indicate the range of perspectives on the meaning of, and approaches to, integration in a CASE environment,
- to raise awareness and understanding of the key aspects of CASE environment technology, and the important role that it plays,

- to showcase work within the Software Engineering Institute (SEI) CASE Environments Project that has made a significant contribution to understanding in this area, and
- to introduce a new model of CASE environment integration that can be used to analyze existing CASE environment, and can provide the basis for constructing a CASE environment with appropriate integration characteristics.

This book is specifically *not* intended to survey the many CASE tools and integration technology products available, to evaluate existing CASE environment technology, nor to select a single integration technology as being "the best." Rather, the core of the book is an examination of the concept of CASE tool integration, and a description of techniques that may be used to analyze and construct integrated CASE environments.

Scope of the Book

To adequately address the complex and interdisciplinary topic of CASE environment integration the book has a wide scope, satisfying the following needs:

- It assembles a diverse set of integration perspectives, representative of the wide range of work currently taking place.
- It includes descriptions of conceptual models and architectures that can be used to gain a better understanding of integration issues, details of practical lessons from the design and construction of CASE environments, and reviews of the existing state of the practice in integration technology.
- It is sufficiently advanced in nature to address the complex problems that are at the heart of the integration problem, yet written with sufficient context to allow educated software engineers to understand and appreciate many of the issues addressed. Hence, the book assumes a certain level of software engineering background of the reader, but not specific prior knowledge of the integration technology discussed.

The book has been distilled from a collection of research papers and technical reports produced by members of the SEI CASE Environments Project. However, significant reworking of much of the material has taken place to ensure consistency, new chapters and sections have been written as appropriate, and a uniformity of style and quality has been maintained throughout the book.

Expected Audience

While the advanced subject matter of the book means that it is not primarily targeted as an introductory text in software engineering, we envisage a number of distinct audiences for this book that make it both useful and important:

- Software engineering researchers — In industry, government, and academe a number of large research efforts are underway in the general CASE environment area. An understanding of the topic of integration in a CASE environment is essential to these researchers, and this book is an excellent reference point for their work.

- Software engineering managers — In both industry and government, software engineering managers make important decisions about tool acquisitions, development project support, and environment technology. Because of the central role of CASE environments in software development, these decisions are important both strategically and financially. This book can help to provide these people with an appreciation of some of the issues that must be considered in analyzing and comparing CASE tools and environments.

- Advanced students — The importance of providing students with an understanding of CASE tool and environment technology is now recognized in many parts of academe. This book is useful as an advanced text for final year undergraduate students of computer science and software engineering, or as part of postgraduate masters' and doctoral programs. Very little material has previously been available that provides to such students a balanced, comprehensive view of the key CASE tool and environment issues.

Acknowledgments

We acknowledge the contributions of Michael Caldwell, Peter Feiler, Fred Long, Jock Rader, and Kurt Wallnau to the efforts of the CASE Environments project, which are reflected throughout the pages of this book. It should be especially noted that Chapter 11 was based on work originally performed by Kurt Wallnau (presently at Paramax) while at the SEI, and that Chapter 12 was based on work performed in association with Jock Rader (presently at Hughes Aircraft Corporation) while a resident affiliate at the SEI.

We also thank Len Bass, Sandy Brenner, Anthony Earl, Fred Long, Hausi Muller, Tom Shields, and Ger Van der Broek for their insightful review comments on earlier drafts of this book, and Sandra Bond for her assistance in copy-editing the final version.

The Software Engineering Institute is sponsored by the U.S. Department of Defense.

Part I: The Problem of Integration in a CASE Environment

It is not an overstatement to suggest that the use of individual CASE tools *in isolation* has often failed to live up to the high expectations of tool purchasers and users. While individual tools provide useful services assisting in specific activities, tools commonly do not work well together to support the sequences of activities and the multitude of users involved in the software engineering process. It is a common hope, both among the authors and in the wider software engineering community, that the use of integrated CASE environments comprised of many tools will begin to fulfill expectations for tool support.

In Part I of this book, we discuss the difficult problem of CASE environment integration, and introduce the main themes of this book.

First, we provide a set of definitions that we use throughout the book, and introduce the problem of CASE tool integration using a detailed hypothetical example.

Next, we discuss previous approaches to understanding integration in a CASE environment, and describe the basic architectural models that have been used.

Finally, we describe our conceptual model of CASE tool integration based on the separation of three levels of integration — mechanisms, services, and processes. The use of this model is discussed, first by examining its utility for gaining a deeper understanding of integration issues, and later as the basis for an implementation of an integrated CASE environment.

Part I consists of the following chapters:

1. Introduction

2. Previous Approaches to Understanding CASE Tool Integration

3. Toward a Better Understanding of Integration

CHAPTER 1
Introduction

1.1 Introduction

Computers have a significant impact on almost every aspect of our lives. Computer systems are used as integral components in the design of many of the artifacts we use and the homes we inhabit. They also control the operation of a number of devices we frequently use, and record information on many of the significant actions we take in our daily lives. The rapid increases in performance and reliability of computer hardware, coupled with dramatic decreases in their size and cost, have resulted in an explosion of uses of computer technology in a wide variety of application domains. A consequence of this trend is that computer software is in great demand. In addition to new software being written, many millions of lines of existing software are in daily use, and require constant maintenance and upgrade. As a result, computer software is very often the overriding factor in a system's costs, reliability, performance, and usability. Software that is poorly designed, implemented, and maintained is a major problem for many companies that make use of computer systems.

These facts have led to increasing attention being placed on the processes by which software is developed and maintained, and on the computer-based technology that supports these activities. Over the past decade or more, this attention has focused on understanding better how software can be produced and evolved, and on providing automated support for these processes where appropriate. One of the consequences of this attention has been the development of the field of *computer-aided software engineering (CASE)*, which directly addresses the needs of software engineers themselves in the use of computer-based technology to support their own development and maintenance activities. The promise of CASE is that automated support for some aspects of software development and maintenance will:

- increase productivity and reduce the cost of software development,
- improve the quality (e.g., reliability, usability, performance) of software products,
- keep documentation in step with software products as they evolve,
- facilitate maintenance of existing software systems, and
- make the software engineers' task less odious and more enjoyable.

Spurred on by these goals is a growing interest in developing products that support software engineers in their tasks. The result is that over the past decade the CASE market has grown into a large and influential one. For example, in a survey of the CASE tool market carried out in 1990 it was found that:

- Over 470 CASE tool vendors could be identified, with new ones appearing monthly.
- The annual worldwide market for CASE tools was $4.8 billion in 1990.
- The annual worldwide market for CASE tools is estimated to grow to $12.11 billion in 1995 [25].

In addition to the CASE market, there is also significant research work taking place worldwide in the CASE area.

1.2 What Is CASE?

Many definitions and description of CASE exist. We choose a broad definition, perhaps the most straightforward one possible:

CASE is the use of computer-based support in the software development process.

This definition includes all kinds of computer-based support for any of the managerial, administrative, or technical aspects of any part of a software project.

1.3 What Is a CASE Tool?

Since the early days of writing software, there has been an awareness of the need for automated tools to help the software developer. Initially the concentration was on program support tools such as translators, compilers, assemblers, macro processors, and linkers and loaders. However, as computers became more powerful and the software that ran on them grew larger and more complex, the range of support tools began to expand. In particular, the use of interactive time-sharing systems for software development encouraged the development of program editors, debuggers, code analyzers, and program-pretty printers.

As computers became more reliable and in greater use, the need for a broader notion of software development became apparent. Software development came to be viewed as:

- A large-scale activity involving significant effort to establish requirements, design an appropriate solution, implement that solution, test the solution's correctness, and document the functionality of the final system.
- A long-term process producing software that requires enhancement throughout its lifetime. The implications of this are that the structure of the software must enable new functionality to be added easily, and detailed records of the requirements, design, implementation, and testing of the system must be kept to aid maintainers of the software. In addition, multiple versions of all artifacts produced during a project must be maintained to facilitate group development of software systems.
- A group activity involving interaction among a number of people during each stage of its life. Groups of people must be able to cooperate, in a controlled manner, and have consistent views of the state of the project.

This view of "programming in the large" resulted in a wide range of support tools being developed. Initially, the tools were not very sophisticated in their support. However, two important advances had the effect of greatly improving the sophistication of these tools:

- Research in the area of software development processes gave rise to a number of software design methods (e.g., Jackson Structured Programming, the Yourdon Method) that could be used as the basis for software development. These methods were ideally suited to automated tool support in that they

required step-by-step adherence to methods, had graphical notations associated with them, and produced a large number of artifacts (e.g., diagrams, annotations, and documentation) that needed to be recorded and maintained.
- Breakthroughs in computer hardware technology gave rise to affordable personal workstations and to personal computers. These machines have relatively large memory storage capacities, fast processors, and sophisticated bit-mapped graphics displays that are capable of displaying charts, graphical models, and diagrams.

We refer to all of the above tools as CASE tools and posit the following definition:

A CASE tool is a computer-based product aimed at supporting one or more software engineering activities within a software development process.

Other authors have attempted to make finer-grained distinctions between different classes of CASE tools along a number of dimensions. The most common distinctions are:

- Between those tools that are interactive in nature (such as a design method support tool) and those that are not (such as a compiler). The former class are sometimes called CASE tools, while the latter class are called development tools.
- Between those tools that support activities early in the life cycle of a software project (such as requirements and design support tools) and those that are used later in the life cycle (such as compilers and test support tools). The former class are sometimes called front-end CASE tools, and the latter are called back-end CASE tools.
- Between those tools that are specific to a particular life-cycle step or domain (such as a requirements tool or a coding tool) and those that are common across a number of life-cycle steps or domains (such as a documentation tool or a configuration management tool). The former class are sometimes called vertical CASE tools, while the latter class are called horizontal CASE tools.

Unfortunately, all these distinctions are problematic. In the first case, it is difficult to give a simple and consistent definition of "interactive" that is meaningful. For example, some classes of compilers prompt the user for information. In the second and third cases, there is an assumption about the ordering of activities in a life cycle that is not the case in some styles of software development (e.g., object-oriented software development, or prototype-oriented development), hence our use of the broader, inclusive definition of a CASE tool.

1.4 What Is a CASE Environment?

The first generation of CASE tool developers concentrated to a large extent on the automation of isolated tasks such as document production, version control of source code, and design method support. While successes have been achieved in supporting such specific tasks, the need for these "islands of automation" to be connected has been clearly recognized by many first generation CASE tool users. For example, a typical development scenario requires that designs be closely related to their resultant source code, that they be consistently described in a set of documentation, and that all of these artifacts be under centralized version control. The tools that support the individual tasks of design, coding, documentation, and version control must be integrated if they are to support this kind of scenario effectively.

In fact, such tools are more often used as components in a much more elaborate software development support infrastructure that is available to software engineers. Figure 1 is an illustration of the main components and users of a CASE environment.[1] It illustrates that a typical CASE environment consists of a number of CASE tools operating on a common hardware and software platform. It also shows that there are a number of different classes of users of a CASE environment. Some users, such as software developers and managers, wish to make use of CASE tools to support them in developing application systems and monitoring the progress of a project. On the other hand, tool integrators are responsible for ensuring that the tools operate on the software and hardware platform available, and the system administrator's role is to maintain and update the hardware and software platform itself.

Figure 1 also illustrates that software developers, tool integrators, and system administrators interact with multiple CASE tools and environment components that form the software and hardware platform of the CASE environment. It is these interactions, among the different CASE environment components and between users and those components, that are the key elements of a CASE environment. In many respects the approach toward the management, control, and support of these interactions distinguishes one CASE environment from another. We can define a CASE environment by emphasizing the importance of these interactions:

[1.] Also called a *software engineering environment* (SEE), a *software development environment* (SDE), or an *integrated project support environment* (IPSE). For this discussion these terms are treated synonymously.

A CASE environment is a collection of CASE tools and other components together with an integration approach that supports most or all of the interactions that occur among the environment components, and between the users of the environment and the environment itself.

FIGURE 1 A Typical CASE Environment.

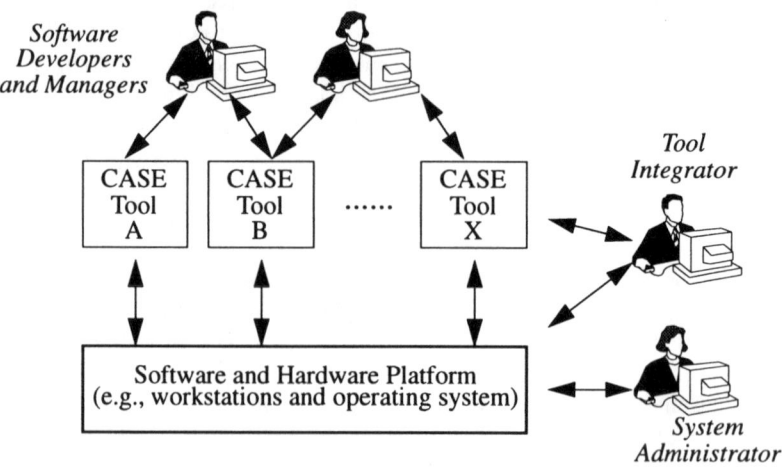

The critical part of this definition is that the interactions among environment components are supported within the environment. What distinguishes a CASE environment from a random amalgamation of CASE tools is that there is something that is provided in the environment that facilitates interaction of those tools. This "something" may be a physical mechanism such as a shared database or a message broadcast system, a conceptual notion such as a shared philosophy on tool architectures or common semantics about the objects the tools manipulate, or some combination of these things.

The range of possible ways of providing the "glue" that links CASE tools together inevitably leads to a spectrum of approaches to implementing a CASE environment. One of the main points we make in this book is that there are many ways to build a CASE environment. While many people concentrate on the selection of CASE tools and components when assembling a CASE environment, they largely ignore the need to support the interactions among those components. We concentrate less on which components should be chosen, and much more on how the selected components can be made to work together effectively. Whether a chosen approach to component interaction is appropriate in a given context will depend on many overlapping factors: the needs of the organization in question, the available resources, and so forth. A detailed assessment of these related factors and constraints is necessary to determine the CASE environment most suited to the problem at hand.

1.5 Expectations About CASE and the Need for Tool Integration

Current interest in CASE tools and environments is based on expectations about productivity, savings, extensibility, and similar features. Current *experiences*, however, suggest that the technology of CASE tools and environments is as yet insufficient to provide all of those promised benefits. In particular, as organizations begin to acquire collections of CASE tools and wish to use them to support their software development, they typically experience one or more of the following problems:

- inability to combine tools easily to cover the complete software development life cycle (e.g., a requirements tool and a design tool with different implementation architectures, supporting incompatible methods),
- misalignment and overlap of tools when they carry out similar services (e.g., two tools, each performing version control in incompatible ways),
- lack of well-defined procedures for moving data from one tool to another and for synchronizing the communication between the tools so that one tool can easily be invoked from another,
- poor management visibility of the progress of tasks within a project and of the intermediate states of artifacts produced by the tools,
- few facilities to support tailoring and adaptation of the tools to different organizations' development needs,
- no well-proven approaches to the introduction and adoption of collections of tools, and
- significant system management and maintenance problems with the installation, operation, and evolution of collections of tools due to the size and complexity of many of the tools and their relative immaturity.

The need is for a reasonable way to assemble sets of CASE tools to minimize the above problems. Case environment *integration* is seen by many people as the key to doing this. A "well-integrated" CASE environment suggests a set of tools and components that are well matched in terms of functionality and operating needs, consistent and uniform in terms of user interaction styles, and interoperable in terms of data transfer and synchronization of services. An integrated CASE environment is one in which most or all of these attributes can be found.

We note that the term integration is difficult to define precisely, a problem that is addressed in later chapters. Indeed, integration in a CASE environment has come to refer to any aspect of an environment that can be deemed to be "good," with the result that it is often very difficult at present to infer any meaning from the term when it is used. For example, a statement from a prominent vendor's marketing brochure claims that the vendor's product facilitates "the complete integration of all tools." It is impossible to interpret this statement without a great deal of explanation and context (unfortunately not to be found in the same vendor's brochure).

1.6 A Hypothetical Example of the Problems of CASE Tool Integration

We now describe a hypothetical example that illustrates a number of the problems of integrating a collection of CASE tools. While we make many simplifying assumptions about the CASE tools, the example nonetheless captures some of the complexity of the issues that must be addressed in creating an integrated CASE environment. The main focus of the example is on the sharing of data between tools through a common data model, although some other aspects of integration are addressed as well.

We assume at the start that there are three independent CASE tools, and that they each have their own internal database for recording data. We describe these CASE tools in terms of the structure of the data that they maintain in that database. We use a version of the Entity-Relationship (ER) notation of Chen [21] for describing these data structures. In this notation, a box is an entity type, with the name of the entity type as the label of the box. The names of attributes of the entity type are placed on the border of the box (the data types of the attributes are omitted for simplicity). Arcs linking boxes represent relationships between entity types. The "crows feet" on the end of an arc indicate that the relationship has cardinality "many" at that end. The arcs are labeled with the name of the relationship (the relationships are bidirectional, but they are labeled in one direction only).

1.6.1 Description of the Toolset

The three CASE tools for this example are a version management tool, a project management tool, and a software bug tracking tool. For the version management tool, the data that are maintained consist of information about *documents* that have many *versions*. A *person* is responsible for creating each version. Each version was also produced by a particular *tool*. Figure 2 shows the version management tool's data structure.

1.6 A Hypothetical Example of the Problems of CASE Tool Integration

FIGURE 2 The Data Maintained by the Version Management Tool.

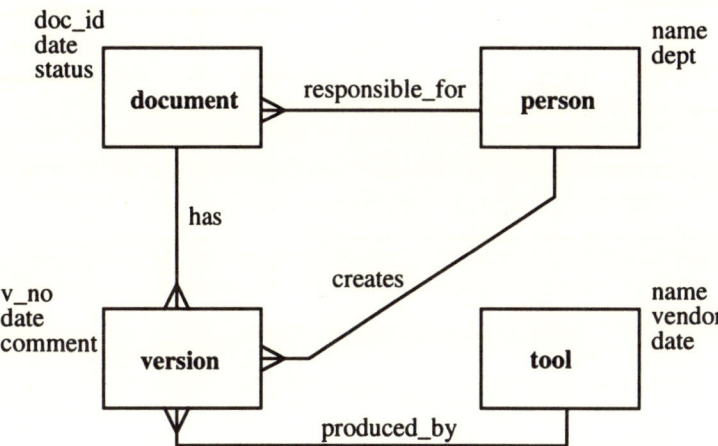

In contrast to the version management tool, the project management tool is interested in *project*s and *product*s and the defects (*unfixed bugs*) that are recorded against each product. A project is assigned a *manager,* and produces a number of products. The project management tool is not concerned with intermediate versions of products, nor bugs that have been identified and fixed. Figure 3 shows the project management tool's data structure.

FIGURE 3 The Data Maintained by the Project Management Tool.

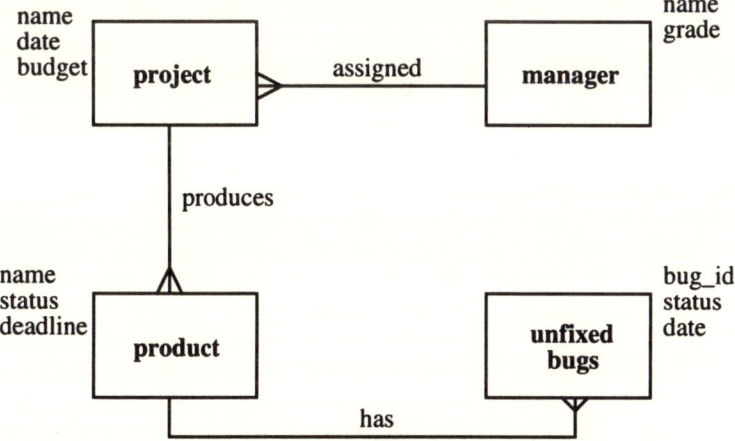

Finally, as shown in Figure 4, the bug monitoring tool is interested in tracking problem reports and their assignment to programs. A *design* may be implemented by many *programs,* each of which may include many *modules.* Each module may have many *bug reports* assigned to it. A bug report may have been tracked to faults in a number of modules. Bug reports are assigned to a *developer* who is in charge of it.

Note that the bug monitoring tool is not interested in projects, but only in the programs produced by projects. Also, because the bugs must be tracked closely, the bug monitoring tool is interested in the details of which modules make up a program.

FIGURE 4 The Data Maintained by the Bug Tracking Tool.

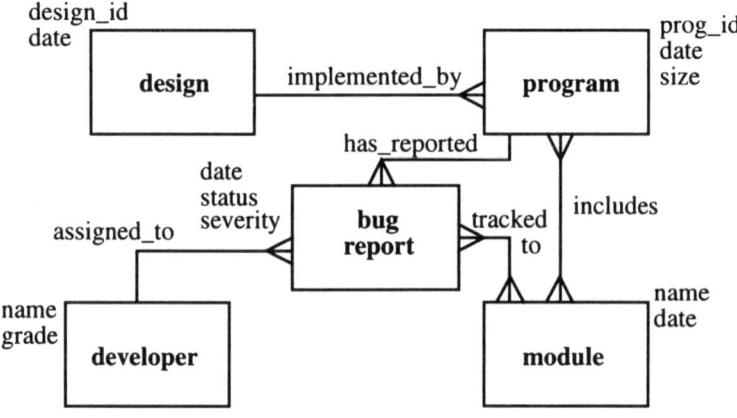

1.6.2 Problems in Integrating the Three Tools

We now consider how to integrate the version control, project management, and bug monitoring tools. These are simple CASE tools performing highly related tasks. In an integrated CASE environment, therefore, it would make sense to ensure that they all work from the same data, and that they all inform each other when changes occur. Use of a common data repository seems an obvious choice for integrating the three CASE tools. A single database, external to all three CASE tools, could hold the shared data that is manipulated by the three CASE tools. This could either replace the tools' internal databases, or could involve some form of import and export from the tools' individual databases.

While this sounds like a straightforward task, we can identify a number of problems that must be addressed before this task can happen. We divide these prob-

1.6 A Hypothetical Example of the Problems of CASE Tool Integration

lems into three main areas: problems imposed by the divergent mechanisms and interfaces of individual tools (mechanism issues); problems imposed by the divergent semantics used by tools (semantic issues); and problems imposed by the process to be supported by the integrated toolset (process issues).

1.6.2.1 Divergent Tool Mechanisms

Among the first problems the tool integrator faces are those relating to the strategies currently being used by the CASE tools to store data and to make that data accessible to other tools. Many (if not most) common CASE tools use proprietary database formats; only a relatively few use databases with standardized interfaces. To compound the problem faced by the tool integrator, many of these proprietary formats are poorly documented by the CASE tool vendors.

While some CASE tool vendors provide import/export interfaces to data, others do not. Even when such interfaces are provided, in many cases the import/export format supported is also unique to the vendor. Only a small (but fortunately growing) number of vendors provide import/export interfaces using a common, publicly agreed interchange format.

In addition to problems concerning the database used and interfaces provided, the tool integrator is often faced with less obvious problems concerning the manner in which a CASE tool commits and rolls back transactions, enforces security, and distributes data across the network. Obviously, if one CASE tool is to rely on the integrity of data from a second tool, transaction, security, and data distribution approaches must be coordinated.

All these issues (and many more) should be addressed when examining how independent CASE tools are integrated. Detailed knowledge of the CASE tools' operation in isolation is a necessary precursor to making them work together.

1.6.2.2 Divergent Tool Semantics

A number of integration problems arise due to the lack of generally agreed semantics concerning the data that are being manipulated. The commonest problem concerns either different names for the same data items, or the same names for different data items. This leads to confusion over terminology (e.g., are a *product* and a *program* the same thing?).

A second issue concerns different notions of which information needs to be stored. Obviously, a CASE tool can (and often does) choose to derive some information at tool start-up. This information may be critical to its integration with other tools, yet may be unavailable in the tool's database.

Finally, since the CASE tools will continue to evolve separately, vendors may change tool semantics and operation (e.g., the bug monitoring tool may decide to include its own notion of versions of bug reports). It is difficult (if not impossible) for the tool integrator to anticipate these changes. However, unanticipated changes are likely to have an impact not only on the manner in which integration is best accomplished, but also on the performance of the integrated CASE environment.

1.6.2.3 The Supported Process

At the process level, the way in which the tools are used have an important influence on how they should be put together. Many issues can only be addressed in light of an understanding of how the integrated CASE environment will be employed in support of a project development process.

Typical examples of issues that arise involve access control and data granularity. With access control, the integrator must determine what types of concurrent access are allowed based on the process to be supported. For example, in determining how to perform the integration, the tool integrator must address questions such as whether simultaneous access will be granted to a manager producing a report on unfixed bugs and the user of the version control tool who is checking out the latest version of a document that includes a previous report on unfixed bugs. For any shared data, the integrator must determine the granularity of the objects to be versioned. The solutions chosen to address these issues will have a significant effect on the performance of the CASE environment.

Other issues concern deciding when certain actions can happen (e.g., when is the project management tool informed of new errors?) and the roles of different individuals in the project (e.g., who is allowed access to the various data elements?)

All these issues have an effect on how the CASE tools should be integrated, and require knowledge of the process that the integrated CASE environment is expected to support. Without this knowledge, the tools are likely to be put together with the goal of minimum integration effort rather than maximum benefit to end-users.

1.6.3 Part of a Possible Solution

We suggest a partial solution to this problem by identifying a common shared schema that all three tools are to use (Figure 5). However, the existence of this shared schema is not in itself a guarantor of integration, but only a means to it. Several other factors are necessary:

1.6 A Hypothetical Example of the Problems of CASE Tool Integration

- Each CASE tool must accommodate this shared schema; this may necessitate extensive rewriting by the CASE tool vendor. The emergence of widely known public schema definitions will become necessary in this regard.
- The process that the integrated CASE environment will support must be defined and represented. This must be carried out by the organization that seeks to use the integrated CASE environment.
- Each CASE tool must use the same set of integration mechanisms in a consistent way. For instance, whatever mechanism for access control to the shared data used by one CASE tool must be used by the others to ensure consistency of access. This may require the existence of conventional protocols, whether actually standardized or simply de facto agreements between the CASE tool vendors.

FIGURE 5 The Data Maintained by the Combined Toolset.

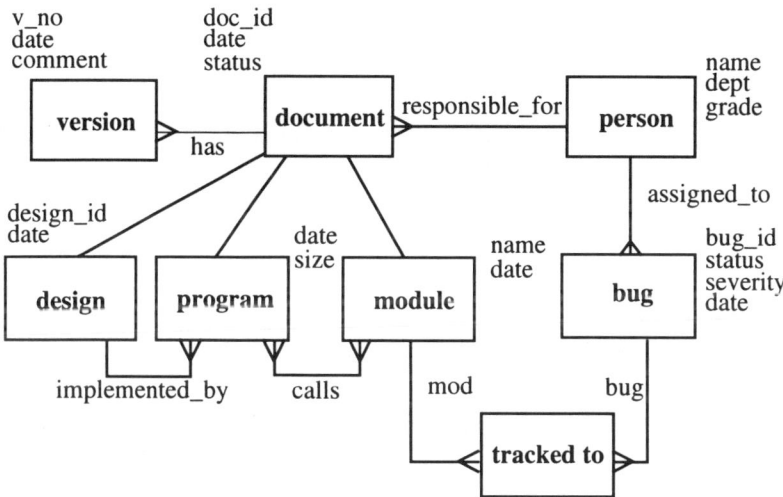

1.6.4 Summary of the Example

Through this very simple integration example we have illustrated a number of problems that must be addressed in putting together three hypothetical CASE tools. The reality of the situation is that the problems of integrating CASE tools will be much more difficult than we have described:

- An underlying problem worthy of note is that the effort of integrating CASE tools is almost certain to increase more than linearly as the number of CASE tools to be integrated increases. For example, integrating six CASE tools is likely to be many times more difficult than integrating three CASE tools. This occurs for reasons analogous to those that dictate that writing a program of one hundred thousand lines of code is much more than twice as difficult as writing one of fifty thousand lines of code — the number of possible interconnections between components increases rapidly, the low-level details become more than a single person can retain, and maintaining consistency becomes much more difficult.

- The CASE tools to be integrated are typically produced by different vendors, each with their own goals, ways of working, problems, and so on. Managing and interacting with multiple vendors to produce an integrated solution is a formidable task requiring solutions to many political, technical, and financial problems.
- The simplifying assumptions that we made will in reality not be possible. The data that a typical CASE tool will store and manipulate are much more complex than in the example, and even a pair of compatible tools, i.e., that use the same interface standard, will often exhibit different conventions or notations in using the standard.
- Our example made the assumption that a CASE tool is relatively well-behaved, and limits its functionality to a single area. In reality, this is seldom the case. Sets of real CASE tools are more likely to overlap a great deal in their functionality, with the result that choices about which CASE tool performs a given service within a CASE environment may call for difficult decisions, and will almost certainly have an impact on the integration scheme. For example, a design tool and a coding tool will each typically implement its own version management approaches, which may well be incompatible.

The scope of the difficulty of CASE tool integration is such that it is not easily achieved without considerable effort. Our aim in this hypothetical example is to convey some of this difficulty by concentrating on the many practical and conceptual issues involved in sharing data between a set of CASE tools. Prescribing that some set of CASE tools should be "integrated" is merely a starting point. Choosing the mechanisms that the integration will use and defining both the relevant services and the process that the integration will support are the necessary and much more difficult steps that must be taken to arrive at a desired goal.

1.7 Summary

Producing complex software systems of high quality, on time, to budget, and with adequate documentation to allow them to be maintained and enhanced is the goal of most organizations producing computer-based systems. CASE has been proposed as one approach that can help to make this happen. However,

1.7 Summary

individual CASE tools that provide "islands of automation" are not sufficient to realize this goal. What is required is an environment for developing software. Such an environment will support the use of multiple CASE tools in a cooperative, synergistic fashion throughout the software development life cycle — in short, an integrated CASE environment.

The role of this book is to provide a context for understanding the concepts fundamental to an integrated CASE environment. The book addresses the topic by focusing on the following viewpoints:

- A conceptual viewpoint that addresses the question, "What does integration mean in the context of a CASE environment?" Previous work in this area together with our own thoughts on this question are presented.
- A mechanistic viewpoint that addresses the question, "How can I implement integration in a CASE environment?" Existing products that support the integration of CASE tools are examined and discussed.
- A practical viewpoint that addresses the question, "What has been achieved and where is the future for integrated CASE environments?" Practical experiments we have carried out in CASE tool integration are described, and an examination of companies using integrated CASE tools is presented together with a commentary on the current state of the CASE environments field.

Integration is a critical factor in providing usable, supportive, comprehensive automated support for software development. It is a concept in need of study, refinement, and explanation. In this book we present an analysis of this important topic, providing valuable information to all those involved in the development of CASE tools and environment, or the use of such an environment to produce software systems.

CHAPTER 2

Previous Approaches to Understanding CASE Tool Integration

2.1 Introduction

CASE tools typically support individual users in the automation of some task within a software development process. Used thus, CASE tools have undoubtedly helped many organizations in their efforts to develop better quality software to budget and within predicted time scales. Further, if tool technology matures according to the current expectations of many industry analysts, then CASE tools offer the potential to revolutionize the way in which much of our software is currently developed.

However, the success of *integrated* sets of CASE tools — i.e., CASE environment — is a more complex issue. The potential for success is great, but is dependent on many factors. Perhaps the most urgent need is for an improved in-depth understanding of the meaning and role of integration in a CASE environment. This is important because it will form the foundation for many of the tasks that will follow. For example, without a common understanding of integration, we will continue to struggle to have the necessary shared concepts and terminology to allow integration products to be described and compared, standard interfaces to CASE environment components to be agreed upon, and objective measures of the effectiveness of integration approaches to be produced.

The focus of this chapter is a review of previous approaches toward defining a common understanding of integration in a CASE environment. We begin by examining the conceptual models of integration that have been developed and that help to understand the main concepts being addressed in an integrated CASE environment. We then look at the main architectural approaches that have been used in constructing a CASE environment, concentrating on the integration that is supported by those architectures.

2.2 Conceptual Models of Integration

The problem of integrating software components to produce a CASE environment is the central focus of this book. It is a problem that has resisted easy solution and offers a highly difficult challenge to the software community. In attempting to resolve some of the complex issues in CASE tool integration, researchers have sought a conceptual framework through which these issues can be more easily understood and communicated between different people.

While there are several ways to attack this problem, one necessary first step is to consider the *properties* of integration to clarify what integration actually means. Another necessary step is to distinguish the mechanistic from the semantic elements of integration, thus separating *how* tools might be integrated (in terms of the underlying mechanisms) from the issue of defining *what* is integrated (in terms of the required semantics).

However, in addition to this simple separation of concerns, a number of more detailed conceptual models have been developed. As exemplars of this work on integration, the following three approaches are of particular interest:

- Integration as a set of attributes that characterize a CASE environment.
- Integration as goals for the relationships between CASE environment components.
- Integration based on a central repository through which CASE environment components share data.

To a certain extent, these approaches are based on different models of what integration actually is. Common to all, however, is the notion that integration is an important aspect of a CASE environment and one needing clear intellectual def-

2.2 Conceptual Models of Integration

inition. The following is an overview of these three approaches; each is elaborated more fully in subsequent subsections.

Integration as a set of attributes (discussed by Wasserman [77]) provides a view whereby integration can be thought of as a set of characteristics of a CASE environment. These characteristics can be seen as independent dimensions (e.g., data, control and presentation) along which integration issues can be examined. This approach has proved useful in providing a basic understanding of the main concepts of integration. Subsequent work has expanded and evolved Wasserman's original set of dimensions. For example, the process and platform integration dimensions are elaborated by Brown and McDermid [14].

A second approach (discussed by Thomas and Nejmeh [75]) treats integration not as a property of a component, but rather as a property of the *relationships* between components. Goals are defined for the properties for each relationship. They then focus on the properties of particular relationships, namely the relationship between a tool and a framework, a tool and a development process, and among tools. This important concept helps to highlight integration issues as being distinct environment characteristics in their own right.

A third view of integration focuses on a central repository as a key mechanism. This use of a central repository is considered by many people to be a preferred strategy for CASE environment integration, and has been the basis of several environmental efforts. The subject of repositories is broad, and can be considered from a number of viewpoints. We consider the repository approach in terms of a set of facets or characteristics necessary to any repository implementation.

We now describe these three conceptual perspectives on integration in more detail.

2.2.1 Integration as a Set of Attributes

A seminal paper by Wasserman viewed integration as a set of attributes that can be applied to a CASE environment [77]. Orthogonal dimensions of integration allow the environment to be assigned attributes in each of the dimensions. Wassermann proposed five dimensions of integration, three of which were discussed in detail. *Control integration* relates to inter-tool coordination; *data integration* relates to information sharing; and *presentation integration* refers to user interface consistency and sophistication.

The essential idea of Wasserman's paper is that any CASE environment can be evaluated for its approach to integration in each of these dimensions. For example, in the data integration dimension, one CASE environment may use a file system, while another uses a database. These would be said to have different data integration attributes. By examining an environment in each of the dimensions, it is then possible to define the set of integration attributes of that environment that characterizes its approach to integration. This allows some measure of comparison of different environments in terms of their integration approach. Figure 6 illustrates three of the integration dimensions proposed by Wassermann. The dimensions are shown as orthogonal, and have gradations marking various points along each of the axes.

The integration dimensions proposed by Wasserman have subsequently been refined and expanded. For example, *platform integration* (system support services) and *process integration* (support for a well-defined development process) have been described in more detail.

In addition, the concept of a multidimensional approach to characterize the integration approach of a CASE environment has been expanded. As discussed by Feiler and Wallnau [76], the dimensional view of tool integration can be enhanced by distinguishing between integration of tools with a framework and integration of tools with a process. Tool-process integration can be subdivided into life-cycle process (how well the tool supports the high-level software production process being used by an organization) and development process (how well the tool supports a particular engineering activity within a life-cycle step). Framework and process integration can be seen as orthogonal to data, control, and presentation integration, the latter categories being concerned with aspects of tool-to-tool integration, the former concerned with the integration of a tool with its environment.

While this multidimensional view of integration has merit in separating a number of integration issues that previously had been confused, it is also somewhat problematic. One question that immediately arises is whether the dimensions are truly orthogonal, and whether they can (or should) be considered separately. It is at least apparent that there is a close and complex relationship between data and control integration. For example, restricting access to shared data is undoubtedly a form of control that synchronizes interaction with the data, while a message sent from one tool to another will most often contain or refer to one or more data items. Another problem with the dimensional view is that a position further along each axis is often interpreted as a "greater" or "better" level of integration. In fact this is not necessarily so. Certainly the mechanisms are more sophisticated in terms of the integration approaches they support. However, the important role played by the semantic agreements between tools (e.g., agreeing on what the shared data, messages, or screen icons actually mean) is not addressed in this view.

2.2 Conceptual Models of Integration

FIGURE 6 Three Integration Dimensions.

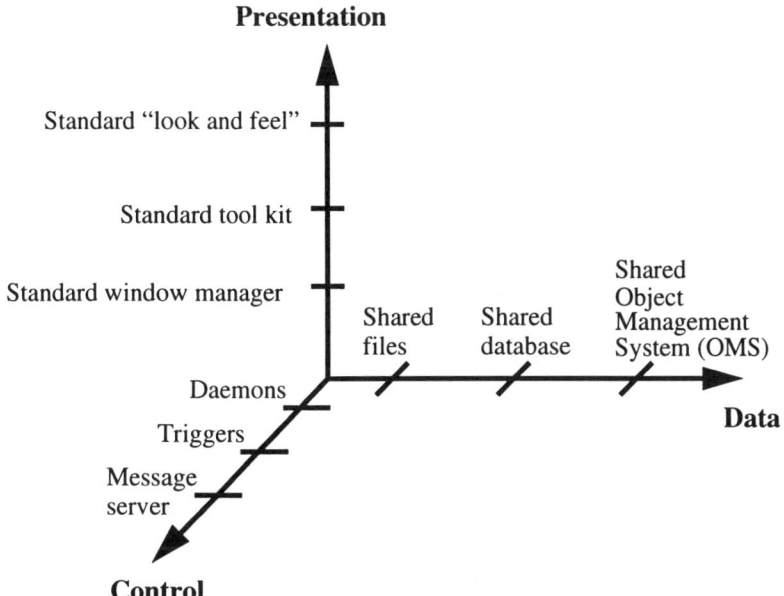

2.2.2 Integration as a Relationship

Work by Thomas and Nejmeh [75] focuses on integration not as a property of a single element, but as a *property of the relationship* between two or more CASE environment components. They take this approach to highlight that integration addresses the way the components interact rather than describing characteristics of a single component. It is this assembly of components that is the key to a well-integrated environment.

Thomas and Nejmeh identify several types of inter-component relationships that are of particular importance:

- *Tool-to-tool relationships.* Thomas and Nejmeh expand on Wasserman's dimensions of integration by discussing the ways in which individual tools interrelate.
- *Tool-to-framework relationship.* As the tools are hosted on some framework component (e.g, a database system or an operating system), the manner in which each tool makes use of the framework's services is significant.

- *Tool-to-process relationship.* How well each tool supports the process being carried out is another relationship of interest. The relationship may be expressed in terms of a tool's support for an individual step within the software life cycle (e.g., requirements definition), and its support for multiple steps (e.g., the requirements, design, and coding steps).

A useful distinction that is made in this work is between "well integrated" and "easily integrable." An environment can be well integrated with respect to how end-users of the environment carry out their application development tasks. For example, there may be a consistent and intuitive user interface for interaction with all tools in the environment. On the other hand, a well-integrated environment is not necessarily easily integrable with respect to how easy it is for the environment builders and administrators to assemble the environment, tune it for particular needs, and replace one tool with another. To a large extent these two views of integration are independent; there is no guarantee that an environment that is easy to assemble is enjoyable and productive to use, or vice versa.

Thomas and Nejmeh's view of integration is illustrated in Figure 7, which shows their notion of integration as a relationship between components, and also identifies various kinds of relationships that may exist.

While the Thomas and Nejmeh view of integration is fruitful, it has at least two limitations. First, the integration relationships are expressed as "goals" that an environment may achieve. Unfortunately there is no discussion in their work about how to achieve these goals, what dependencies lie between them, and what trade-offs must be made. Second, a tool is not equivalent to an end-user service. Rather, a tool may implement part of a service, or many services. Hence, in using this approach to analyze a CASE environment composed of a number of tools, there is no guidance on which of the many possible tool relationships are of most interest. While an integrator could use this approach to consider the potential relationships between every pair of tools in the environment, there is little direction in addressing the environment as a whole. Unfortunately, in a real environment, the potential relationships between a pair of tools are heavily influenced by the other components of the environment.

2.2 Conceptual Models of Integration

FIGURE 7 Integration Relationships Between Environment Components.

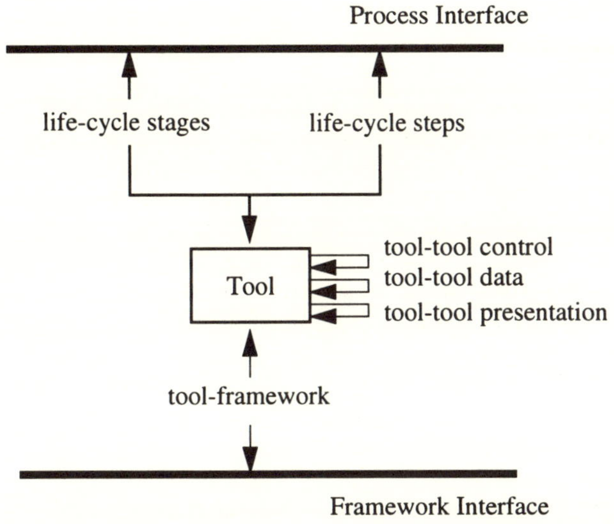

```
                    Process Interface
          ▲                   ▲
          │                   │
    life-cycle stages    life-cycle steps
          │                   │
          └──────┬────────────┘
                 ▼
              ┌──────┐  ── tool-tool control
              │ Tool │  ── tool-tool data
              └──────┘  ── tool-tool presentation
                 ▲
                 │
            tool-framework
                 │
                 ▼
                    Framework Interface
```

2.2.3 Integration Based on a Repository

The notion of integration based on a central repository is widespread throughout the CASE community. There is a pervasive belief on behalf of many people that a repository of some sort at the heart of a CASE environment should be the primary means of tool integration.[1] We first examine what is meant by a repository, briefly examine the current state of the practice, and then address some issues needing resolution in the repository approach to integration.

2.2.3.1 Characteristics of a Repository

The very term "repository" is the source of some confusion. The reason is partially that the various communities currently producing software (database, management information system (MIS), CASE tool vendors, etc.) have each adopted this idea in slightly different ways. Hence, there is confusion in addressing the issue across these domain boundaries. We take perhaps the widest view of a repository, and specifically discuss four facets, or characteristics, of a repository. These are:

---

[1]. While there is some debate over this viewpoint, it is nevertheless a well-established position in many government agencies.

- a data storage mechanism,
- an interface to persistent data,
- a set of schemata, or information models, and
- a concept of operations to manipulate the data.

For the remainder of this book, any reference to "a repository" is to a system incorporating all four of these characteristics.

There are many data storage mechanisms, ranging from simple file systems to complex database systems; in all cases, this mechanism is responsible for safekeeping of persistent instances of data. The mechanism may be central or distributed across a number of sites, and the instance data may also be either centrally stored or replicated to improve availability.

Regardless of how the data are stored, there will be interfaces that allow access to that data. There may be multiple interfaces to the same data; conversely, the same interface may provide access to different data storage mechanisms. Additionally, the interfaces may exist in different forms. For example, an interface to which programmers write applications may be complemented with a graphical interface to allow end-users to directly query the data themselves.

A description of stored data is called a schema. A schema typically records information about the different types of data in the repository and how those data are interrelated. The schema will itself be stored somewhere (often with the instance data itself) and will require an interface to access it (often the same interface as the instance data). The schema information may be specific to a particular application domain or may be more general to a wide set of domains. As a description of all the data stored in the repository, the schema has an important role to play. In effect, a representation of the schema acts as the definition of the data stored in the repository, explains the design of the data structures, and can be used as the basis for determining access control on the data. Due to this central role, the accuracy of the schema as a representation of a real-world application domain is critical to the success of the repository.

Finally, some understanding of the use of the data is required. There are a number of components to this. First, a set of operations to manipulate the data must be available. These may be held separately from the data as a set of application routines.[2] Second, the typical patterns of interaction with the data must be con-

---

[2.] However, a basic notion of object-oriented approaches to repositories is that operations should be closely bound to the data that they manipulate. Hence, they represent operations within the repository.

2.2 Conceptual Models of Integration

sidered (e.g., the frequency of change of the data items). This is generally found in a concept of operations document that describes typical scenarios in which the data are used. The concept of operations is often specific to a particular organization and the way it does business, though attempts have been made to define more generic ones. It is the concept of operations that determines how the data in the repository are accessed, by whom, at what frequency, and so on. This information is critical to tuning the repository for performance.

2.2.3.2 The State of Repository Technology

Taking each of the four characteristics of a repository in turn, we can examine a selection of products and standards currently available and in use with respect to these characteristics.

In spite of considerable developments in object management systems (OMSs), the use of file systems, particularly those based on UNIX, is still a widespread mechanism for data storage. Relational databases are also frequently used, particularly in the management information system domain, and object-oriented databases are currently receiving a great deal of attention, with a small number of production-quality systems now available. Operational use of entity-relational object storage systems such as implementations of the portable common tool environment (PCTE) is as yet rare.

For repository interfaces, the Structured Query Language (SQL) and UNIX (Posix) standards are well established, and most tools and systems are written to these interfaces. There is a great deal of activity in developing new interfaces, particularly to facilitate CASE tool portability across different CASE environments. The Institute of Electrical and Electronic Engineers (IEEE), American National Standards Institute (ANSI), International Standards Organization (ISO), and the European Computer Manufacturers Association (ECMA) and other standards bodies all have efforts in this area. While there is relatively little actual use of most of these developing interface standards, a growing number of CASE tool vendors are beginning to make commitments to some of them.

At the schema level, there have been a number of attempts to define generic information models that can be used as the basis for semantic agreements between tools across an application domain. There is a great deal of research taking place in this area, with "enterprise modeling and integration" being the phrase that unites much of this work. To date, none of these generic schemata has achieved wide success, although the IBM AD/Cycle Information Model and ISO Information Resource Dictionary System (IRDS) represent extensive efforts in this area.

2.2.3.3 Issues Concerning Repositories

The existence of a repository within a CASE environment is itself not a guarantor of integration, but merely a mechanism that facilitates it. There are many other issues that must be resolved. These issues are of two main categories: syntax issues (e.g., naming, notation, conventions), and semantics issues (e.g., what is stored, where it is stored, what it means). Thus, supposing that two tools might share data stored in a repository, the tools must first come to agreements on the storage mechanism, the interface, the schema, and the operations. As an example, two tools might decide to use an Oracle database, and that SQL will be the common interface. In such a case, there is still the need to share a common schema for the tools to have a common understanding of the information stored in the database, and to agree on what operations will be permitted to change the data. While the fourth characteristic of a repository (a shared set of operations) is not a necessary condition for integration at a functional level, it is important to the correct inter-working of the tools as they must synchronize their actions on the data.

2.2.4 Summary

The need to provide a deeper conceptual understanding of the integration aspects of a CASE environment has led to a number of efforts to characterize integration in terms of:

- attributes along a number of orthogonal dimensions (e.g., data, control, presentation),
- goals of the relationships between CASE environment components, and
- the repository of data that is shared between the components of the CASE environment.

Each of these approaches provides insight into the issues, but none of them individually provides a sufficiently rich picture of the full range of concerns.

2.3 Evolution of Integrated CASE Environment Architectures

In parallel with efforts to obtain a better conceptual understanding of integration issues within a CASE environment, there has been interesting progress to obtain an improved practical understanding of how CASE environments can be constructed. In particular, a great deal of attention has been paid to the problem of defining an appropriate architecture of a CASE environment. An examination of these architectural styles can provide further insight into the integration concerns of a CASE environment.

2.3 Evolution of Integrated CASE Environment Architectures

Two independent traditions have led to the current state of the practice in CASE environment architectures. The first tradition focused on the development of an integrated project support environment (IPSE) that supports the entire software process based on a comprehensive set of shared mechanisms that facilitate tool coordination and interaction. This tradition reflects the vision that formed in the 1970s and was perhaps most clearly expressed in the early 1980s in efforts such as the Ada Stoneman report [16] and the environments that were based on that model. The second tradition, that of coordination among independent CASE tools, began with the development of single-user tools that exploited the hardware advances that were being made — graphical workstation technology, faster processor speeds, and larger main and secondary storage. Early CASE tools of this type have evolved to support groups of users, and to address a wide range of engineering activities. For example, a number of CASE tool products are available that provide support for small teams of engineers who are developing software designs in multiple notations, automatically generating code fragments from those designs in a programming language, and producing documents describing the software and its design.

The IPSE path has concentrated most of its attention on the development of generic CASE environment infrastructure technology (usually called "environment frameworks") to provide strong software support for large-scale software development efforts. The different classes of environments shown in Figure 8 (based on a taxonomy in Dart et al. [24]) provide some insight into the historical and conceptual basis of the first-generation IPSE concept. This taxonomy categorized early approaches into four categories, based on the approach toward integration in an IPSE. In one category it is the focus on the support for a central language that is the key (e.g., the Ada Programming Support Environments); in the second category it is provision of a set of tool-kit components that can be used in multiple combinations to support different software development styles (e.g., UNIX); the third has support for one or more methods of development that form the focus of the environment (e.g., structured design environments); and the fourth is based on the use internally of a single program representation with a structured editor as the main interaction approach (e.g., Gandalf [35], or Cornell Program Synthesizer [67]).

FIGURE 8 The Evolution of CASE Environments.

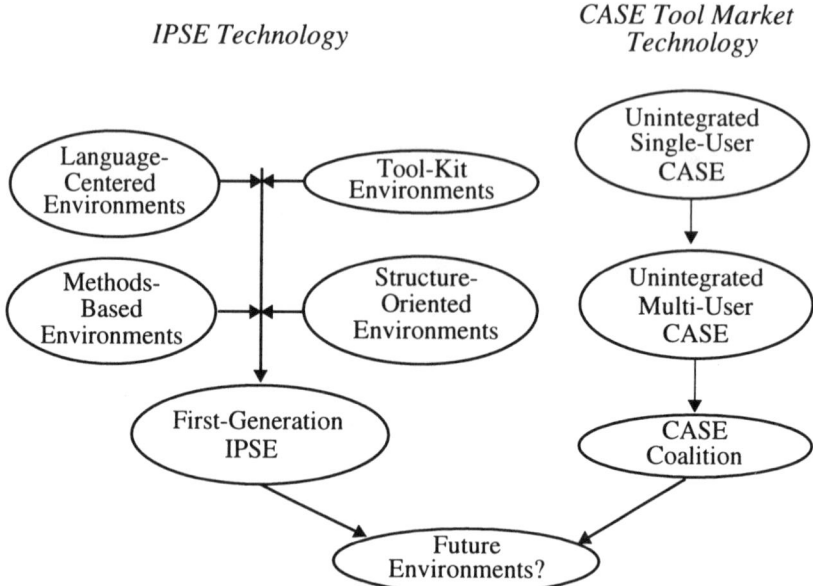

Separate from the IPSE path, a different approach was championed by individual CASE tool vendors, and was driven primarily by market forces. Initially, these CASE vendors focused on their own products as the basis of a complete solution. Gradually, they began to realize that no single tool could encompass all of the engineering and management tasks involved in building software systems. As a result, CASE vendors began to band together and produce multivendor "CASE coalition" environments covering a much wider range of functionality than was provided in any single CASE tool.

These two trends reflect generally distinct approaches to the problem of integration. The IPSE approach is historically older, but is considered more costly and difficult to achieve. At present, and as a result of a fast-developing market for individual CASE tools, there has been a notable shift away from the IPSE approach (i.e., monolithic, centralized environments) toward the CASE coalition approach (i.e., more loosely coupled, tool-centered environments).

As is discussed in subsequent sections of this chapter, neither architectural approach provides a complete solution. Each is learning from the other, and the distinctions between the two are beginning to blur. Table 1 summarizes the

2.3 Evolution of Integrated CASE Environment Architectures

essential characteristics of IPSE and CASE architectural approaches to building a CASE environment.

TABLE 1 Comparison of IPSE and CASE Approaches

Characteristic	IPSE	CASE Coalition
Environment Architecture	central OMS large-grained tools	multiple private OMS tool-function access
Integration Model	data-oriented integration	proprietary data and control-oriented integration
Process Support	centralized, explicit large-grained process support	localized, implicit fine-grained process support

In the following sections we first examine the IPSE and CASE coalition trends in more detail. In the next chapter we suggest a new model of CASE tool integration, and examine it in light of these existing approaches.

2.3.1 The IPSE Approach

The IPSE can be seen as an attempt to synthesize key aspects of language-centered, structure-based, method-based and tool-kit environments into an organic whole. The IPSE concept, depicted in Figure 9, owes much of its original characteristics to the Stoneman report [16], which described the requirements and architecture of Ada Programming Support Environments (APSEs).

In Figure 9, IPSEs are characterized by (logically) centralized object management services and possibly centralized support for software process management. IPSEs evolve through changes to the OMSs, amendments to the data model specification, and the addition of new tools. Software process support can be in the form of dynamic process control, such as in the ISTAR contracts [26], or static process control, such as in the Software Life-Cycle Support Environment (SLCSE) data model [69].

FIGURE 9 Elements of the IPSE Concept.

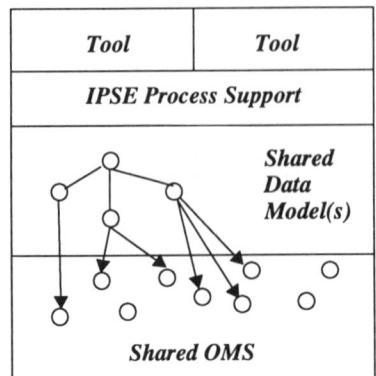

Although the Stoneman requirements were couched in terms of software environment support for Ada software development, the pedigree of these concepts can be found in earlier language- and structure-oriented environments such as Gandalf [35] and InterLisp [72]. Stoneman went beyond these environment efforts to also address the important issues of scale and complexity that characterize modern software-intensive systems. Thus, Stoneman and the environments that followed the Stoneman architectural vision — such as ISTAR [26], PCTE (Portable Common Tool Environment) Added Common Tools (PACT) [73], and Environment of Advanced Software Technology (EAST) [5] — all include a strong element of software process support.

The IPSE approach, and especially its reliance on a framework of common capabilities, is a highly generalized approach. While the implementation details vary considerably among IPSEs, they tend to share some fundamental characteristics. These include their large size, together with a comprehensive approach to integration; the development of complex data management technologies called object management systems; and the need for tailoring the environment for a given process or project. These characteristics each contain some significant drawbacks; we examine each of them in turn.

2.3.1.1 Large-Scale Comprehensive Solutions

First-generation IPSE efforts such as the Ada Language System (ALS), Ada Integrated Environment (AIE), and SLCSE [69] were undertaken by large organizations with substantial financial and technical resources at their disposal. Thus, these efforts were able to mount a full frontal assault on the IPSE problem, which resulted in engineered, fully specified IPSEs. However, it is pre-

2.3 Evolution of Integrated CASE Environment Architectures

cisely this comprehensiveness that has been a major obstacle in gaining widespread acceptance of IPSE technology.

The obstacle lies in the fact that a comprehensive environment solution affects almost every aspect of the environment's construction, its performance, and its use. For instance, the often-stated IPSE goal of achieving transportability of tools across different IPSE installations led to IPSE framework definitions spanning all infrastructure services that may be required by tools, essentially requiring the definition of a virtual operating system interface. This has adverse consequences on the cost and complexity of IPSE frameworks, as well as on the ultimate performance of the IPSE in its target setting. Additionally, IPSE users are confronted with an unfamiliar interface to computer services, which implies the need for significant training, overcoming of cultural biases, and other major technology-transfer problems.

2.3.1.2 Development of Object Management Systems

The problem of managing persistent data in an IPSE raised challenging questions regarding data management technology. While conventional file systems provided support for important services such as data distribution and versioning, they did not support associative naming schemes and data structuring techniques to capture semantic relationships among data. Existing database technology, however, supported associative naming and capture of semantic information, but did not adequately support distribution, versioning, and long transactions. Thus, several first-generation IPSE efforts defined a new class of data management systems, popularly called object management systems. These blurred the distinction between database and file system. The IPSE framework interface specification, the common APSE interface set (CAIS-A), and the portable common tool environment (PCTE) provide sophisticated OMS operations as major components of the interfaces they define. However, implementing OMS technology has proved quite difficult, both at the level of understanding essential OMS requirements, as well as in achieving adequate performance in the implemented systems.

2.3.1.3 The Need for Tailoring

IPSE frameworks needed to be made sufficiently generic to suit the requirements of a variety of different users. This included support not just for the range of potential user roles that exist in the development of any one system, but support also for the development of systems across different application domains. The desired degree of generality resulted in the specification and implementation of IPSE frameworks that still required substantial tailoring on the part of customer organizations. This tailoring is most evident in the area of IPSE support for software development processes — a key requirement of IPSEs. Since processes vary across corporate-level organizations, across organizations within corporations, and even across projects, process support provided by IPSEs tended to be far shallower than that which could ultimately be supported by many of the existing CASE tools.

In combination, these characteristics, or rather their adverse limitations, resulted in slow acceptance of IPSE solutions by potential customer organizations. Their comprehensiveness, technological complexity, and need for tailoring proved sufficient disincentives for even large organizations. This has resulted in reluctance by CASE vendors to target their software to IPSE framework specifications — a task requiring significant effort, given the breadth and complexity of IPSE interfaces. The lack of CASE tool support in IPSEs, particularly when measured against the proliferation of tools in the stand-alone CASE market, has further reinforced customer reluctance regarding IPSEs, resulting in a kind of "Catch-22" for would-be IPSE vendors.

2.3.2 CASE Coalition Approach

CASE coalitions are in many ways the inverse of IPSEs. Where IPSEs provide a central set of capabilities and monolithic tools, CASE tools participating in a coalition typically provide their own databases. In addition, tool services are separately accessible. Thus, while IPSEs support data-oriented integration via OMS services, CASE tools participating in a coalition define their own integration models and proprietary services, frequently relying on remote execution and other forms of control-oriented integration. Similarly, while IPSEs provide explicit support for software processes, especially large-grained processes such as the life-cycle process, CASE tools participating in a coalition support finer-grained processes in an implicit, localized fashion. The development of CASE coalition environments is actually a "bottom-up" as opposed to a "top-down" aspect of IPSEs. This bottom-up aspect of CASE coalitions actually betrays their origin: they began to be produced as a reaction to customer demand for integrated CASE solutions, and as a reaction to the realization that no individual vendor can produce all the tools necessary to support modern software engineering processes.

While extremely useful for many purposes, there are also some negative aspects of coalition environments. They are composed of tools that were developed in isolation, and these tools often project their own idiosyncratic views of the software development process. The key problems with coalition environments are a lack of generality, poor evolvability, and residual egocentrism of tools, as reflected in uneven, ad hoc software process support.

Although coalition environments are not perfect, they can provide a near-term pragmatic bridge between customer demands and the ideal integrated CASE

2.3 Evolution of Integrated CASE Environment Architectures

solutions. An example of a vendor coalition is the Interactive Development Environment's Software Through Pictures, CodeCenter, and Frame Technology's FrameMaker coalition integration. The vendors of these tools have provided mechanisms to allow designs produced by the design tool to be easily embedded in documents within the documentation tool, and for code stubs to be generated from the design tool for use within the coding tool.

Figure 10 depicts coalition environments as consisting of several tools from different vendors integrated with each other, and making use of both public and proprietary tool interfaces. Coalition environments are characterized by specialized "point-to-point" integration of tool services offered by coalition participants. Coalition environments evolve laterally through point integration of new tools. Difficulties in achieving data interoperability among multiple private OMSs has resulted in a proliferation of integration techniques, with emphasis on control-oriented programmatic tool interfaces. Process models supported by CASE coalitions are implicit and embedded in the hard-wired integration of tool services.

FIGURE 10 Coalition Environments.

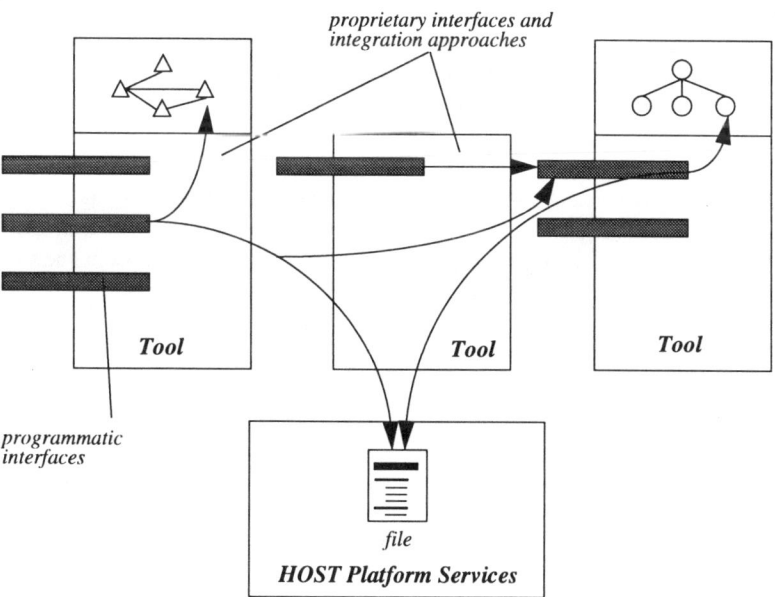

Coalitions of CASE tools tend to have several characteristics in common. These include: idiosyncratic behavior of individual tools; a least-common-denominator approach to framework services; and a tendency toward localized process support. We examine each of these below.

2.3.2.1 Idiosyncratic Tool Behavior

The key characteristic of coalition environments is the degree to which the coalition member tools continue to behave in an egocentric manner. That is, tools developed in isolation have often evolved idiosyncratic concepts that have an impact on software development processes (e.g., multi-user support and version control). In coalition environments, the tools do not surrender such concepts in favor of common process models, but instead continue to project their own process models. Further, tool egocentrism is often revealed in integrations in which one or more tools act as the central integration element, or environment driver. This tendency exaggerates the idiosyncratic differences between tools.

2.3.2.2 Least-Common-Denominator Approach to Services

The CASE tool industry evolved coincidentally to (and in some isolation from) the IPSE framework efforts described earlier in this chapter. Due to their independent nature, and also due to the relatively limited resources of typical CASE vendors, tool vendors have felt the need to balance the depth and breadth of services provided against the availability of their tools on a number of popular computer platforms. The pressure to maximize product availability across a variety of hardware platforms has produced a tendency toward least-common-denominator platform services; this in turn results in a high degree of tool independence.

This tendency toward limited use of common services reduces the dependency of tools on high-level services (such as object management) that may not be available on a sufficiently large base of installations. As a consequence each tool tends to re-implement critically important services such as data and configuration management in ways that are not standard across tools, and not accessible by other tools. Another consequence is a reduced dependency on the presence of other CASE tools, while at the same time encouraging tools to become more egocentric.

These least-common-denominator and isolationist tendencies combine to present a chaotic image of potential CASE environments. Tools implement duplicated services, rely on a non-standard set of platform services, and provide non-standard, idiosyncratic services to the end-user. It is not surprising, then, that the CASE vendors themselves must become intimately involved in the integration of their tools not with other tools in general, but with specific selections of tools, leading to strategic alliances between some CASE vendors.

2.4 Summary

This characteristic of CASE coalition environments raises some troubling questions regarding the scalability of these environments to large-scale development efforts and their evolvability over time to include new tools or new versions of old tools.

2.3.2.3 Localized Process Support

For coalition integrators, the choice of which tool services to integrate often depends upon what processes the integrated toolset is intended to support, and how the tools should support these processes. For example, CASE vendors involved in a coalition must determine whether module interface specifications generated by a design-tool should be automatically imported into a programming tool's database. Conversely, they could decide that changes to these specifications in the programming tool should be automatically re-imported into the design tool. The decision will be reflected in the "hard-wired" integration strategy adopted by the coalition vendors. Hard-wired, proprietary coalition integrations typically result in software process support that is implicit and inflexible, and hence difficult to evolve.

Each of the CASE tools involved in a coalition will embed some notions of the processes in which they were expected to be used. As CASE tool integration takes place in a point-to-point fashion, there is no explicit, overall process that is maintained, with the result that the supported processes are difficult or impossible to manage and evolve over time. The recent interest in control-oriented integration frameworks is the result of the attempt to generalize the control notion in the form of a message passing approach to tool synchronization, offering greater flexibility over the processes being supported.

2.4 Summary

In this chapter, we have examined conceptual approaches to understanding integration in a CASE environment, and the trends in CASE environment architectures for the implementation of those integration concepts.

The previous conceptual approaches involved three different views of integration of a CASE environment. Each view provides us with a useful perspective on integration:

- The *attribute* view allows various aspects of integration such as data, control, and presentation to be examined separately through the creation of a set of orthogonal dimensions.

- The *relationships* view ensures that attention is focused on the interaction of components, particularly the interactions between tools, between a tool and the framework, and between a tool and the process being enacted.
- The *repository* view highlights the important role in integration played by data sharing, with the repository notion embodying a range of factors.

These three views are illustrative of the complexity of the integration concept in CASE environments. They highlight the many ideas that are bound up in the notion of integration in a CASE environment, and the difficulty that arises in interpreting statements such as "product X is an integrated CASE tool."

The two primary architectural approaches to the construction of CASE environments, the IPSE approach and the CASE tool coalition approach, illustrate two very different ways of embodying integration concepts in a CASE environment. In the IPSE approach it is the importance of common services and mechanisms that is the basis of an integrated CASE environment. In the CASE coalition approach it is the point-to-point connection of individual CASE tools that ties together the comprehensive functionality offered by the CASE tools.

We have been taking a new view of integration in a CASE environment. This view builds on the strengths of the previously described approaches, and attempts to synthesize them within a conceptual framework that points the way toward a greater understanding of the integration problem, and a method for constructing an integrated CASE environment that results in a solution that matches an organization's needs. We can characterize this new approach as "integration as a design activity." The approach focuses on three levels of interest in a CASE environment: mechanisms, services, and processes. This view of integration separates the issues of abstract functionality (as defined by end-user services) from those of implementation (as defined by the mechanisms chosen for the actual framework and tools). It also considers that integration is seen as the means to support different aspects of an organization's development processes. The essential thrust of this work is to view any integration activity in some context, which will necessarily affect the nature of the integration that is achieved. In particular, the premise is that integration must be designed into an environment within the context of the environment users' needs and constraints.

CHAPTER 3

Toward a Better Understanding of Integration

3.1 Introduction

The need to provide better automated support for software engineering activities has led people to concentrate attention on the problems of integrating the many different components that can be found in a typical CASE environment. In the previous chapter we reviewed some of the work that has taken place to try to provide a greater shared understanding of the meaning of integration, and to build integrated CASE environments. We have synthesized some of the best aspects of this previous work to develop a model that helps to provide a more comprehensive view of integration, and can be readily applied to different environment needs. The model attempts to provide a set of concepts for understanding a range of integration issues, a vocabulary that can be used to clearly separate different integration aspects, and an organizing framework that helps to relate many of the important issues in CASE tool integration.

An attraction of our model of integration is that it also can be used as the basis of a CASE environment architecture in which the integration characteristics of the environment are defined, understood, and amenable to change. In this chapter we describe this model in detail, discuss how it can help in considering the design and construction of a CASE environment, and analyze the kinds of CASE environments that will result from realizing implementations of this model.

3.2   A New Conceptual Model of Integration

The previous chapter highlighted a number of shortcomings with previous conceptual models of integration in a CASE environment. The discussion pointed to the need for a better understanding of the issues involved in designing, constructing, and using an integrated software development environment, regardless of the available technology.

Here we propose a new conceptual model for understanding integration in a CASE environment that we believe can be used to improve our understanding in this area. In this model we distinguish three levels at which we are concerned with the integration of a CASE environment. The central one consists of the *services* available to environment end-users. The second level consists of the *mechanisms* that implement the end-user services. The third level of interest is that of the *process* that encodes the set of goals and constraints of a project or organization, providing the context in which the end-user services must be related. This model is illustrated in Figure 11.

Looking at these three levels in more detail, we see that the *mechanisms* level includes the architectural concerns and the technology components that will implement the integrated CASE environment. Integration at this level addresses implementation issues, including the software interfaces provided by the environment infrastructure (e.g., operating system interfaces), the software interfaces provided by individual tools in the environment, and the specific integration mechanisms that will be used to connect the various CASE environment components. This level also includes many architectural concerns of the tools, such as their internal structure (e.g., client/server) and data management structure (e.g., derivers, data dictionary, database). The question, "How does this CASE environment connect the various components?" can be answered at this level. The mechanisms level is concerned with the technology available and the techniques that can be applied to connect the different CASE environment components.

3.2 A New Conceptual Model of Integration

FIGURE 11 A Three-Level Conceptual Model of CASE Environment Integration.[1]

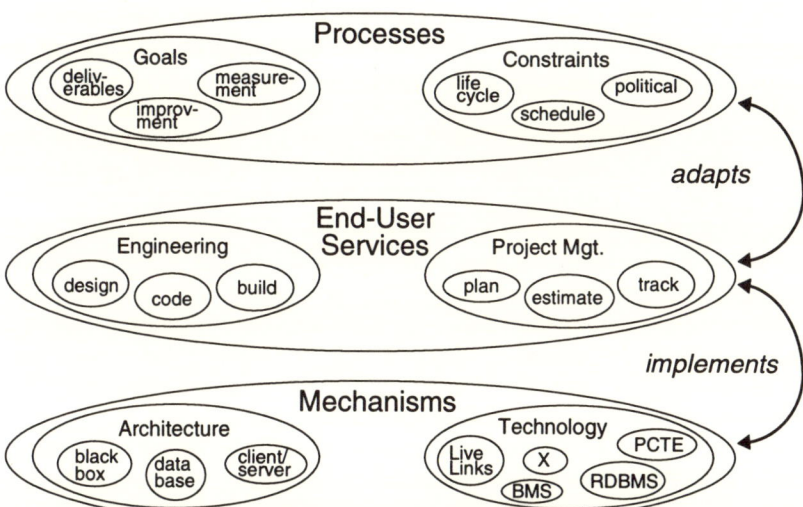

The *end-user services* level corresponds to an abstract description of the functionality that the CASE environment offers to the end-user. Integration at this level can be regarded as the specification of which services are provided by a CASE environment, and how (at an abstract level) those services relate to each other. For example, integration concerns at this level may include defining the relationships between the version control and the data management services, or describing the way in which a specification and a design service are related through traceability of design components. The basic question, "What does this CASE environment do?" can be answered at this level by describing the abstract functionality of the CASE environment.

The *processes* level corresponds to the use of end-user services in the context of a particular software development process. Integration at this level can be regarded as a kind of process specification for how software will be developed. This specification can define a view of the process from many perspectives, spanning individual roles through larger organizational perspectives. For example, the way in which design documents gain approval before implementation is allowed to begin is a process constraint that affects the way in which end-user

---

[1]. Note that this figure illustrates examples of the elements at each level, and is not intended to be exhaustive.

services are integrated. Another example is the bug tracking and version control process that must be followed when errors are found in existing code. The question, "Which activities does this CASE environment support?" can be answered at this level. There may be a wide range of activities supported, with many degree of freedom in the use of the CASE environment, or the environment may be specific to a small number of well-defined processes.

As we have noted, integration issues must be addressed within each of these three levels. However, there are also integration relationships that span the levels, though in different ways.

The relationship between the mechanism level and the end-user services level is an implementation relationship — end-user services may be implemented by different mechanism services, and conversely, a single mechanism may implement more than one end-user service. Hence, the abstract functionality of a CASE environment at the end-user services level can be described in terms of the mechanisms that implement those services.

The relationship between the end-user services level and the process level is a process adaptation relationship. The processes that are to be supported act as a set of guidelines and constraints for the combination of end-user services. For example, the way in which the design and the coding service interact is a function of the development process that is to be supported. Also, the way in which they interact in support of a classic waterfall style of software development may be very different from their interaction in support of a prototype-oriented style of development.

This three-level model provides a context in which to discuss many facets of CASE environment integration that previously have been treated in a relatively ad hoc manner. The functionality required from a CASE environment can be related to the CASE tools and integration technology that realize it. The organizational and development processes that constrain and guide the use of CASE environment services can be discussed in terms of their effects on those environment services. Hence, this model provides a powerful conceptual framework for understanding and discussing many aspects of integration in a CASE environment. We use this three-level model as a working context for understanding integration, and expand on its meaning and application in the rest of this chapter.

For the moment, however, existing integration technology and implementation architectures do not closely match this somewhat idealized model of integration. For example, many CASE tools embed process constraints that dictate and limit the ways in which they can be used. Constraints should logically be separate from the end-user services implemented by those tools to allow the tools to be combined in multiple ways supporting a wide variety of processes. Similarly, the end-user services supported by a CASE tool are often closely coupled to that tool's particular implementation techniques. Currently, the ways in which many CASE tools are implemented constrain their use and application.

We can speculate on the realization of an implementation of a CASE environment that more closely matches our three-level model. Such an implementation would draw together the best elements of current IPSE and CASE work. We refer to a realization of this approach as a *federated environment*. We discuss the realization of this model of a CASE environment later in the chapter.

3.3 Integration as a Design Activity

Much of the work we have carried out is focused on how a CASE environment can be designed and assembled with its integration characteristics in mind. In particular, the aim has been to develop an approach that considers integration as a key factor that influences many of the design decisions that take place while assembling a CASE environment. If this view is adopted, then the most important factors in constructing the CASE environment are considerations of how integration is embodied within the CASE environment, decisions concerning what trade-offs need to be made in its assembly, recording the reasons for the design decisions that are made, and measuring the results of the design activities when compared to the stated needs for the environment.

The basis of this view is a separation of the mechanistic level issues (how the interrelationships among components are implemented) and semantic level issues (what services are provided, and how those services are related). However, of equal importance is a description of the context in which the environment will operate. This is a description of the software development processes that are being supported by the environment. This results in the three-level view of integration — end-user services, mechanisms, and process — that was presented earlier.

With this view of integration as a design activity in mind, and having the conceptual framework provided by the three-level model, it is possible to sketch the outline of a method for assembling an integrated CASE environment.

The first step in this approach is to analyze and record the processes that are to be supported, and the constraints on the organization in carrying out these processes. For example, an organization may have a suitable approach to designing, coding, and testing individual software modules that has been institutionalized throughout the organization. This approach must be documented to produce a process model of the description of the practices as they currently take place. Connections between this process and related practices (e.g., the methods for system building and system integration testing) must then be defined.

Given this context in which to work, the next step involves the description of required CASE environment services that will be used in support of these processes. At an abstract level, the CASE environment services can be discussed, and the interrelationships defined. For example, design, coding, and software module testing services may be required from the CASE environment. Based on the processes being enacted by an organization, the ways in which these services must interact to support those processes can be defined.

The next step is to choose CASE environment components that can realize the services required. CASE tools can be selected with a detailed knowledge of the processes that need to be supported and the necessary connections that are required with other CASE environment components. For example, instead of the imprecise statement, "I need a testing tool," an organization is now able to express its needs in more detail: "I need a testing tool that will support these activities, and that will allow these services it provides to interface with these other services from my design and coding tools." Integration technology such as databases and message passing systems may be required to facilitate the construction of the CASE environment. Again, these can be selected and evaluated with a much clearer understanding of the requirements that they must satisfy.

While these steps are described in sequential fashion, in most instances there will be significant feedback and iteration between the steps. For example, changes to the processes may be made to accommodate the tools available, or tool selections may be amended to accommodate new requirements. However, the important point to note is that such changes can now take place within a context that has documented why such changes are necessary, provides a basis on which such decisions can be rationalized, and maintains a history of why the CASE environment architecture has evolved to be how it is. In most current CASE environments, the conceptual framework necessary to facilitate these actions does not exist.

3.4 Realizing a Federated CASE Environment

Considering integration as a design activity encourages an approach to CASE environment construction that is based on a set of documented decision on the trade-offs that will need to be made. The three-level model of integration provides the conceptual framework within which this design approach can operate.

3.4 Realizing a Federated CASE Environment

We now consider what kind of CASE environment would result from the application of this approach. We call a realization of this approach a "federated environment" as the approach indicates an environment architecture that has focused particular attention on the connections necessary among the environment components.

There are three key premises in this realization. The first is that the resultant CASE environment is, whether implicitly or explicitly, focused on one or more development processes. The second is that whatever integrating mechanisms might be available, it is likely that for the foreseeable future no one single integrating mechanism will prove sufficient. Rather, several integrating mechanisms are likely to cooperate in providing the integration necessary to support a given process. The third premise is that different degrees of integration can (and should) exist between different components of a CASE environment. We discuss each of these premises in the section below.

3.4.1 The Focus on Process

The process (or processes) offers a top-down overview of the environment and especially its level of integration. This means that it is of little use to describe the integration of tool A with tool B *unless these two tools are expected to interact in support of a particular process.* For instance, while one certainly could claim that "the compiler is integrated with the project management tool," it is not possible to determine whether the integration is of value. Even when the integration could be valuable, some sort of process description needs be present. It might not be evident what it means to integrate a compiler with a project management tool. But this could be meaningful given some context provided by a process description: "After each compilation, a message should be sent to the project management tool announcing the success or failure of the compilation; the project management tool then updates the appropriate attributes in the project database." In this context, the statement is more comprehensible, and there is even some indication both of a needed framework mechanism to allow communication among tools and also of some necessary functionality of one of the tools (i.e., the project management tool must be able to update a database; this could in turn be accomplished through an internal database to the tool, or via another message to an external database).

3.4.2 Cooperating Integrating Mechanisms

As discussed in later chapters, there are many different integrating mechanisms in current use. These mechanisms tend to fall into one of two categories. The first is essentially data-centric; such systems are often called "repository-based systems." The second type of integrating mechanism is based on a control paradigm, and allows synchronization and communication between independent CASE environment components.

Although claims have been made that one or another of these mechanisms is sufficient, it is apparent that both data and control mechanisms are needed within any extensive CASE environment. CASE environment components typically need to both share information and synchronize their actions on these data. There is no reason why different integration mechanisms cannot be used for each of these tasks, provided that their interaction is well understood. An in-depth understanding of the processes being supported by the CASE environment can provide much of the information required to define their interactions.

3.4.3 Different Degrees of Integration

Given any reasonably diverse set of tools, and given the context of a typical software development process, it is very likely that the required relationship between one pair of tools will be different from the required relationship between another pair. For instance, the relationship between a compiler and a debugger might require a large amount of sharing of data, internal representations of programs, symbol tables, and so forth. On the other hand, the relationship between an editor and a spell checker might require only that each has knowledge of ASCII and the underlying file system.

Such differences in the requirements for integration between CASE environment components leads inevitably to different implementation approaches toward integration of those components. In fact, variations in the degree of integration are also the de facto situation of many existing CASE tool coalitions: if the vendors of a design tool and a documentation tool have agreed to share some internal data structure, then any third-party tool that is integrated with them will necessarily be so in a more limited way.

Given these facts, we suggest that in a real-world situation, a CASE environment could be composed of groups of CASE tools that are integrated in different ways to support different needs. In effect this produces a CASE environment architecture consisting of loosely coupled collections of tightly integrated CASE environment components. Figure 12 illustrates this concept.

Couplings between some groups of CASE environment components will in some circumstances be very tight (e.g., frequent data interchange, detailed semantic agreements, complex synchronization of events) and in other circumstances will be very loose. The determination of the degree of integration may vary. The requirements and constraints of the processes being supported will dictate whether tight or loose integrations are appropriate. Furthermore, some integrations will be tight because of the use of coalitions of CASE tools supplied by the CASE vendors, while others will be the responsibility of third-party CASE environment integrators, or of the end-user organization itself.

FIGURE 12 An Example of a Federated Approach.

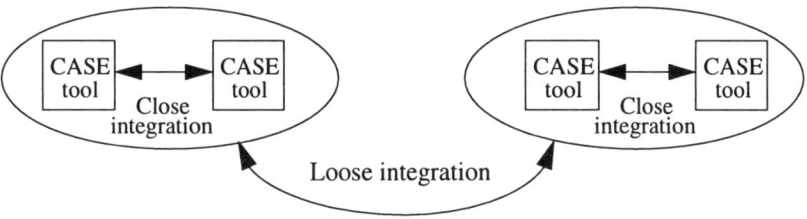

3.5 Summary

Previous attempts at developing conceptual models for understanding integration aspects of a CASE environment concentrated on static approaches to analyzing the properties and relationships of existing systems. While much can be learned from these models, what many people would like is not only the ability to analyze certain integration characteristics of an existing CASE environment, but also the ability to construct a CASE environment to suit their integration needs, and to be able to evolve that environment in a controlled way as those needs change. In this chapter we have proposed a model and an approach to constructing a CASE environment that will help to satisfy these desires. The model separates three different integration concerns — end-user services, mechanisms, and process — and allows each of these to be examined in isolation. It also allows relationships among these three concerns to be discussed and analyzed.

We have described this model and illustrated the use of the model as the basis of an approach to constructing a CASE environment that considers CASE environment integration to be a design activity. We then considered the realization of a CASE environment based on this approach.

The remainder of this book uses this three-level model as an organizing framework for discussing many of the ideas that are important in providing a deeper understanding of CASE environment integration. The integration concerns of interest at the three different levels of the model are discussed in detail in separate chapters, followed in subsequent chapters by discussion of the lessons we have learned in a set of experiments that we undertook to try to explore different aspects of our approach to CASE environment construction and analysis. In the final chapters of the book, we consider the reality of the current state of the practice in CASE tool integration and take a look toward the future.

Part II: Service, Mechanism, and Process Level Integration

In Part II of this book, we examine each of the three levels of the CASE tool integration model defined in Part I.

We begin with a discussion of the service level of integration. This discussion focuses on describing an abstract conceptual model of a CASE environment that highlights integration needs. The definition and use of a service-based model of CASE environments is then discussed in detail.

Following a discussion of the service level, the mechanism level is considered. First, the different (mechanistic) dimensions of integration and the relationship between those dimensions are discussed. Then, two of those dimensions (data and control) are examined in detail, with emphasis given to the various mechanisms that are becoming available to provide support along each dimension.

Finally, the process level of integration is discussed, and the effects that process considerations have on CASE tool integration are examined.

Part II consists of the following chapters:

4. A Service-Based Model of a CASE Environment

5. Properties and Types of Integration Mechanisms

6. Data Integration Mechanisms

7. Control Integration Mechanisms

8. The Role of Process in Integrated CASE Environments

CHAPTER 4
A Service-Based Model of a CASE Environment

4.1 Introduction

We have already described our three-level model of CASE tool integration in which services, mechanisms, and process all participate. In this chapter, we focus on the services aspect, and examine what we actually mean by "service." We also consider the variety of services typically found in an environment, and the interrelationships between services and other aspects of an environment (i.e., interfaces between services). The vehicle for this examination is an abstract description called a "reference model."

We use the term reference model to characterize a model of a system taken from a purely conceptual standpoint. Such a conceptual model permits consideration of alternative implementations of a service, adding new implementations, and so on. We note the potential for confusion here, since the term reference model is often implicitly concerned with the notion of architecture; in many cases a reference *model* is understood to refer to a reference *architecture*.

We do not use the term in this way. Our understanding of the term is closer to the concept of a "feature catalog"; it is explicitly not intended to identify an architecture, but rather is intended to provide a common reference point from which the functional capabilities of actual implementations can be described. This view is consistent with our separation of services (described in the reference model) both from the mechanisms that provide those services and also from the processes that they support.

4.1.1 Background to the Project Support Environments (PSE) Reference Model

The reference model we use as our exemplar is the one developed by the U.S. Navy Next Generation Computer Resources (NGCR) Program. As part of the work of the NGCR, the Project Support Environments Standards Working Group (PSESWG) defined an environment reference model as its starting point for selecting interface standards. The working group examined many existing efforts (e.g., the Software Technology for Adaptable, Reliable Systems (STARS) Program, the National Institute of Standards and Technology (NIST) Integrated Software Engineering Environment (ISEE) working group), synthesized many aspects from them, and eventually created an entirely new document called *A Reference Model for Project Support Environments* [63].

Per the PSESWG, the aim of an environment reference model is to describe from a purely conceptual view point what functionality an environment can be expected to provide. A reference model is explicitly not intended to define the physical architecture of an environment. A reference model is, however, intended to help understand integration issues in an environment, and to provide a basis for identifying interface areas. Where possible, such interfaces may be standardized, thus improving the ability to:

- understand, compare, and contrast available technology,
- relate users' requirements to actual implementations, and
- assess the ease (or otherwise) with which different software tools and products can be integrated.

The PSESWG approach is consistent with our separation of services from mechanisms. It presents a view of an environment that is not contingent on how the services are currently provided. It also accepts, to a certain degree, the notion that an environment provides some functionality as part of the framework and other functionality within particular tools that populate the framework. (While this division is convenient, it is not immutable. In many cases this is an artificial division based on a particular choice of implementation architecture. In other cases it is a pragmatic split based on currently available software and hardware.) A service-based model avoids binding to any particular current environment architecture. Finally, the PSESWG approach does not focus on a particular commercial tool, product, or environment.

4.1.2 The Importance of Interfaces

As noted above, in addition to distinguishing between mechanistic and semantic issues, another goal of PSESWG was to highlight the need for the reference model to expose the *relationships between the services* of an environment as of equal importance to the services themselves. PSESWG therefore also considered the concept of *interfaces* and *interface areas* (i.e., collections of interfaces) as being of great importance to tool integration. There are many interfaces that must be considered in tool integration, not just the interface between two environment services. For example, the interface between a service and an end-user making use of that service, interfaces internal to a service, and an interface between an end-user service and the framework services that support it must all be considered. The ability to identify these interfaces cleanly, and thereby analyze their characteristics, is a major attraction of the PSESWG service-based approach.

4.2 Overview of the PSE Reference Model

The PSE Reference Model is a conceptual description of the functionality that may be provided by a CASE environment. This description is general and is bounded neither by a particular application domain nor by any specific life-cycle paradigm for a development project. This is in contrast to an actual, implemented environment that is constructed of particular components (i.e., software and hardware) and that typically does reflect a chosen life-cycle paradigm, at least implicitly.

4.2.1 The Centrality of Services in the Reference Model

The central notion of the PSE Reference Model (and also of this book's model of integration) is that of a *service*. In contrast to a service, we also can observe both the actual software component that provides this service (often called a *tool*), and the human work (often called a *task*) for which this service is necessary. We can also distinguish between those services that are commonly visible at the level of the end-user and those services that commonly provide an environment's infrastructure. Each of these concepts is integral to a full understanding of the reference model; we now examine them in greater detail.

When described from the conceptual point of view, an environment's capabilities are referred to as *services*, which are abstract descriptions of the work that can be done. Some of these services are of direct interest to an *end-user* while others comprise an underlying infrastructure, or *framework*, comprised of relatively fixed capabilities that support processes, objects, and user interfaces.

When described from the opposite, or actual view, i.e., when a realized environment is considered, the components that directly support an end-user are generally called *tools*. Although no single definition for "tool" will suffice, that of the IEEE glossary [39] is useful:

> ***A tool is a computer program used to help develop, test, analyze, or maintain another computer program or its documentation.***

As in the conceptual view, the components that comprise an actual infrastructure are referred to as the *framework*. The same term, framework, is thus used in both a conceptual and an actual sense, and its precise meaning depends on the context.

Finally, when an environment is considered from the vantage point of how it supports human activities, then either the environment will provide a *service* to a human user, or a human user will perform some *task* with the aid of the environment. For instance, one can speak of the *task* of testing software, or of using a software testing *service*.

As noted previously, these different views of an environment result in subtle differences in the meanings of key terms. In particular, there is a different meaning for service when it is contrasted with *tool* and when it is contrasted with *task*. In the first case, a tool is an actual realization of one or more conceptual services. While there is no strict correlation between tool and service (because one tool may realize many services, or one service may be realized by many tools), there are relatively straightforward correlations between a tool's functions and service descriptions. In the second case, a task and a service provide complementary views of the same activity. For instance, one might consider that the environment provides some capability (e.g., an environment's testing service), or one might consider that a human user performs some task using the environment (e.g., the human activity of testing). Whichever view one takes, both refer to the same notion (i.e., a human using a piece of software to test the output of an engineering process).

In brief, services are abstract capabilities of the environment, tasks make use of and provide context for those capabilities, and tools are the actual executable software components that realize environment services. Figure 13 illustrates the

4.2 Overview of the PSE Reference Model

distinction between these concepts. *Service* can be contrasted with *tool* along an axis of conceptual versus actual, or it can be contrasted with *task* along an axis of capability versus activity.

FIGURE 13 Relationships of Tools, Tasks, and Services.

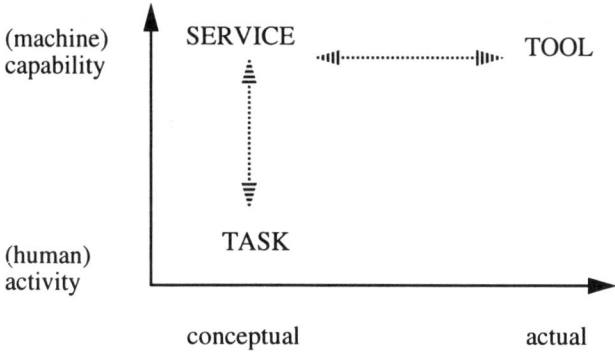

4.2.2 Differences Between Conceptual Models and Actual Environments

The separation of the "conceptual" world of the model from the "actual" world of existing tools and environments is of fundamental importance. The conceptual viewpoint that governs the reference model provides an abstract description of the functionality that may be found in an environment. An actual viewpoint would describe a particular realization of the conceptual view in terms of an environment architecture with specific tools and standards. There is a mutually reflective relationship between the conceptual and the actual views, i.e., between the environment reference model and existing environments: one may either consider the model to be abstracted from many environments, or may regard a particular environment as a realization of the model.

Since the reference model is conceptual as opposed to actual, the service descriptions tend neatly to partition the functions of an environment. When an actual environment is examined, however, these neat conceptual groupings are seldom found. Real software components span various service groups, with many components considered to be end-user tools also providing capabilities properly regarded by the reference model as framework services. The likelihood of this functional overlap is the reason that a conceptual model is necessary: one of its principal values is that it provides a common conceptual basis against which to examine many different environment implementations. Figure 14 illustrates the distinction between conceptual service descriptions, having no duplication of functionality, and a set of actual software components, many of which may overlap in their functional capabilities. As the figure shows, tools may duplicate other tools' functionality, and a tool often provides both framework and end-user services.

FIGURE 14 Relationship Between Conceptual and Actual Worlds.

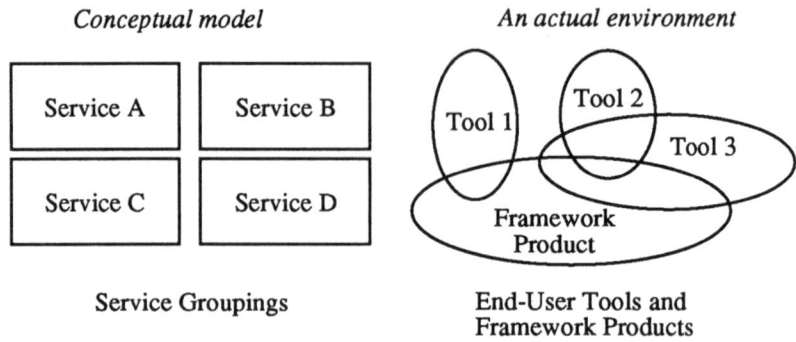

Note that even if actual environments show this mixing of framework and end-user functionality, it is nonetheless true that framework services tend to be a relatively fixed set of infrastructure services found in most environments, regardless of domain or tool content. Some of these ideas have been further explored in the work of Brown and Feiler [12][13].

4.3 Description of Reference Model Services

The reference model is a catalog of service descriptions spanning the functionality of a populated environment. The service descriptions are grouped in varying ways, either by degrees of abstraction, granularity, or functionality. The highest-level division classifies services either as end-user or framework services. The former includes services that directly support the execution of a project (i.e., services that tend to be used by those who directly participate in the execution of a project such as engineers, managers, and secretaries). The latter services pertain to users who facilitate, maintain, or improve the operation of the computer system itself (e.g., a human user performing such tasks as tool installation), or the services be used directly by other services in the environment. End-user services are further subdivided into technical engineering, project management, technical management, and support services. The first

4.3 Description of Reference Model Services

three groups partition the execution of a project into engineering, management, and a middle category that partakes of both. The fourth group, support services, is orthogonal to the other three, since it includes capabilities potentially used by all other users, such as word processing, mail, and publication.

Figure 15 shows the relation of these service groups. Framework services form a central core with a potential relationship to all other services in the environment. Support services underlie the other end-user services. The remaining three groups, technical engineering, project management, and technical management, surround the framework services and make use of the support services. In addition, services from these three groups may have relationships with each other. It is not the intention that the boundaries of the parts of this drawing explicitly indicate interfaces, since this figure is drawn at the level of service *groups*, not of individual services. Thus, it must be stressed that while a drawing such as this attempts to suggest in a very general manner how the high-level service groups relate to each other, there is an express intention to avoid any sort of architectural implication. The reference model is a conceptual, not an actual, model, and no architectural choices are intended by this figure.

FIGURE 15 A Graphical Depiction of the Reference Model Service Groups.

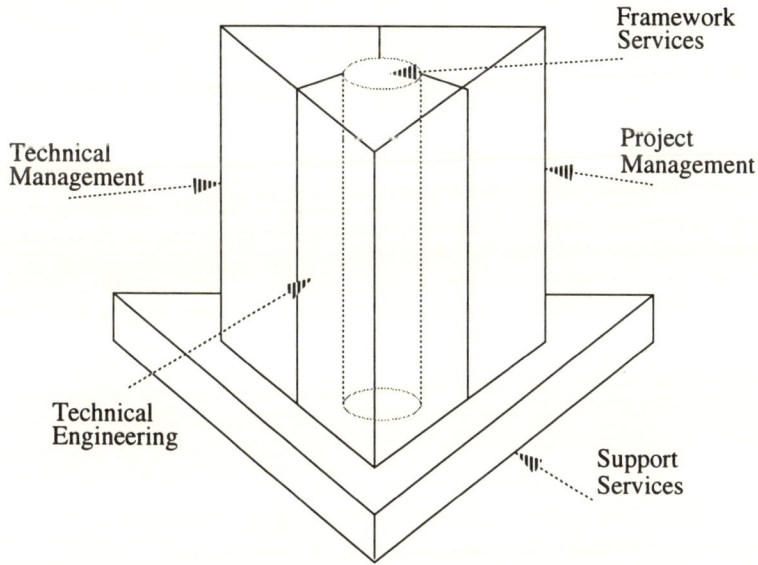

Each of the end-user service categories (technical engineering, project management, technical management, and support services) is further subdivided by engineering domain, by user role, or life-cycle phase. Technical engineering services focus on the technical aspects of project development. These services support activities related to the specification, design, implementation, and maintenance of systems. Project management services are relevant to the overall success of the enterprise. These services support activities related to developing and executing a project, including such things as scheduling, planning, and tracking the project's overall progress. These activities span the lifetime of a project from inception through deployment and maintenance. Technical management provides services that are closely related to engineering activities. However, these services pertain to activities that are often equally shared by engineers and managers. The operations of these services do not clearly fall into one or the other category, but fall into a middle category that partakes of both technical engineering and project management. Support services focus on tasks and activities common among all users of an environment, regardless of the domain, role, or life-cycle phase in which the activity is taking place. Support services are needed by virtually all users of the computer system.

4.3.1 Technical Engineering Services

These services are subdivided by specific engineering domains (e.g., software engineering). In addition to "traditional" engineering domains, the reference model also considers life-cycle processes to be an area for which an engineering discipline is appropriate, and services related to that domain are included here as well. Within an engineering domain the processes used in the life cycle of a project define a series of tasks, each requiring services for its support.

The following services are defined in the reference model: system engineering services (including requirements engineering, design and allocation, simulation and modeling, static analysis, testing, integration, reengineering, host-target connection, target monitoring, and traceability); software engineering services (including requirements analysis, design, simulation and modeling, code verification, software generation, compilation, static analysis, debugging, testing, build, reverse engineering, reengineering, and traceability); and life-cycle process engineering services (including process definition, process library, process exchange, and process usage).

4.3.2 Project Management and Technical Management Services

There are two categories of management services: project management and technical management. Services in the project management category include those relevant to planning and executing a program or project. Services in the technical management category provide a managerial complement to engineering activities in the areas of configuration management, reuse, and metrics.

4.3 Description of Reference Model Services

The following project management services are described in the reference model: planning, estimating, risk analysis, and tracking.

The following technical management services are defined in the reference model: configuration management, change management, information management, reuse management, and metrics.

4.3.3 Support Services

These services include those associated with processing, formatting, and disseminating human-readable data, including several common text and figure processing services, as well more specialized publishing, user communication, and presentation services. They also include administration services that provide support for use of the environment itself.

The reference model describes the following support services: common support services (including text processing, numeric processing, figure processing, audio and video processing, calendar and reminder, and annotation); user communication services (including mail, bulletin boards, and conferencing); administration services (including tool installation and customization, PSE user and role management, PSE resource management, PSE status monitoring, PSE diagnostic, PSE interchange, PSE user access, and PSE instruction).

4.3.4 Framework Services

Framework services comprise the infrastructure of an environment. They include those services that jointly provide support for applications, for CASE tools, and that are commonly referred to as "the environment framework." Since 1989, NIST has sponsored a series of workshops developing a reference model specifically for environment frameworks. The product of that group is a document published jointly by NIST and the European Computer Manufacturers' Association (ECMA), and is commonly known as the *NIST/ECMA Frameworks Reference Model* [62]. This document contains detailed descriptions of 50 framework services. The PSESWG elected essentially to use the NIST document in its entirety, and the PSESWG Reference Model simply contains abstracts of the more extensive descriptions found in the NIST/ECMA document.

The reference model defines the following framework services: object management, process management, communication, operating system, user interface, and policy enforcement. In addition to these services, the NIST/ECMA Reference Model contains services related to framework administration and configuration; these are included in the end-user section of the PSESWG Reference Model.

4.3.5 Rationale for the Service Groupings in the Model

In the widest sense, all users of the computer system are ultimately participating in project execution. However, the reference model distinguishes end-user services as those that are directly related to project execution. Using the example previously cited, i.e., tool installation versus engineering activities, installing a tool clearly can facilitate the eventual engineering process. However, services specifically related to tool installation are conceptually different enough from services that directly support high-level engineering activities that the reference model considers the classification of tool installation appropriately as a framework service and not as an end-user service.

There are other criteria by which services are grouped in the reference model. Often a collection of services provides the functionality needed to support a common resource. For example, there are 21 services in this reference model related to accessing data objects in a common repository. These services are all considered part of the object management services group. Since these services are related by creating, accessing, manipulating, and using objects from a repository, their classification as a single group allows for a better conceptual understanding of the requirements imposed on any realization of these services and ultimately on any standards that address these services.

Another motivation for grouping some services together might be the roles individuals take in using them. Thus, the activities that go into designing and producing executable source programs will use services that are grouped under the heading of software engineering. In this case, the group is determined by the users of the service rather than by the management of a common resource.

The boundary between service groups, particularly the boundary between end-user and framework services, is a dynamic one that changes over time. There is a general tendency for greater functionality to be gradually assumed by the underlying framework. For instance, historically most operating systems have included a directory structure and file system for data storage; a relational database is only occasionally added to a basic operating system.

In the future, however, relational or object-oriented database functionality may be part of every operating system. It is precisely this growth of functionality that leads toward the notion of "framework," in contrast to the notion of "operating system."

4.4 Uses of the Reference Model

While our particular interest in the reference model is related to our examination of CASE tool integration, there are also some immediate and pragmatic uses for the reference model, particularly in defining or characterizing an integrated environment. We now consider some of these, including: choosing interface areas for potential standardization; producing mappings and comparisons based on the reference model; describing the integration requirements of a system; and defining tool and environment architectures. We briefly examine each of these potential uses of the reference model.

4.4.1 Choosing Interface Areas for Potential Standardization

Having described an environment in terms of its services, we can now focus on the interfaces between those services, with a goal of identifying and understanding the interfaces within an environment where standardization is both possible and desirable. To realize interaction among services we must distinguish both the semantic aspects of the interface (i.e., the process aspects), and the mechanistic aspects (i.e., the use of different services to provide those semantics).

Interfaces among end-user services generally reflect the semantics of interaction among those services. Typically, these interfaces can be expressed in a number of forms, such as domain data models, service functions that can be requested by end-users or by other services, or behavioral models describing the behavior of the service based on external input. These interfaces may be provided by the framework services in different ways, depending on the architecture of the environment. For example, data in a domain data model may be accessible through a common data storage service, or may be imported and exported from one end-user service to another via a communication service.

An important point to emphasize is that within the end-user services there are a number of different interface *areas* that may be of interest. We describe elements of this range by first considering interfaces within one service, then among services. For example:

- Interfaces that permit two instances of one end-user service (e.g., different entity-relationship (ER) design editors, or different C compilers) to interoperate, or to allow one instance to be replaced by another.
- Interfaces that permit different services within one life-cycle step to work together (e.g., cooperation between compilers and debuggers, or between ER design editors and design analyzers).
- Interfaces between two specific steps in a life-cycle domain. These are interfaces that typically require some form of mapping or transformation to con-

vert representations defined in one step into those required by another. These can be interfaces within an engineering domain (e.g., a mapping between identifiers in the coding language and the design language), or interfaces within a management domain (e.g., a mapping between work breakdown structure (WBS) and schedule elements).

- Interfaces to an engineering domain, or to the management domain. These would define the use of the services within the context of higher level organizational policies. Particular life-cycle and project models would be represented as data models and behavioral models within the environment. In fact, services from individual engineering steps, as well as management services, may interface with the life-cycle model. Similarly, individual management services, as well as engineering services, may interface with the project model.
- Interfaces between management and engineering services. Typically, management services must interact with individual engineering services and engineering domains. For example, performing the management service of metrics analysis requires the collection of metrics information within individual engineering steps, together with metrics gathering at the life-cycle level.

4.4.2 Mapping Environment Implementations to the Reference Model

A key activity within the PSESWG work is the validation of the reference model through its application either to an interface standard or to existing tools and environments. This activity is commonly called a mapping. Although producing a mapping is an extremely useful exercise, it is not a simple task. First, the complexity of most environments means that performing a mapping activity is a non-trivial undertaking. When done properly, the effort involved can consume several labor weeks. Second, both the system to be mapped and the reference model must be well understood by the individual doing the mapping, and there are few people with the needed combined expertise. Third, based on the quality of existing mappings [66], it is evident that detailed mapping guidelines, examples, and perhaps even training are fundamental to promoting consistency across mappings.

In addition to mappings, the reference model permits different products to be compared directly with each other, using a common vocabulary and a common reference point. Such comparisons are especially useful because they distinguish products' abstract functionality (e.g., end-user services) from their implementation mechanisms (e.g., framework services). Thus, the separation of end-user and infrastructure services means that in using the model, particular tools and frameworks can be characterized as providing more or less equivalent end-user services using different infrastructure services. For example, the end-user service of inter-tool communication might be realized via different infrastructure services — a remote procedure-call mechanism, message server facilities, data sharing with triggers, and so on. Hence, different ways of implementing common end-user functionality can more easily be represented and analyzed.

4.4.3 Describing the Integration Requirements of a System

By defining a system's services, the reference model can be used as a basis for describing the integration requirements of a system. The advantage of doing this is that these requirements can be described in an abstract way, in terms of required services and the interfaces necessary among and within those services. This is independent of particular implementation constraints, which can then be examined in the light of the abstract requirements.

As an example, when considering the integration of a number of tool products with a particular framework product, the reference model can help in a number of ways. For example, it can help determine the amount of overlap in providing the same services; identify the sets of interfaces provided by the products; look for patterns of commonality among the tool services; and derive an integration strategy that takes into account integration alternatives, desired degree of tightness of integration based on the process to be supported, and the need for flexibility to accommodate product heterogeneity, product replacement, and adaptability of process over time.

4.4.4 Defining Tool and Environment Architectures

The implementation of services and their corresponding interfaces are an architectural consideration. Since the reference model is explicitly a purely conceptual device, there is also the need to analyze existing architectural models using the language and service categories of the reference model as the common basis from which they can be described. By performing such analyses, common interfaces across a set of architectures will become apparent, and details of the selections of interface standards at those interfaces can be compared. Concurrent activities in examining the requirements for environment interfaces and in collecting descriptions of candidate environment standards also contribute to this goal.

The reference model and the interface areas identified by it should be able to accommodate a number of different tool and environment architectures and tool integration approaches. This is important because of the many different possible realizations of services. In particular, tools and environments may cooperate in different ways to provide some, or all, of the services defined. For example, an individual tool product typically provides a number of different services within the one tool. Often it may only offer an interface to a subset of those services. Similarly, tools may implement those services in different ways. For example, a tool may implement all of its services itself and only rely on platform services to support its operation, or it may utilize other tools and services in its implementation (e.g., a relational database).

There are also several approaches to the actual interoperation of mechanisms among tools. One common way to allow tool interoperation is through the tools' use of the same instance of a data storage service (e.g., an ER data model provided as part of the platform services) and the same user interface management system (e.g., the Motif/X Window System provided as part of the user interface services). However, even when sharing these mechanisms there are different possible levels of interaction. For example, even though two tools may use the same instance of the data storage service with an ER data model, they may not have an agreed domain data model. Similarly, even having agreed upon a domain data model, one tool may be using an ER conceptual schema with an underlying relational implementation, while the other maintains the data internally in an object-oriented database. Each of these alternatives offers a different degree of integration and uses a different set of interfaces.

4.5 Summary

This chapter has described in outline a service-based environment reference model. The purpose of the model is to characterize environments through distinguishing the services they make available, and the interfaces provided within and among those services. The main characteristics of the model are:

- The separation of end-user services, as perceived by environment end-users, and infrastructure services, which support those end-user services. These are constrained with the context of the development process being followed by a particular organization.
- A framework that can reflect current environment standardization efforts, identifying the areas in which sufficient work is taking place and those in need of most attention.
- The definition of a base model with ample scope for future development to suit new requirements within particular application areas.

Finally, we reiterate that in presenting the main elements of a services reference model, we have abstracted from notions of tools and frameworks toward the higher-level concepts of services and interfaces.

CHAPTER 5
Properties and Types of Integration Mechanisms

5.1 Introduction

A central theme of this book is the three-level approach to CASE environment design and construction that distinguishes conceptual issues (the services) from implementation issues (the mechanisms) and stresses the need for a design context (the process) that the CASE environment must support. Previous chapters have discussed this theme, as well as provided insight into a conceptual model that identifies and classifies the services that might be found in a CASE environment.

However, regardless of the service model or conceptual approach selected, environment builders must eventually face the bottom-line decision of how to actually carry out tool integration. The choices they face in terms of potential mechanisms are numerous and include a full range of selections that provide varying degrees of effort and integrated capability.

In this chapter, we first consider the properties of integration by continuing the discussion of integration as a relationship (see Section 2.2). In this discussion (Section 5.2), we highlight properties that are addressed by various integration mechanisms.

Later sections of this chapter focus on the specific relationship between two particular classes of integrating mechanisms: those based on the sharing or transfer of data between tools (data integration), and those based on synchronization and communication between tools (control integration).

5.2 Properties of Integration

In Section 2.2 we introduced the concept put forward by Thomas and Nejmeh that integration can be considered by defining the properties required of the relationships between different environment components. Their definition of integration is exclusively a conceptual view, and is independent of the particular technology being used to implement that integration. This definition considers four classes of integration and identifies properties important in achieving integration in each of these classes:

Data Integration

- *Interoperability.* How much work must be done for a tool to manipulate data produced by another?
- *Non-redundancy.* How much data managed by a tool are duplicated in or can be derived from the data managed by another?
- *Consistency.* How well do two tools cooperate to maintain the semantic constraints on the data they manipulate?
- *Exchange.* How much work must be done to make the nonpersistent data generated by one tool usable by another?
- *Synchronization.* How well does a tool communicate changes it makes to the values of nonpersistent, common data?

Control Integration

- *Provision.* To what extent are a tool's services used by other tools in the environment?
- *Use.* To what extent does a tool use the services provided by other tools in the environment?

5.2 Properties of Integration

Presentation Integration

- *Appearance and behavior.* To what extent do two tools use similar screen appearances and interactive behaviors?
- *Interaction paradigm.* To what extent do two tools use similar metaphors and mental models?

Process Integration

- *Process step.* How well do relevant tools combine to support the performance of a process step?
- *Event.* How well do relevant tools agree on the events required to support a process?
- *Constraint.* How well do relevant tools cooperate to enforce a constraint?

These distinctions are useful mostly because they permit separate consideration of each of these conceptual dimensions in its own right. When considered in light of actual integration mechanisms, however, these distinctions present certain difficulties. This is because integration from a *mechanistic* perspective is more difficult to separate into these clear and distinct categories. Thus, while it is tempting to regard a particular integration mechanism as falling completely into either the data, control, presentation, or process category, such an approach is misleading on a number of practical levels. Whenever integration takes place through some real integrating mechanisms, then:

- data are shared between the agents,
- controlled interaction between the agents takes place,
- presentation of information and an interface to operations must exist, and
- the integration takes place in the context of some process, whether explicit or otherwise.

For example, to embed a diagram produced by an analysis and design tool into a document being written using a desktop publishing system, it must be possible to:

- embed the text and graphical representation of the diagram in the document flow,
- synchronize the transfer and sharing of the design,
- present an interface that allows the embedding to take place, and
- perform the embedding in a manner consistent with the organization's process and documentation standards.

If we consider an integration mechanism to be a means toward sharing information between real tools or agents, then any realistic mechanism in an actual situation emphasizes all of the above dimensions, though to a greater or lesser degree.

We need therefore to consider the essential differences between these dimensions. This distinction is most difficult between the data and control dimensions. We focus on these two in the next section.

5.3 The Relationship Between Data and Control Integration

It is critical to ask whether there are any *distinguishing* characteristics between data and control integration. (i.e., what unique attributes of data integration per se are significant when considering integrating mechanisms?). We also must consider the parallel set of questions concerning the distinguishing characteristics of control integration. As we consider these questions, it becomes apparent that data and control are, if not aspects of the same thing, at least interrelated. We note that there are some features that distinguish data and control and other features that suggest that they overlap in some fundamental ways.

For instance, it seems that at the most basic level, data and control are different: data are an artifact over which control is exerted. We also observe that data and control have different characteristics of interest. For instance, the data stored by tools are commonly persistent, have a definite size and location, and exist in a specified format. On the other hand, control is often time-dependent and transient. Control is also distinguished by a source, a target, and often by an agent that acts to facilitate control.

While these sets of characteristics differ, data and control have important interactions. For instance: something that is the source of control will have a location and a size, which are characteristic of data. Similarly, some data is not persistent and are clearly temporal. Even data that are persistent will exhibit temporality (in the sense of versions) and accesses to them must be synchronized. Further, while the notion of "format" is typically associated with data, any agent that exerts control (e.g., part of a messaging system) will need to do so using some agreed-upon arrangement of the control message, a shared knowledge of parameter placement, and similar issues that are usually considered data format issues. In addition, these control messages must themselves be defined, communicated, and stored.

These differences and similarities make it difficult (and perhaps impossible) to define an integration mechanism that is either entirely data-oriented, or entirely

5.3 The Relationship Between Data and Control Integration

control-oriented. As we examine integration mechanisms, we see that they will exhibit characteristics of both data and control integration. We see that data integrating mechanisms must necessarily exhibit at least some rudimentary control integration: if two tools are sharing data, there is at least the simple notion that one will write them before the other reads them. In the same vein, if two tools are exchanging messages, there is at least a common understanding of the format and information content of the message that is sent.

We can conclude that the essential difference between mechanisms that integrate data and control lies in the *intention* and the *emphasis* of the mechanism. That is:

- Data integration mechanisms emphasize storage and persistence, common data structures, and shared understanding of those structures.
- Control integration mechanisms emphasize a common communication approach between components and a shared understanding of the events that initiate interaction.

Data-centered systems are sophisticated and explicit about which data structures are shared, about which relationships exist between those structures, and about which views of those structures have been defined. They are less sophisticated in enacting sequencing of access; this is often implicitly accomplished through locking and transaction semantics. By contrast, in a messaging system, it is the temporal and synchronizing aspects that have the major emphasis. Environments built on such systems are sophisticated and explicit about how synchronization takes place through notification and requests, while data sharing is typically not much more than a reference to a shared file through a globally known file naming scheme.

It is necessary to note that these characterizations in no way suggest preference: one approach is not better than the other; both have their strengths and weaknesses, and either may be more appropriate in one context as opposed to the other. Similarly, neither type of system is necessarily easier to implement than the other; both require detailed agreements over the semantics of the items being shared and sophisticated mechanisms capable of encoding and enforcing those agreements.

In fact, as both control and data integration mechanisms become more mature, it is likely that the distinctions between them will become increasingly blurred. We already see this tendency in some object-oriented systems, where the distinctions between data and control mechanisms that interact with the data are closely interwoven.

In a typical object-oriented system, objects are manipulated through a public interface (called a method) by sending messages. The message sent and the type of the object identify the method to be invoked. Using this approach, one tool can invoke an operation by sending a message to another tool that causes the second tool to manipulate or share data, providing the second tool makes such an interface (method) available. Clearly, such tool interaction shows characteristics of both data integration (i.e., a shared understanding of the data manipulated by the tools) and control integration (i.e., a shared understanding of the mechanisms whereby one tool can invoke another).

5.4 Presentation Integration

In later chapters of this book we deal with the issues of data and control integration in some detail. However, we do not provide such a detailed analysis of presentation integration. We take this approach for a number of reasons.

First, the human-computer interface (HCI) is a complex topic in its own right and is being addressed in detail by a large community of HCI experts. If we take the approach that a CASE environment is just another application system with a significant human interaction component, then many aspects of the work of the HCI community can be directly applied to the use of a CASE environment. For example, studies carried out by the HCI community on the effect of user interface design on the productivity of software engineers is particularly relevant to the design and implementation of a SEE. Rather than repeat these issues here, we refer interested readers to texts other texts (see, for example, [2]).

Second, there is little useful work on presentation integration as it is unique to the use of a CASE environment. Most often in the CASE community the notion of presentation integration is treated in a much less detailed and informed way than either data or control integration. To some extent this is a result of the CASE community deferring to the HCI community. However, there is also an extent to which this phenomena is a result of the background and interest of most of the CASE community. Solving data sharing, event synchronization, and tool interaction issues has necessarily been the primary concern of this community. Perhaps this is an illustration in support of the complaint by the HCI community that in most application domains the user interface is too often considered as an afterthought.

As a result, we summarize the presentation aspects in this section, while dealing with data and control integration in much more detail in the chapters that follow. We examine presentation integration from the perspectives of services, mechanisms, and process.

5.4 Presentation Integration

5.4.1 Services for Presentation Integration

At a functional level, the presentation integration of a CASE environment can be discussed in terms of the behavior available at the environment's user interface. In particular, from this perspective the consistency of the behavior presented by the different environment components is of concern in describing presentation integration.

While behavior at the user interface could be interpreted in many ways, it is almost always viewed by the CASE community as a "look and feel" issue. That is, presentation integration is achieved by ensuring the same visual appearance of the user interfaces of each of the components (e.g., menus with similar options and consistent design of icons) and by having similar effects occur when the same interaction takes place (e.g., double clicking on the trash can icon has the same effect no matter which CASE environment component is being executed).

The way this consistency is achieved is through defining style guides for user interface design. These may be specific to the design of a particular CASE environment, or common across a range of environments. An example of such a set of guidelines is the X/Open guide.

5.4.2 Mechanisms Supporting Presentation Integration

The main interest of presentation integration from a mechanistic perspective is the sophistication of the mechanisms that are provided, and the consistency of their use throughout the CASE environment.

In terms of sophistication of mechanisms, the reduced cost and better performance of bit-mapped graphics workstations has led to a move toward graphical user interfaces rather than text-based interfaces. In most UNIX-based systems this is now interpreted as the use of the X Window System and the Motif tool kit. In PC-based systems it is the use of Windows. These allow each of the components in the CASE environment to present a graphical windows, icons, mouse pointer (WIMP) interface to the user. Such graphical interfaces are considered to be easier to use and to increase user productivity.

In terms of consistency of mechanisms, the expectation is that if all the components use the same mechanisms, then it is more likely that there will be some measure of consistency between the interfaces of the components. This consistency of user interfaces across tool boundaries will hopefully make the CASE environment easier to use and more productive.

5.4.3 Process Aspects of Presentation Integration

Providing a single, consistent way to access and execute the various CASE tools that form a CASE environment is a particularly important aspect of user interface interaction that is often distinguished as a special case of presentation integration. This view of presentation integration takes the approach that user interaction with CASE tools should be restricted to a single process to ensure that the tools can only be accessed by the appropriate people in a project, and so that the tools are executed with the appropriate version of the data to operate on.

One way for a CASE environment to do this is to insist that there is a single way for all users to access the environment. For example, a user logs into the environment and is presented with a list of tasks that are available to be carried out. The user selects a task and is given the set of tools and documents appropriate to that task. The user may execute only those tools, and only with those data. This kind of interface provides a consistent presentation of the CASE environment's functionality to the users, and reduces the number of errors that can be made due to use of incorrect versions of data and tools. Examples of analogous approaches to this have been implemented in many environments including ISTAR, Aspect, and the STARS environments.

5.4.4 Summary of Presentation Integration

Presentation integration in a CASE environment can be viewed from a number of perspectives. We have highlighted the service, mechanism, and process aspects that are most commonly found today.

Clearly, there is much more to the user interface aspects of an environment than we have discussed here. The large body of work that the HCI community has produced has direct relevance to the design and implementation of a CASE environment, and many of the ideas, techniques, and tools it has developed are used in this domain.

5.5 Summary

If we intend to actually integrate CASE tools, we need to begin serious consideration of the mechanisms that are available to help us do that. Several such mechanisms are available.

In this chapter we have identified the various classes of mechanisms that support CASE tool integration, but have focused on two broad classes of mechanisms (those supporting data integration and those supporting control integration) that are particularly important to our integration activities. How-

5.5 Summary

ever, we have agreed that the two approaches are employed to varying degrees in any specific integration mechanism. What separates data from control approaches is their different emphasis on particular services and sophistication of the services offered.

Most database systems emphasize the data aspects of integration, and provide extensive support for data storage, retrieval, and update. Synchronization and control of data are typically less well developed. In a message-passing system, the converse is true. Controlled interaction of components is supported through an extensive set of operations. However, support for the data being controlled is much less well defined.

In the subsequent chapters in this section, we discuss the general characteristics of integration mechanisms that have a strong data and control emphasis (Chapters 6 and 7, respectively). In addition, we describe specific mechanisms and discuss their strengths and weaknesses.

CHAPTER 6
Data Integration Mechanisms

6.1 Introduction

Data integration is a basic need for a CASE environment because individual tools operate on data that are of interest to other tools. For example, many CASE analysis and design tools produce code templates representing the interfaces between system components. These templates are of interest to tools that assist in code generation since they specify an interface between system components that ideally is maintained during the implementation process. Likewise, changes made to these interface descriptions during the implementation process often have an impact on the design of the system as reflected in the analysis and design tool.

Many approaches have been developed to facilitate the sharing of data between components of a CASE environment. These approaches differ both in the mechanisms used to provide this support and in the degree of support provided.

In this chapter we consider some concepts central to the problem of data integration, discuss the major strategies adopted to provide data integration, and analyze the strengths and weaknesses of these strategies. Finally, we discuss particular mechanisms that reflect these strategies.

6.2 Key Issues for Data Integration

If environment components are to share data, then two issues must be addressed. First, agreements must be made between components concerning what data are stored, where, and how they are accessed. Second, the components must share a common understanding of the meaning of the data. We refer to the first issue as data persistence, and the second issue as data semantics.

These two issues provide the backdrop for our discussion of the principal types of mechanisms for data integration. One type of mechanism focuses on different storage strategies, and the second type of mechanism focuses on semantic agreements. Although we consider each separately, no mechanism exclusively addresses only data persistence or data semantics. In practice, all mechanisms address both data persistence and data semantics to varying degrees.

6.3 Data Persistence

There are two basic strategies that support storage and sharing of persistent data. The first involves data import and export, whereby tools maintain separate databases for their unique data, and sharing is accomplished by some translation from an internal form to an external form to make it available to other tools. The second involves the use of a common data store, through which all tools access and manipulate data through a common mechanism. Again, while in theory these two strategies represent a clear dichotomy, in practice most practical attempts to provide for data integration incorporate a combination of the approaches.

6.3.1 Import/Export with Separate Databases

The use of an import/export mechanism with separate databases is a direct and often expedient mechanism for sharing data among heterogenous tools and databases. It is especially useful for third-party integrators. This strategy involves the output of data from the database of one tool to make it available to a second tool.

6.3 Data Persistence

Typically, data sharing occurs only in the form of *data extraction* (i.e., export-only); once data are extracted from the first tool's database and manipulated in the second tool, changes to those data are not automatically reflected in the first tool. There is no innate reason why tools cannot interact such that the changed data are automatically exported back to the original tool (i.e., a fully automated import/export strategy). However, such interaction is complex and rarely attempted.

An unfortunate characteristic of export-only strategies is the difficulty of maintaining consistency between related data in the tools. The task is frequently manual, and inconsistencies often develop with even the most careful processes. However, many organizations have found that the problem is tractable when the volume of data or number of tools involved is small, but grows unmanageable with larger volumes of data and numbers of tools.

Tighter and more highly automated import/export style integration between even two tools often requires extensive modification to both tools, since few CASE tools are initially designed with the needs of other tools in mind. Even attempts to consider the needs of other tools may be unsuccessful, since the resulting designs often represent a compromise between the integration requirements of a number of tools, and therefore do not offer ideal integration support for any specific tool.

At the core of all import/export-based integrations is the premise that individual tool databases remain distinct and under control of individual tool vendors. While the degree of integration that can potentially be achieved in this manner is quite high, in practice import/export integrations are often limited by the practical interests of the vendors, who wish to minimize the changes they make to their individual tool.

In spite of these limitations, import/export approaches remain the choice of most CASE tool vendors. Such approaches encompass the least risk for vendors, particularly at a time when common data store technologies are just becoming available. By maintaining control over their own tool database, vendors are avoiding potentially damaging commitments. At the same time, CASE tool vendors are strengthening their import/export linkages with other carefully selected tools. However, such linkages often remain explicitly under the control of the individual vendors.

6.3.2 Common Data Store

The use of a common data store as a mechanism for achieving tool integration represents the main alternative to import/export integration. Common data stores appear in a number of guises, including:

- as a proprietary data store in a tightly integrated toolset from a single vendor,
- as a traditional database used to accumulate data from multiple tools, and
- as a common object base developed explicitly to support the needs of tool integration.

Tightly integrated toolsets (such as compiler-linker-debugger units) from a single vendor often operate on common data structures such as a symbol table. The central data store is often proprietary, and the data format is not readily available to all. In such a case, the specific tools operating on the common data structure are also closely related by their interaction in support of a single software engineering activity (e.g., the edit-compile-debug cycle).

General purpose commercial databases may also be used to facilitate data integration between tools. Commercial databases have been adapted as a repository for the data from different and heterogenous tools. Such integrations share a number of characteristics, including: a focus on a limited and well-defined activity such as document generation or requirements traceability; inclusion of a limited range of tool data (normally that needed to address the specific activity); and a primarily one-way movement of data from the tools to the database (but not back again).

Recently, a number of efforts have been made to develop object management systems (OMSs). As with conventional databases, such systems provide a common repository for tool data. However, their design and implementation are targeted specifically toward the needs of CASE tool integration. Object management systems also often extend the range of functionality in the areas of security and process control, and include explicit support for distribution. The most recent efforts in this area have included explicit support for object-oriented methods and languages.

A number of questions remain to be addressed before such object management systems gain widespread acceptance. Tool vendors have expressed concerns about the general immaturity of object management systems, as well as OMS performance, costs of porting tools, and lack of customer interest in the technology.

Of these questions and problems, it is the state of customer interest that will likely determine whether a particular OMS technology (or in fact OMS technol-

6.3 Data Persistence

ogy in general) becomes a preferred agent of data integration. A recent investigation of integrated tool users suggests that few are currently considering migration toward OMS technology [61]. Rather, it appears that many users are attempting to integrate tools by using the import/export capabilities provided by tool vendors.

6.3.3 Comparison of Import/Export and Common Data Store

The integration characteristics of the import/export approach and the common data store approach are compared in Table 2. The characteristics against which the two approaches are compared represent an amalgamation of those proposed by Thomas and Nejmeh [75] and Brown [7] as desirable for data integration of software engineering tools.

TABLE 2   Comparison of Import/Export and Common Data Store

Data Integration Characteristic	Import/Export Approach	Common Data Store Approach
Interoperability (effort to manipulate data produced by another tool)	Managed to varying degrees by agreements between tool vendors.	Managed by common schema and data interfaces.
Non-Redundancy (degree of data duplication)	Limited to some by the specialization of tools. Some redundancy is tolerated and managed by import/export of relevant data items.	Minimize redundancy through careful schema design.
Data Consistency (maintenance of semantic constraints)	Data are guaranteed consistent only at the point of import/export. Automatic update only in limited situations.	A single copy of the data assures data consistency.
Data Exchange (of non-persistent data)	No implicit approach.	No implicit approach.
Synchronization (communication of changes to non-persistent data)	No implicit approach.	No implicit approach.

Data Integration Characteristic	Import/Export Approach	Common Data Store Approach
Extensibility and Flexibility (support for changes)	Published data interfaces and event definitions.	Schema modifications and multiple views.
Security (restricting of access)	Security on a per-tool basis.	Security via a centralized policy and mechanism.
Concurrency (support for multiple users)	Concurrency is on a per-tool basis. Discrepancies between tools are reconciled by import/export of data	Provided by pessimistic locking of data items in the common data store to prevent concurrent access.
Transaction Integrity (maintaining consistent state in the data in the event of failure of a particular action)	Transactions between tools are often user-initiated and last only for the import/export process. Verification that the transaction occurred as expected is mostly a manual process.	Transaction logging with rollback.
Configuration Management (support for multiple versions and configurations of data objects)	Configuration management is commonly provided on a per-tool basis.	Configuration management is centralized and provides for configurations of data across tools.

Some general conclusions can be drawn from this table:

- Both the import/export approach and the common data store approach require a set of common conventions shared by the involved parties. In the case of the import/export approach, these conventions are often ad hoc, and are shared by only a few tool vendors. Thus, there may be a tendency for proliferation of different conventions and integration approaches. Common conventions between a few tools are relatively easy to identify and accept, however. In the case of the common data store approach, the conventions tend to be more comprehensive, cover a wider range of potential data integrations, and are open for wider participation by many CASE tool vendors.

However, agreements on these conventions are harder to reach since the needs of a much larger tool vendor (and user) community must be met.
- Since the identification of wide-ranging conventions is so difficult, tool vendors may limit efforts to import/export integrations with tools supporting common and well-understood activities. Motivation to create more wide-ranging, process-specific integrations is likely to come from a third-party user or integrator, since such integrations will likely entail the use of a collection of tools with a range of relationships (both loosely and tightly related) for a more variable set of processes.
- Import/export style integrations are potentially troublesome for large-scale software engineering activities, since large projects have a particular need for centrally managed security, concurrency, transaction integrity, and configuration management. These concerns tend to be supported more by the common data store approaches.
- For the management of non-persistent data (data exchange and data synchronization), neither approach adequately addresses the problem. The management of non-persistent data is closely related to the area of control integration, and therefore points to the need for a tight relationship between these integration approaches.
- Most importantly, there is no general answer as to which approach is better. That will depend on the tools and integration technology available, as well as on the needs of the organization. Wasserman recognized the importance of the relationship of the tools to the software process needs of the organization, and termed it process integration [77]. Thomas and Nejmeh extend Wasserman's analysis and identify dimensions of process integration [74]. Carney and Brown discuss this issue, and provide a mechanism for determining the appropriate integration based on a specific process defined in terms of a usage scenario [9].

6.4 Semantic Mechanisms for Data Integration

Semantic mechanisms for data integration are generally involved with recording information about the data shared among tools. One general type of semantic mechanism focuses on recording high-level information about the relationships among data. Shared schemata and information models represent two examples of this approach. A slightly different type of semantic mechanism addresses lower-level notions, particularly data formats.

6.4.1 Common Schemata

Data are often stored according to a structuring mechanism known as a schema. Typically, a schema identifies the types of objects (or items) represented within the data, some characteristics of those objects, and the types of relationships between objects. Information about object and relationship types is commonly represented without regard for the actual physical location of the data; a schema can be used to represent relationships among data stored in a single physical database or distributed across multiple databases. Therefore, a schema can be a useful mechanism to identify data types and relationships regardless of whether the data are to be stored in a common object store or distributed across multiple tool databases.

In many systems, the schema is also used to determine the manner in which an object can be accessed. One typical approach involves the following of "links" (often relationships). Depending on the particular paradigm supported, a schema may also maintain information concerning operations on the object.

Since a schema provides a means for a tool both to structure and to access data, it follows that sharing a schema across several tools is a means to integrate them at the semantic level (i.e., regardless of whether they use an import/export or a common data storage strategy). Such shared schemata are often referred to as "information models," since they focus on the meaning of the data to be shared.

Unfortunately, the development of common schemata that meet the needs of a wide range of tools has not been easy. To develop a common schema, tool vendors (and users) must first agree on the basic paradigm to be used; common paradigms include relational, entity-relationship, and object-oriented. Potentially, the closer the chosen paradigm is to that supported by an individual tool, the less work involved in modifying that tool to support the common schema. Thus, tool vendors are motivated to support their own particular paradigm.

In addition, tool vendors intending to identify a shared schema must agree on the type and granularity of data to be represented in the schema. If primarily coarse-grained (large and complex) data are represented, the data needed by a specific tool may not be available in a readily accessible format; additional processing (parsing) of the data may be required to extract the relevant information. However, tool vendors often prefer this approach since it commonly requires fewer modifications to the tool that primarily creates and manages the data. On the other hand, if fine-grained data (data approaching the smallest meaningful unit) are represented in the schema, additional burdens may be placed on tool vendors to comply with the common schema, as well as on tools using the data, which may be forced to reassemble fine-grained units into more complex units.

6.4 Semantic Mechanisms for Data Integration

When tool vendors accept a common schema, they also must relinquish some degree of freedom to modify the data structure used by their particular tool, since any changes to structure potentially affect other tools that use that data. Agreements must be reached concerning who can change the schema and when and how it can be changed. Since many tool vendors view their unique schema and data as a primary commercial advantage over their competitors, they are not always willing to give up control of schema changes.

6.4.2 Common Data Formats

A somewhat different semantic mechanism is seen in the use of common data formats for integration. Common data formats can represent either a consensual agreement to store all data in the specified format at all times, or to extract a subset of the data and make it available (in the common format) at specific times. In both cases, the focus of the mechanism is less on the *meaning* of the data to a human observer and more on the conveying of semantic information based on the structure of the data.

For instance, two tools that share a common data format in the form of a common file structure will (by definition) be able to parse each other's files due to the known structure of the data. Frequently, the common structure will maintain clues to the semantic content of the data, for example, by identifying a specific piece of data by position within the data file. However, identifying the location and semantic value of a particular piece of data often requires parsing of the data file, leading to an adverse impact on performance.

In practice, the complexity of the semantic information that can be transferred by using common data formats is quite high. However, in developing a common format, tool vendors must balance the quality and quantity of the semantic information that can be represented against the ease of translating to and from the common format (particularly if it differs from the tool's internal format). Put simply, interpreting the encoded semantic information becomes increasingly difficult as a format becomes increasingly complex.

As with the common schema approach, control of the evolution of the common data format can be a particularly difficult problem. If the common data format is controlled by a third party such as a standards organization, the format will likely represent a compromise between the positions of many vendors. Subsequent updates to the format will likely require additional compromises, and therefore may be slow in coming and provide only minimal enhancements to functionality. On the other hand, if the common data format is proprietary (even if the format is published), changes may occur at a rate that taxes the resources of the user, particularly if the user has performed additional integrations based on the common format.

6.4.3 Summary

In spite of approaching the problem of sharing semantics of data from different directions, both common schemata and common data formats may ultimately require parsing of data by tools to extract semantic information However, the two approaches tend to focus on different dimensions: schemata focus on the meaning of data (up) toward human intelligibility, and formats tend to focus on the meaning of data (down) toward machine readability.

6.5 Other Factors for Data Integration

Before examining some examples of actual data integration mechanisms, we note two other issues: characteristics of the data that are to be stored and integrated, and the influence of process constraints over the choice of integrating mechanisms.

6.5.1 Characteristics of Software Engineering Data

Most commercially available databases have been developed specifically with the needs of applications such as banking and personnel management in mind. As a result, these databases have been tailored to be highly efficient for these and similar management information system (MIS) applications. However, Bernstein [3] and Masurka [47] have concluded that CASE environment needs dictate that new approaches to data management are required. A summary of the different needs of commercial database and software engineering database support is provided in Table 3.

Because of these differing characteristics, interest in alternative database approaches, such as object-oriented and entity-relationship database management systems is particularly strong in the software engineering and CASE environments communities.

6.5 Other Factors for Data Integration

TABLE 3 Comparison of Commercial and Software Engineering Databases (derived from Brown [7])

Commercial Database	Software Engineering Database
Relatively static schema which can be determined a priori	Continuously evolving schema including data about the environment itself.
Fixed length data items	Variable length data items
Small number of entity types with a large number of instances of each type	Large number of entity types with fewer instances.
Single values for data items	Multiple versions of data items with dependencies and relationships between versions recorded.
Many short transactions that can be used as the basis for data locking to prevent concurrent access	Long transactions that cannot be conveniently used for data locking.

6.5.2 Process Constraints on Data Integration Mechanisms

Knowledge of the data, even specific domain knowledge about the data, may still be insufficient when considering integrating mechanisms. It is also necessary to determine whether the integrating mechanisms are appropriate for the specific process needs of the organization. Some process needs are likely to affect the mechanisms chosen in terms of both the supported methodologies and the granularity of the data to be integrated.

As an example, large software projects place additional demands on tools and tool data. The long duration, large staff, and iterative nature of large software projects require that tools and tool integration address additional requirements, including:

- Extensibility and flexibility, so that tools from various vendors can be added and deleted from the integrated toolset. This requirement is necessitated by the long duration of large software projects, as well as by the long life of the resulting systems that rely on the toolset.
- Security mechanisms that limit the damage from careless and unauthorized manipulation of tool data.

- Concurrency control, so that multiple users of tool data are provided timely access, but prevented from damaging the data or invalidating the work of others. Concurrency control for data is particularly important and difficult as the degree of data interoperability and exchange increases.
- Transaction integrity, which allows operations on data shared between tools to be committed or rolled back as a single unit. For integrated tools maintaining a high degree of data consistency and exchange, maintaining transaction integrity requires tight cooperation in committing and rolling back transactions.
- Common configuration management, which requires that versions of the data from individual tools be grouped into configurations of related data.

In summary, data integration occurs using some specific mechanism, among several tools, and in the context of some process. It can best be considered a design activity that weighs all of these factors in choosing a data integration mechanism.

6.6 Examples of Actual Integration Mechanisms

Within the last few years, the number and range of mechanisms designed to support data integration in a CASE environment have grown rapidly. A few of these mechanisms have been standardized by assorted international organizations. Other mechanisms represent the proprietary efforts of tool vendors to support integration of their tool with others. As suggested previously, these mechanisms do not represent a pure implementation of a common data store or import/export approach to data integration. Rather, they are characterized by the emphasis the approach places on centralized versus decentralized (import/export) data control. Subsequent sections of this chapter present a sample of these data integration approaches.

6.6.1 Common Data Store: The Portable Common Tool Environment (ECMA PCTE)

ECMA PCTE is an interface specification of facilities that can be used by software tools.[1] It was standardized by the European Computer Manufacturers

---

[1] The facilities of ECMA PCTE go beyond those necessary for data management alone, and include capabilities for process control, security, network management, auditing, and accounting. PCTE attempts to provide an integrated (though not necessarily complete) set of environment services in these areas. This chapter focuses particularly on the data management capabilities of PCTE. A general overview of PCTE can be found in Long [45].

6.6 Examples of Actual Integration Mechanisms

Association [59], and has been submitted to the International Standards Organization (ISO). It exists as an abstract specification, using formalized English and some formal notation, and also in language bindings (to C and Ada, at present, with a C++ binding being developed). No full implementation of the ECMA specification is yet available, though implementations of earlier versions of the specification, particularly a version known as PCTE 1.5, have existed as products for several years. In the following discussion, "PCTE" refers to the ECMA standard unless otherwise noted.

PCTE facilities are designed to enable tools to store data, and to retrieve and manipulate that data. The PCTE data management system is called the *object management system* (OMS) and is of the entity-relationship-attribute type.

Basic data items in PCTE are called *objects*. An object may, but need not, have *contents*. An object's contents can be thought of as corresponding to a file in a traditional operating system. PCTE provides facilities to read and write object contents. An object may have *attributes* attached to it. These are pieces of information associated with the object. There are facilities to set, read, and modify attributes on objects. PCTE distinguishes between *primitive objects* and *composite objects*. A primitive object has no components whereas a composite object is a collection of primitive objects and other composite objects. *Version control* operations for both primitive and composite objects are built into the system.

PCTE's OMS also allows *links* from one object to another. Thus, an arbitrary network of linked objects may be built up. Links may also carry attributes. Facilities are provided to create and delete links and to traverse links. This latter facility allows users and tools to navigate within the network of linked objects and, hence, to access objects in the OMS.

Objects, links, and attributes have a type associated with them. The type model can be used to ensure the integrity of certain data in the database. For example, the typing structure can prohibit a document object from being written to by an object representing test data.

Object, link, and attribute types are defined and managed in *schema definition sets* (SDSs) (which are themselves stored in the OMS), and the type model is represented by objects and links in the OMS. An object type may inherit properties from several other object types. Inheritance is not a characteristic of link and attribute types. An SDS usually contains a collection of related type definitions associated with some tool or use of the OMS. PCTE provides facilities for adding, removing, and modifying SDSs.

A running program in PCTE always has associated with it a *working schema*. A working schema is a composition of SDSs. A process can access only those objects, links, and attributes whose types are defined in SDSs included in its working schema. This working schema mechanism controls the visibility of the process into the database at a given time, thereby aiding security and access control. However, an executing tool may reconfigure the working schema by adding or removing SDSs.

Tools may be integrated into PCTE using one of three strategies:

- Foreign tool encapsulation.
- File-level integration.
- Structured integration.

Foreign tool encapsulation. This strategy allows data exchange or communication of PCTE tools with other tools running on the native operating system. Encapsulation most often involves transferring data from a non-PCTE tool into the PCTE OMS and back again (Figure 16). Using this approach, tool data are represented as the contents of a PCTE file object. The PCTE object may be versioned and linked to other objects in the object base in the standard manner. To use the tool, the contents of the PCTE object are copied to the file system. At the end of tool processing, the tool data are replaced in the repository, potentially as a new version.

FIGURE 16 Foreign Tool Encapsulation.

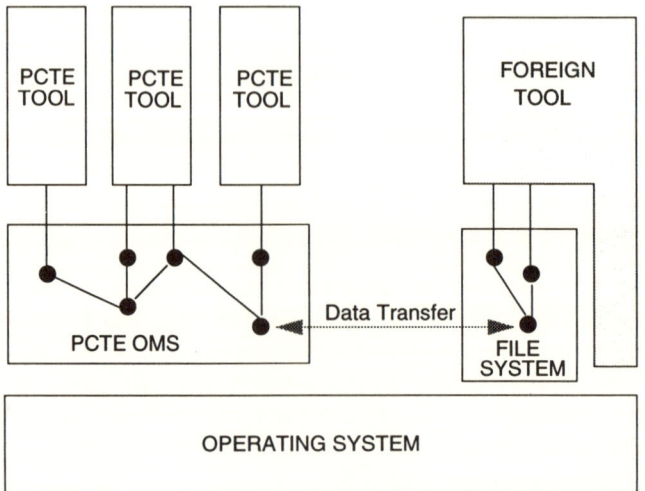

6.6 Examples of Actual Integration Mechanisms

File-level integration. Tools integrated into PCTE at the file level use the contents of PCTE objects exactly as they would use files in a conventional operating system. The functionality of the tool is not decomposed, and the process structure of the tool is not altered (Figure 17).

File-level integration allows the tool's data to be stored in the OMS where they can be explicitly linked to other related data. For example, a documentation tool could be integrated in this way, and documentation produced by it could be explicitly linked to the source code to which it relates. Tools such as browsers and document generators can be developed to follow links to related objects.

It is comparatively easy to implement or port a tool to PCTE in this way. Most of the concepts of PCTE do not need to be understood by the person doing the implementation or porting and, essentially, all that is needed is to replace traditional file input/output by object contents input/output.

FIGURE 17 File-Level Integration.

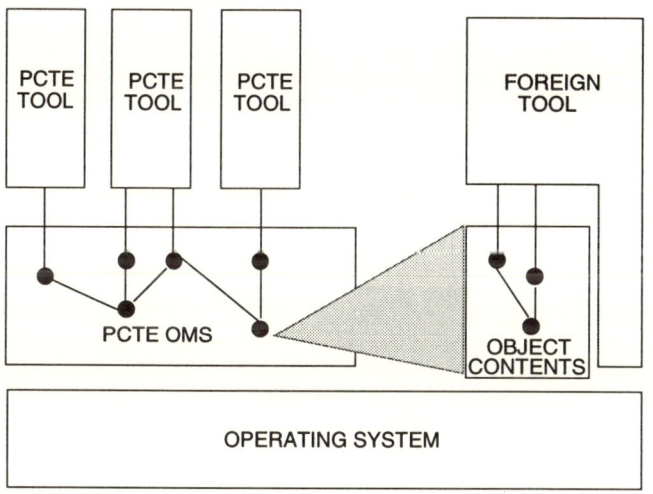

Structured integration. For structured integration with PCTE, the data and process structure of a tool are represented in the OMS (Figure 18). For example, the internal structure of a document or piece of code could be represented in the OMS by having separate paragraphs or procedures stored as the contents of separate objects, and relationships between components explicitly represented through the object typing and inter-object links. This means that other tools (for example, browsers) have direct access to this structure without having to parse an entire document or program.

An important consideration for structured integration is the granularity of the data to be represented in the contents of PCTE objects. In some applications, the designer may want to explicitly represent data structures down to a very fine level where each object is only a few bytes in size. In such cases, it can be expected that there would be frequent accesses to the database to retrieve and update these "fine-grained" objects. However, there is some debate as to whether the overhead associated with access to a PCTE object effectively precludes representing objects requiring many accesses per second.

In any case, for structured integration with PCTE, a tool will have to be written from scratch or extensively revised from a traditional operating system-based tool. Such a transition would require a major (re-)engineering effort.

FIGURE 18 Structured Integration.

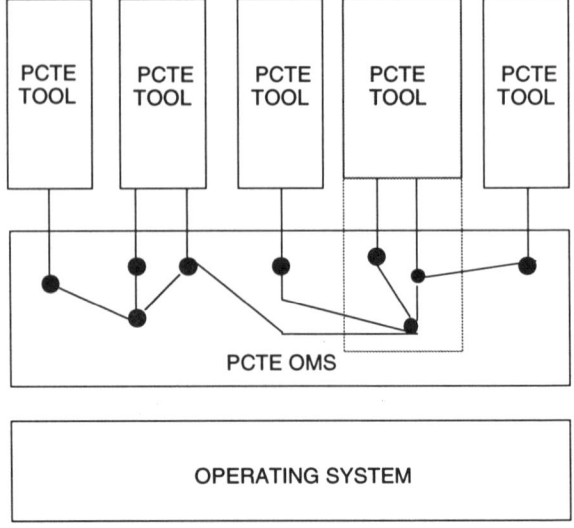

6.6.2 Common Data Store: A Tool Integration Standard (ATIS)

ATIS (A Tool Integration Standard) is a tool interface approach that forms a baseline for a number of activities aimed at providing a set of standard interfaces for aspects of CASE tool integration. The original approach leading to the

6.6 Examples of Actual Integration Mechanisms

ATIS specification was developed by Atherton Technology and subsequently modified by Atherton and other industry parties [17]. Implementations of ATIS variants are available from Digital and Atherton. In addition, the ANSI committees X3H4 and X3H6 are considering parts of the ATIS technology as a baseline for standardization.

ATIS is based on an object-oriented data model. The model identifies *object classes*, which are abstract data types related to each other to form a hierarchy. New object classes *inherit* the properties and behavior of the super-type.

The basic data item of the model is an *object*, which is a specific instance of an object class. Objects have a state, which is indicated by the value of the attributes of the object.

Objects also incorporate a set of behaviors that are appropriate to the object class. The set of behaviors for an object are defined by its *methods*. Methods can have *preambles* and *postambles*, which are themselves methods. When a method is invoked, its preamble is invoked prior to the execution of the method, and the postamble is invoked subsequent to the execution of the method.

To communicate with an object, a *message* is dispatched to the object. Each object understands a specific set of messages that is mapped to its methods. An object can accept or reject a message; if it accepts a message, it invokes the correct method to satisfy the request.

As with PCTE, ATIS provides support for versioning, configuration management, and access control of data.

Two types of tool integration are identified in the ATIS documentation [1]:
- Encapsulation.
- Porting.

Encapsulation. Encapsulation with ATIS is similar to foreign tool encapsulation with PCTE. No source-code changes are made to the tool. The tool's data are not decomposed into ATIS objects. However, objects derived from the existing ATIS types may be used to store the data artifacts generated by the tool.

In encapsulation, the data of the tool are not directly managed by the ATIS repository. Rather, tool data are stored in the repository and exported and re-imported prior to and after tool use. Commonly, a wrapper is built around the tool to automate the import and export process.

Users of encapsulated tools benefit from the version control capabilities provided by ATIS. Since the (imported) tool data are stored in the repository, multiple versions can be maintained via ATIS versioning capabilities.

Porting. For porting, the source code of the tool is modified to make full use of ATIS services to create and modify objects, as well as to perform a range of other activities. Porting can be accomplished at a variety of levels, depending on the depth of the integration desired.

For deep integration with ATIS, the data structure of the tool can be decomposed into objects of appropriate granularity for integration needs. In addition, the process structure of the tool can be modified such that individual routines are called when a method is invoked.

Full integration often requires that new object types, methods, and messages be created as appropriate for the tool's data and operations. An object of the appropriate type is created for the tool, allowing the ATIS-based system to invoke the tool as a result of a message. The tool is invoked by the ATIS system, and its data input and output files are managed by the system.

6.6.3 Common Schema: The Information Resource Dictionary System (IRDS)

The Information Resource Dictionary System (IRDS) is a data dictionary standard that is intended to support consistent (across tools and systems) entity-relationship-attribute modeling for "real-world" concepts and data such as persons, events, or quantities [71]. IRDS does not represent the actual value of the data, nor does it dictate an implementation approach within a database system. Rather, it is intended to provide a consistent format for describing the structure and relationships of data within the database system. For this reason, IRDS is sometimes discussed as a standard for specifying "meta-data."

By defining a consistent format for meta-data, IRDS is intended to:

- improve identification of information resources that could be shared within and across organizations,
- reduce unnecessary application development in situations where other suitable applications already exist,
- simplify conversion efforts by providing consistent documentation, and
- increase portability of skills resulting in decreased training costs.

The IRDS standard defines a four-level data architecture containing:

6.6 Examples of Actual Integration Mechanisms

- an IRD schema description layer, which identifies the meta-data types for entities, relationships, and attributes,
- the IRD schema layer, which defines basic entity, relationship, and attribute types (e.g., the entity-type "user," the relationship-type "record-contains-element," and the attribute-type "length"),
- the IRD data layer, which identifies instances of the types defined in the schema (e.g., "Finance Department" and "Personnel Department" are instances of the entity type "user"), and
- the actual data in the production database (e.g., "0131" represents a specific department). The IRDS specification provides no functionality at this level, but rather includes it in the IRDS data architecture to provide context.

While IRDS provides no interfaces for access to the tool data in a system (since it is not a database system and is not intended to store tool data), it does provide interfaces to build an IRD schema specifying the structure and relationships within tool data. IRDS also provides interfaces to support the importing/exporting of IRDs (note this does not involve the transporting of data between, for example, individual tools, but rather the transporting of a *description* of the data).

Recently work has begun by an ANSI committee on the evolution of IRDS toward object orientation. The evolution of IRDS is also being discussed in ISO committee. One key (and unresolved) issue is whether a new IRDS will maintain an almost exclusive focus on meta-data, or whether the parameters of the standard will be redrawn to include a focus on actual tool data.

6.6.4 Common Schema: The IBM Information Model

The IBM Information Model is a component of an IBM product called the Repository Manager, which originally was conceived as part of the AD/Cycle strategy for mainframe-based development environments. The Information Model works in conjunction with the Repository Manager Model (providing basic capabilities from which to build up the Information Model) and the Business Model (developed by the end-user from the capabilities provided by the Information Model) to provide a customized model for an organization.

The Information Model is based on the entity-relationship paradigm and is intended to support application development, particularly in the domain of information systems. The model was developed by IBM in conjunction with CASE tool vendor partners and is intended to be extendable by third-party vendors.

The model is divided into submodels that address particular classes of information system objects. The submodels are themselves composed of primitives that are relevant to the particular class of objects being represented. Submodels include the Enterprise model, which provides a conceptual view of an organization's business, and the Technical model, which embodies a physical view of this same information, providing technical details about databases and files.

Together, the two submodels are intended to represent five major types of information:

- high-level planning information, such as goals and critical factors,
- high-level data structure information, identifying major entities and attributes,
- high-level process information specifying the organization's activities,
- low-level data and program information, providing information about data constructs, source modules, and other low-level development data, and
- project management information such as estimates of effort, project activities, and project tracking information.

In response to the decline in interest in mainframe computing and the rise of distributed, network based development environments, IBM has announced the migration of the AD/Cycle approach to workstation-based computing environments. This new strategy is termed AD/Platform. It is unclear what (if any) changes will be made to the Information Model with this change in strategy.

6.6.5 Common Data Formats: The CASE Data Interchange Format (EIA CDIF)

EIA CDIF represents an effort of the Electronics Industry Association (EIA) to define the specific formats for data that are transferred between CASE tools [55]. Such transfers can entail exchange of information regarding both the presentation of the data and the semantics associated with the data.

The use of EIA CDIF as a common format for data transfer between tools is intended to eliminate the need for custom data transfer formats and to replace them with a single, common format. The underlying assumption is that tool databases remain distinct, and the tools import/export data using a common format.

EIA CDIF provides models for the transfer of both presentation and semantic information. The EIA CDIF presentation model defines a standard means for representing the graphical diagrams associated with case tools. The "starter" set of concepts provided by the interim standard is useful for representing data for

6.6 Examples of Actual Integration Mechanisms

the common "node and edges" style graph. The semantic model provided by the interim standard is limited, but provides the necessary capabilities to model and transfer the semantic meaning of data for common data flow and entity-relationship formats, along with objects and data structures.

The EIA CDIF technical committee has also defined a framework that identifies four levels of compliance with the EIA CDIF standard. The capabilities at each level are defined as follows:

- Level 1, in which a tool can parse EIA CDIF-compliant data files, and the tool's output files are themselves EIA CDIF compliant and therefore can be parsed by other EIA CDIF-compliant tools. In simple terms, the tool does not reject EIA CDIF syntax and encoding, but cannot necessarily use data in this format.
- Level 2, in which the tool's output file can be made equivalent to the input file of another tool after transforms and deletions to the input data are performed. All transforms and deletions must be documented. This means that if a tool cannot directly use information from the input file, it will either discard the information, or transform it into a usable form.
- Level 3, in which the tool's output file is equivalent to the input file of another tool after deletions. Transformation of data does not occur.
- Level 4, in which the receiving tool "understands" and retains all EIA CDIF semantic and presentation information, and can reproduce it completely in its output file.

Although EIA CDIF is a mechanism to support import/export style data integration, interest in EIA CDIF has also been generated among parties interested in a common persistent data store approach. EIA CDIF is being discussed within this community as a mechanism for transferring data between different implementations of data repositories (e.g., between two different implementations of PCTE-compliant data repositories).

6.6.6 Import/Export: An Example from Current Practice

An approach to data integration favored by many vendors involves providing capabilities within a tool to export data in a format directly usable by another tool. Often these formats are proprietary (though documented) so that each additional integration requires generation of information in a different format.

As an example of this approach, we briefly examine an integration strategy used by a commercial tool vendor. Cadre Technologies, the supplier of the Teamwork analysis and design tool, has worked with a number of providers of document publishing systems to automate portions of the document generation process.

Interfaces are available between Teamwork and a number of document publishing systems including Interleaf, Frame, Scribe, and VAX Document.

The Teamwork document interface capability, called Teamwork/DPI (for Teamwork/Document Production Interface) includes templates for the common Data Item Descriptions (DIDs) for the DoD standard documentation process (DoD-STD-2167A). Using the provided templates, the Teamwork/DPI user specifies the structure of the document to be generated by defining Teamwork structure charts identifying the relevant information. This activity is accomplished directly from the Teamwork user interface.

Once the structure of the desired document is defined, the user initiates the actual generation of the document, again from the Teamwork user interface. The Teamwork/DPI capability, using the template fleshed out by the user, accesses the Teamwork database to extract the desired information (both pictorial and textual) and to output it in a format amenable to the documentation tool selected. This activity in itself is a strong example of the export of data in a format that facilitates eventual import into the partner tool.

On the document side of the integration, the Teamwork-generated document is indistinguishable from other documents. The user can edit the generated document with the facilities of the documentation system.

Unfortunately, changes to pictures and text made within the documentation system are not necessarily reflected back in the Teamwork model that serves as the source of the information, since there is no automatically created "backward" link. Necessary changes to the document that have an impact on information in the Teamwork model must be made through Teamwork rather than through the documentation system, if consistency between the model and document is to be maintained.

However, a "live" or "active" link capability does exist within some documentation systems that allows information in the generated document to be connected back to the source (in this case a Teamwork model). These live or active links are primarily a control integration mechanism, but do provide a degree of data integration by combining data interchange standards and conventions with remote procedure calls to allow the displaying and editing of "linked" objects in the document [76]. Unfortunately, such links are created on an individual and manual basis.

While such "linking" provides a useful degree of data integration, it suffers from a number of deficiencies in practice. A primary problem arises because of the nature of the generated (primarily DoD-STD-2167A) documents, in which the same information may appear in many different places and formats. Therefore, each specific instance of information generated for a documentation tool by the analysis and design tool may require multiple links within the documentation tool. Even if a single edit operation in the documentation tool causes an active invocation of the analysis and design tool, any changes will not be automatically reflected in all parts of the document. As a result, the only way to insure consistency of the document is to modify the source model and regenerate the document. However, Teamwork does possess a comparison capability to allow the user to identify and mark differences between two versions of a document produced with Teamwork/DPI.

Secondary problems include the cognitive dissonance that may result from the use of two distinct and different user interfaces (Teamwork and the documentation system), as well as the potential for problems with versioning and configuration management of the original model and resulting document.

In spite of these problems, this and similar approaches represent the most practical alternative for both users and tool vendors. For users, time and effort saved in the generation of documents can be substantial, although setting up the tool(s) to generate acceptable documents can be difficult and time-consuming [61]. For vendors, such point-to-point attempts at integration may represent a less risky (although expensive) alternative until some form of alternative data integration strategy (such as a common data store) gains favor in the software engineering community.

6.7 Summary

In this chapter, major strategies for supporting data integration have been identified. These strategies include a common data store, import/export of data between tools, a common schema, and common data formats. In addition, a number of mechanisms reflecting these strategies have been discussed, including ECMA PCTE, ATIS, the IBM Information Model, IRDS, CDIF, and an example from current practice.

Although each of these strategies and mechanisms has been discussed independently, in practice no single mechanism or strategy will solve all data integration problems. The various strategies and mechanisms can work in concert to provide greater flexibility and integration than would be possible with any one alone. For example, although we classify PCTE as a common data store using a common schema, an import/export mechanism with common data format would be useful to transfer data between individual PCTE-compliant implementations. In fact, CDIF has been mentioned within the PCTE community as providing these capabilities. As an additional example, while we place IRDS in the category of a common schema, it is clearly useful in supporting data modeling for both common data stores and for individual tools using the import/export approach.

While it is possible that specific mechanisms will fall out of favor and be replaced by other more sophisticated mechanisms, it is likely that the basic strategies of common data storage, common data formats, common schemas, and import/export of data will be maintained. It is likely that future mechanisms (like current mechanisms) will be understandable when viewed from the perspective provided by these basic strategies.

CHAPTER 7
Control Integration Mechanisms

7.1 Introduction

Controlling and coordinating tool interactions in a CASE environment require an approach to tool integration that is sufficiently flexible and adaptable to suit different user needs, as well as simple and efficient. These conditions will ensure that new tools can easily be integrated and that their productivity is not significantly impaired. As discussed in the previous chapter, one traditional approach toward tool integration has been based on data sharing, often through a common database in which all tools deposit their data. While this approach can provide a high level of control and coordination between tools, it also imposes a significant overhead on the tools, both because of poor performance of existing database mechanisms when used in this way, and because of the necessary agreement required between the tools to define a common syntax and semantics for their data (e.g., a common data schema).

Another approach to integration has been called *the control integration approach*. This approach is based on viewing a CASE environment as a collection of services provided by different tools. Actions carried out by a tool are announced to other tools via control signals. The tools receiving such signals can decide if the other tool's actions require that they take any actions themselves. For example, when an editing tool announces that changes have been made to a source file, a build tool may receive this information and initiate a new system build. In addition, one tool may directly request that another tool perform an action by sending it a control signal. For example, the build tool may request that the source file be compiled by a particular compiler. Hence, the primary means of coordination between tools is through the sending and receiving of control signals.

In the rest of this chapter, we examine the notion of control integration in a CASE environment, review a number of existing systems, and analyze those systems to identify their differences and to reveal interesting future directions for this work.

The reviewed systems do not represent an exhaustive examination of systems implementing a control integration approach. Rather, they are illustrative of the range of sophistication of such systems.

The chapter is organized as follows. Section 7.2 introduces the concept of control integration. Section 7.3 describes a control integration technique employed by a number of CASE environments known as the message passing approach. Four such environments — FIELD, SoftBench, ToolTalk, and CORBA — are reviewed in Section 7.4 and analyzed in Section 7.5. The chapter concludes with a summary in Section 7.6.

7.2 Integration in a CASE Environment

The previous chapter described in detail a number of approaches to CASE tool integration based on shared data. There are clear advantages to these approaches in terms of their central control of all operational data, allowing tools to share information in an unambiguous, well-defined way. However, there are also problems associated with shared data approaches:

- A definition of the common data stores and schemas must often be agreed to a priori. This requires the development of an understanding of both the structures and the semantics of those structures as they will be produced or used by all tools to be integrated. Difficult as this is, it is made considerably worse when, at some time in the future, a new tool needs to be integrated. For exist-

7.2 Integration in a CASE Environment

ing tools not to be affected, only consistency-preserving additions to the common data definitions are permitted.

- A common data store is often a large, complex resource that must be controlled, managed, and maintained. This can occupy a great deal of time, money, and effort on behalf of the organization using the CASE environment.
- To support a large common data store, a complex software system will typically be required. This will add to the cost and complexity of the CASE environment itself and have an impact on overall system performance. In some documented cases, this overhead has been far from negligible, and has significantly impaired the usability of the CASE environment.
- It is difficult to reach an agreement on a common data format that provides for tight integration of data yet supports the needs of many tools.

These factors have lead to the development of much simpler, less demanding approaches to tool integration. While these simpler approaches may reduce the level of support, the corresponding costs involved in introducing, using, and maintaining the CASE environment are also reduced.

One approach that is of particular interest is based on a control integration approach. In this approach, rather than communication among tools primarily taking place via shared data structures, tools interact more directly by requesting services of each other. When one tool requires some action to be taken, it can request that another tool perform that action, rather than directly implementing (and possibly duplicating) that functionality itself. Implementing this approach results in a CASE environment architecture in which tools can be viewed as collections of services. Each tool performs a small, well-defined set of functions, and provides access to its services through a programmatic interface. One way to visualize the control integration approach, as illustrated in Figure 19, is as tools communicating via messages.

FIGURE 19 Integration Through Message Passing.

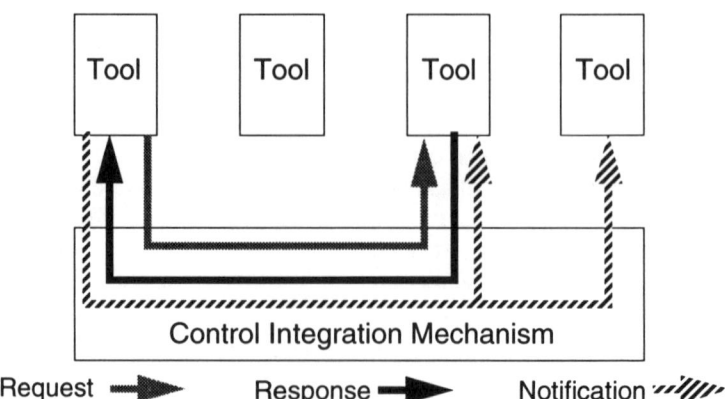

We now look in more detail at the control integration paradigm by describing an architectural approach to a CASE environment based on message passing.

7.3 The Message Passing Approach

In the message passing approach, tools in a CASE environment communicate by passing messages informing other tools of their actions and requesting services from the other tools. For meaningful communication to take place among the tools, appropriate mechanisms need to be in place to allow the communication, and an agreed-upon protocol must be established among the tools to ensure that messages are sent at the necessary times and that their meaning can be interpreted upon receipt.

The mechanistic aspects of the architecture are provided by a *message server* or *message broker*, which is responsible for distributing all messages among tools. The message may contain some indication of which tool, or set of tools, should receive the message, and may define a scope (e.g., local host) for which the message is applicable. Typically, however, the message server has no knowledge of the semantics of any message.

If, however, the approach is to be effective, tools must agree on both the syntax and semantics of the messages they send to each other. The messages themselves generally have a very simple format — each message contains sufficient information to identify the sender, recipient, and the operation being requested (with any necessary parameters such as the names of the files that are being

7.3 The Message Passing Approach

manipulated). Semantic agreements among tools may be very simple (e.g., agreeing to inform each other whenever they start or stop execution), or very complex (e.g., agreeing to a large number of fine-grained events). For example, between a configuration management (CM) tool and a design tool, the syntax and semantics of a version check-in operation, or event, may be agreed to allow the design tool to issue such an operation at the end of each design session and for the CM tool to respond in the appropriate manner. Achieving these syntactic and semantic agreements among tools is essential for meaningful communication.

An important point to emphasize in this process is that the tools that are sending messages essentially broadcast them to all tools by sending them to the message server. The tools do not need to know which other tools are currently running to send messages, and hence are unaffected by changes to executing tools in the environment. It is the responsibility of the message server to selectively forward messages to appropriate tools (a process that is sometimes called *selective broadcast* or *multicast*) and to initiate execution of a tool to handle the current message if necessary.

7.3.1 Inserting a Tool into a Message Passing Architecture

Inserting a tool into a message passing architecture typically involves the following actions:

- Conversion of a subset of the input to, and output from, a tool into message responses and requests. Message *events* must be defined that initiate some part of the tool's functionality upon receipt of a particular message, and messages must be transmitted when the tool performs a particular action or reaches a particular state.
- While not central to the message passing approach, modification of the tool's user interface can also be applied to provide a common "look and feel" for all the tools in an environment. To aid the visual consistency and ease of use of the tool, a window-based interface with buttons and menus can be constructed.

In fact, we can distinguish at least three levels of integration of a tool into a message passing architecture, each with different costs and potential benefits:

- *Basic level.* Tools provide a minimum set of messages. This may simply be the messages to indicate that the tool has started and stopped, and to allow the status (e.g., active or inactive) of a tool to be queried. This level can typically be accomplished without modifying the source code of the tool via some form of tool wrapper or envelope.

- *Functional level.* Tools provide a message interface to access some parts of their functionality. Each tool vendor decides which services implemented by the tool can be accessed via the message interface. Some changes to the tool's source code will be required to implement the interface.
- *Standardized level.* Tools support a standardized set of messages. This implies that tool vendors agree on such a set of messages and the semantics of each message. The environment users then have a measure of independence from individual tool differences for particular classes of tools.

The remaining task is to write the application routines that dictate the connections and sequencing of events that model a particular development scenario. For example, part of a typical software development scenario could be that the action of quitting from the source code editor initiates the following events:

- A CM tool is called to record the saved source code as the latest version of the software.
- A metrics tool is invoked to collect and store information about the new source code module.
- A new object module is generated from the source code by invoking the compiler.

The application routines necessary to implement such a scenario would initiate events, test the values returned in response to those events, set up the appropriate control structures, and so on.

7.3.2 Comparison of Message Passing with Point-to-Point Tool Connection

The most prevalent way in which tools are currently interconnected is via direct point-to-point connection between the tools — one tool makes direct calls to the interface(s) of another tool. Where access to the source code of the tools exists (e.g., when the tool vendors themselves implement the integration), the tools are often amended to use those interfaces. Otherwise, some translation and filtering routines may be used to implement the integration.

In both cases, the disadvantage of the point-to-point integration is that the integration is targeted specifically toward those tools and the particular interfaces provided by those tools. Thus, a design tool that wishes to integrate with three different CM tools typically offers three different versions of its integration software, each targeted at one of the CM tools. Furthermore, there is the ongoing problem of maintaining the integrations as the products evolve.

The message passing approach attempts to overcome these shortcomings by generalizing and abstracting the tool interconnection service in the form of a message server. Hence, the necessary communication among tools is more explicit, visible, and controllable. Agreements among the tools on when and what to transfer are still required, but the message passing approach provides the mechanism and forum within which such agreements can be made, documented, and allowed to evolve.

7.4 Examples of the Message Passing Approach

A number of CASE environment framework implementations have been based on the principles described above. In this section we describe three such implementations — FIELD, SoftBench, and ToolTalk, as well as one specification (CORBA). Two other prominent implementations, Digital's FUSE and IBM's WorkBench/6000, are derivations of FIELD and SoftBench, respectively. It should be noted that some of the problems discussed relative to the messaging systems outlined in this section are being addressed in later initiatives (see Section 7.5.3).

7.4.1 FIELD

Developed by Steven Reiss at Brown University, the FIELD[1] environment is the origin of much of the work on the message passing approach [64][65]. The initial implementation was available at the end of 1987.

The FIELD environment was developed for use at Brown University with the following basic aims in mind:

- To establish the principle that highly interactive environments as seen with many PC-based packages can be developed for large-scale programming with equal success.
- To experiment with the extensive graphical capabilities of current workstations to enhance the quality and productivity of software development.
- To provide a platform for tool integration at Brown University capable of supporting the teaching of programming and as the basis for further research.

---

[1]. FIELD stands for "Friendly Integrated Environment for Learning and Development."

The two basic components of FIELD that support these aims are the use of a consistent graphical user interface as a front-end to all tools and a simple integration mechanism based on message passing.[2]

7.4.1.1 The Message Server

The message server, Msg, corresponds very closely to the general description given in Section 7.3. Msg acts as the central message server to which messages are passed as arbitrary length text strings. This ensures that no fixed protocol for messages is predefined, encouraging tools to form their own collaborations by sharing knowledge of message formats. In addition, by allowing the user to amend Msg easily, different approaches toward creating, transferring, and parsing messages are encouraged. It is claimed that the power of this approach is a consequence of the flexibility that it provides.

In FIELD, the message server is implemented as a separate UNIX process, communicating with other processes via sockets. The implementation is approximately 2,000 lines of C code comprising the server, a client interface, and a pattern matcher.

7.4.1.2 Messages

There are a number of interesting characteristics of the messages sent and distributed in the FIELD environment.

First, FIELD distinguishes two broad categories of messages — commands and information messages. Commands are sent to a particular tool or class of tools requesting that some service be performed. Information messages are typically more widely broadcast to inform all other interested tools of some event that has just occurred. Second, messages may be sent synchronously or asynchronously. In synchronous transmission, a tool sends a message and waits for a response. In asynchronous transmission, once a tool sends a message, it resumes normal operation. As can be expected, command messages are normally synchronous messages and wait for an acknowledgment or response to be returned from the command, while information messages are asynchronous.

As a result of the above, message formats take one of two forms, corresponding to the two kinds of messages:

- Commands contain the name of the recipient, the command name, the system name, and the arguments to the command.

[2.] While the graphical front-end aspects of FIELD are interesting and important to its use, we concentrate on the integration mechanisms.

7.4 Examples of the Message Passing Approach

- Information messages contain the name of the sender, the event causing the message, the system name, and the arguments to the message.

In both of the above cases, the system name is used to allow the message server to distinguish between different invocations of the same tool.

7.4.1.3 Summary of FIELD

Reiss's FIELD environment is an interesting example of the message passing approach to integration, and a number of successes are claimed for it, including support for the development of a system of greater than 100,000 lines of code [65].

However, there are two areas of concern. One is that there are a number of unsubstantiated claims made by Reiss about the FIELD environment. For example, Reiss states that the level of integration in FIELD is sufficient for almost all applications and that complete integration is not necessary. This is a very strong statement to make without any substantive discussion. At best it must be considered an interesting hypothesis to examine. In fact, the testing of this hypothesis may be the key to many of the problems being addressed in tool integration. In particular, it is unclear what level of integration is required, and indeed, whether an environment can be justified in providing only one level of integration, no matter which tools are being integrated, where they fit in the development life cycle, how they are to be monitored by management, and so on. We return to this crucial point in Section 7.5.

It is also worth noting that FIELD has so far been directed at *programming*. From FIELD's point of view, it remains to be seen if the same mechanisms can scale up to *project* support — supporting technical and managerial aspects of software development, covering much more of the development life cycle, and supporting simultaneous multiple access to the system. Some of these aspects are described in the papers on FIELD as "work in progress."

At a more pragmatic level, Reiss recognizes the problems with performance of the current FIELD implementation suggesting various possible optimizations. However, he also points out that much of the problem lies in the layering of the FIELD environment directly on top of UNIX, and the problems of attempting to use batch-based tools in an interactive mode. This leads to the possible conclusion that tools must be designed and implemented with message passing integration in mind to exploit the message passing mechanism properly. If true, this conclusion has important implications for tool vendors.

7.4.2 SoftBench

The SoftBench environment, a product of Hewlett-Packard (HP), was expressly developed to provide an architecture for integrating CASE tools as part of HP's CASEdge initiative [20][40]. SoftBench is based on a control approach to integration comprising three main functional components:

- Tool communication.
- Distributed support.
- User interface management.

Here we concentrate on the first of those components, tool communication, which employs a message passing mechanism based on the one used in FIELD. Hence, the general approach used is as defined earlier for FIELD. In the description that follows, we concentrate on the main differences from the FIELD approach.

7.4.2.1 The Message Server

In SoftBench, the message server is known as the Broadcast Message Server (BMS). It is this component that forms the core of the SoftBench product. In most respects it is similar in operation to FIELD's Msg, with messages being received by the BMS for distribution to all tools that have registered interest in those messages. There are, however, the following points to note with the BMS:

- The BMS has the concept of a tool protocol. This is the abstract notion of a set of operations that are available for each class of tools. For example, the class of "debug" tools would have a protocol that included operations such as "step," "set-breakpoint," and "continue." Ideally, any new tools that are added to the "debug" class will fully support the associated protocol. This will ensure that a calling tool can rely on a client tool providing a well-defined set of operations without knowing which tool from the required class is invoked. This greatly increases tool independence, or "plug compatibility."

- All SoftBench tools send a notification message whenever they perform certain actions. This approach allows triggers to be defined that are fired when notification of events is broadcast (e.g., system builds following file updates, or automatic collection of metrics data).

- Existing tools not developed to use SoftBench can be adapted for use with the SoftBench environment using HP's *Encapsulator* tool. Through the Encapsulator, the user develops an envelope within which the tool can execute and send and receive messages. The encapsulation is written in an Encapsulation Description Language (EDL), or in C or C++ linked with a library of Encapsulator operations.

7.4 Examples of the Message Passing Approach

- When executing, if a tool sends a message requesting a service that no currently executing tools can provide, the SoftBench Execution Manager will automatically look for a suitable tool and execute it. The request for the service is then forwarded to that tool.

7.4.2.2 Messages

In SoftBench, messages are strings of text that follow a consistent format. In particular, there are three kinds of messages — request messages (R), success notification (N), and failure notification (F). Each has the following components:

- *Sender.* The tool that sent the message. This is left empty in SoftBench as all messages are broadcast to the BMS, so the originator is not required.
- *Message-id.* A unique identifier constructed from the message number, process identifier, and host machine name.
- *Message type.* One of R, N, or F.
- *Tool class.* The class of tool (e.g., "debug" or "edit").
- *Command.* The name of the operation or event.
- *Context.* The location of the data being processed. It is formed from the host machine name, the base directory, and the filename.
- *Data.* A list of arguments to the command.[3]

Hence, there is a single, well-defined format for all three types of SoftBench messages.

7.4.2.3 Summary of SoftBench

The SoftBench environment is a very exciting recent development in the integrated CASE marketplace. Indeed, the product has already received enthusiastic support, with over 25,000 reported sales.

Based on the descriptions of SoftBench available, we make the following critical observations:

- At least initially, SoftBench is a "program design, build, and test" system, *not* a complete software development environment. Part of the reason for this lies in the choice of tools that HP has made to integrate with SoftBench — program editor, static analyzer, debugger, program builder, mail tool, and CM interface. However, it is interesting to postulate that there is a more fundamental reason than this. In fact, it may be the case that the approach works best, and tools are more readily integrated, when there is an obvious and

---

[3.] Note that all data arguments are by reference to avoid copying of data.

clear relationship between the tools. The set of program development tools available fall into this category. It is not at all clear that integrating, say, technical and managerial tools, or documentation and development tools, would be nearly as "clean" or as "convenient." We discuss this point in more detail later in this chapter.

- No details at all are given about the implementation of SoftBench. In particular, it would have been reassuring to have seen performance figures for the use of SoftBench in the context of a large, multitool environment. As nothing is mentioned, it must remain an open issue, particularly given Reiss's earlier comments regarding poor performance in FIELD.

7.4.3 ToolTalk

A recent offering from Sun Microsystems is the ToolTalk service, described as "a network spanning, inter-application message system" [31][33][32]. Initially, ToolTalk 1.0 is implemented on top of SunSoft's ONC Remote Procedure Call (RPC) mechanism, and runs on SunOS 4.1.1 or later.

In abstract terms, ToolTalk shares many of the characteristics of the SoftBench product. Perhaps the most noticeable difference is the object-oriented emphasis that has been used in describing the ToolTalk service. For example, the ToolTalk service is said to manage "object descriptions"; the messages of ToolTalk are described as "object-oriented messages"; and one of the main advantages claimed for the ToolTalk service itself is that it provides both a solution to today's integration problems and a migration path to tomorrow's object-oriented architectures.

7.4.3.1 The Message Server

The message server in ToolTalk is a special process called *ttsession*. Each user session has its own instance of the ttsession process.

Programs interact with the ToolTalk service by calling functions defined in the ToolTalk application programming interface (API). This allows applications to create, send, and receive ToolTalk messages.

7.4.3.2 Messages

In ToolTalk, the messages have a more complex format than either FIELD or SoftBench, and more information (e.g., data types) can be conveyed within them. Processes participate in message protocols, where a message protocol consists of a description of the set of messages that can be communicated among a group of processes, a definition of when those messages can be sent, and an explanation of what occurs when each message is received.

7.4 Examples of the Message Passing Approach

A message consists of a number of attributes. These are:

- *An address*. This can be the address of a procedure, process, object, or object type. Thus, the receiver of a message can be of any of these types, providing a great deal of flexibility.
- *A class*. There are two kinds of message classes — notices and requests. A notice is a message that provides information about an event (such as start up of an editor, or termination of an editor), while a request is a call for some action to be taken (such as a build request). For a request message, the process making the request may continue while the request is handled (e.g., a window-based application can continue to handle window events, mouse clicks, and so on), or may wait for an appropriate reply.
- *An operation*. An operation is the identifier for the actual event that has occurred, or the requested action.
- *A set of arguments*. Any parameters to the event or action are listed.
- *An indication of scope*. Messages have a particular scope within which they are valid, limiting their potential distribution. The possible values for a message scope in ToolTalk are *session* (all processes with the current login session), *file* (a particular named file), *both* (the union of session and file), *file-in-session* (the intersection of session and file).
- *A disposition*. The disposition tells ToolTalk what action to take if a handler cannot be found.
- *A state*. Some messages are returned to the sender to indicate that the message server has, or has not, been able to find a recipient.

Within the defined scope of a message, the receivers of that message are obtained by matching the message's attributes with the message patterns registered as being of interest to each of the processes (i.e., tools).

7.4.3.3 Summary of ToolTalk

There are a number of observations that can be made about ToolTalk in comparison with the SoftBench product. We highlight the following:[4]

- There is no mention of any generally available tools that have been integrated with the ToolTalk services. While there is much discussion of the ease with which existing tools can be integrated through these services, no tools are actually named. The only example used is an Electronic Design Automation (EDA) system [32]. The tools integrated were very specialized and appear to have been integrated to support a fixed life cycle of tool interac-

---

[4.] These observations are broadly consistent with a similar review carried out internally within Hewlett-Packard [53].

tion. The reason that little information on tools is given stems from a marketing decision that Sun has made to provide ToolTalk as a message passing layer that can be purchased in isolation from any tools. Separately available is a CASE environment called *SPARCWorks*, a set of tools that makes use of the ToolTalk product.

The decision to market ToolTalk in this way may be a distinct advantage to Sun in the longer term, when customers have a better understanding of the ToolTalk product, and there are many tools and CASE environments available to choose from that operate on ToolTalk. However, in the short term this decision may cause confusion and misunderstanding if application developers purchase ToolTalk only to find that no tools are provided with it to help evaluate and become familiar with the ToolTalk product.

- The amount of work required to integrate a new tool with the ToolTalk service is also not discussed. There is no equivalent to SoftBench's Encapsulator, and Sun has not announced any plans to provide such a capability. As a result, to integrate tools into ToolTalk without amending the tools' source code, it is necessary to write routines in the C (or C++) programming language. A wrapper for an existing tool would thus consist of the use of a graphical user interface generator such as Sun's DevGuide to allow a window-based interface for a tool to be constructed, and the necessary calls to ToolTalk using the UNIX operating system calls of "fork" and "exec" with subsequent communication via UNIX pipes.

  While it is claimed that knowledgeable UNIX and C (or C++) programming personnel will find the writing of a tool wrapper for ToolTalk to be an easily managed task, the Encapsulator libraries provided by SoftBench appear to be a way to make the task of tool encapsulation more accessible to SoftBench users, with the ability to write wrappers in the C (or C++) programming language if necessary.

- As with SoftBench, ToolTalk does not have a notion of groups of users collaborating on a project. Messages are sent to processes or are session-based. However, ToolTalk does have a way for users to collaborate through the notion of "file scoped messages." In file-scoped messages, users specify a file or directory that they are interested in. ToolTalk maintains a record of which users are interested in which scoped files. When a message is sent scoped to a file, ToolTalk forwards the message to all the user sessions interested in that file. A demonstration of multiple simultaneous editing of a shared file has been produced to illustrate the use of this scoped file concept.

- ToolTalk is essentially "free." When one obtains a version of the Sun version of UNIX on a workstation, then ToolTalk is provided. The result is that more people are likely to experiment with the technology for tool integration. Also, in providing a ToolTalk interface to their tools, tool vendors are able to make assumptions about the availability of ToolTalk on certain platforms, encouraging them to use the services provided.

7.4.4 CORBA

The Common Object Request Broker Architecture (CORBA) is intended to provide a common interface that allows applications to exchange information in an object-oriented computing environment. CORBA allows for transparent access to applications operating on multiple computing platforms, requiring that each platform support a compliant Object Request Broker (ORB). Unlike FIELD, SoftBench, and ToolTalk, CORBA is not an implementation of a message passing system. Rather, it is a specification for communication between clients (requesting a service) and objects (providing a service). CORBA is endorsed by the Object Management Group (OMG), an organization that includes major computer manufacturers (e.g., Digital, Sun, Hewlett-Packard, and IBM) as well as software providers (e.g., Microsoft, SunSoft, Object Design) among its members. Implementations of CORBA and CORBA-compliant tools are now available.

CORBA is far more ambitious than FIELD, SoftBench, and Tooltalk, particularly in terms of the services it provides for execution within a heterogeneous and distributed environment. It is intended to facilitate interconnection of multiple object systems. The original CORBA specification is the result of the combined efforts of Digital Equipment, Hewlett-Packard, Hyperdesk, NCR, Object Design, and SunSoft. A subsequent revised specification was released in 1992. A revised CORBA 2 is anticipated in the future.

The basis of CORBA is a typical object model where a client sends a message to an object to request a service. A request contains information identifying the desired service, the target object, (optionally) input and output parameters to the service, and information about the context of the request. A request to perform a service may result in some value being returned to the requesting client, or an exception indicating that an abnormal condition occurred.

7.4.4.1 The Message Server

The message server capability of CORBA is called the Object Request Broker (ORB). The ORB is responsible for the mechanisms required to find the object toward which a request is directed, to prepare the object to receive the request, and to communicate data making up the request. The ORB is also responsible for returning the results of the request to the client.

Two interfaces are provided specifically for the use of the client application to make requests of objects: Interface Definition Language (IDL) stubs and

Dynamic Invoke. A single interface, the IDL Skeleton, is provided to allow the ORB to invoke target objects. The Object Adaptor interface provides a further set of services to target objects. The ORB interface provides a set of common utilities to both the client and objects. The relation of these interfaces to clients and objects is diagrammed in Figure 20 and discussed in the following paragraphs.

FIGURE 20 CORBA Structure.

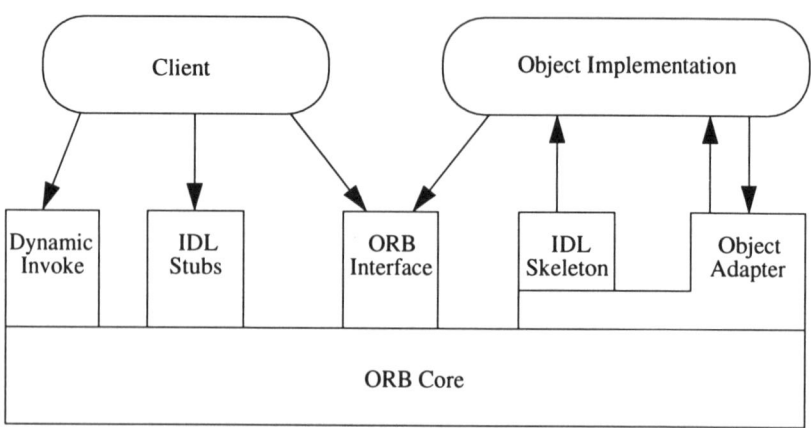

IDL stubs provide an interface that is specific to the services provided by an object. To use an IDL stub, the client must know precisely what object and object services are required prior to execution. The interface for a particular object service is unique to that service. The client invokes these routines via normal programming language calls, and the required IDL stub to access the object interface is bound to the client at compile time.

On the other hand, the Dynamic Invoke interface allows for the dynamic construction and execution of requests for services during execution. This interface is identical across all implementations of an ORB. However, the interface requires that the client provide information about the target object, the operation to be performed, and parameter and context information. Clients can receive this information from, for example, invocations on other objects or data stored in files. In addition, clients can access information about all the objects and operations available to them by querying the Interface Repository. The Interface Repository represents IDL information in a runtime format and allows a client to invoke objects and operations that may not have been known at compile time.

7.4 Examples of the Message Passing Approach

A request is handled by the ORB in a manner that makes the type of invocation transparent to the target object. The ORB locates the appropriate target service, transmits parameters, and invokes the target via an IDL skeleton.

The target object may obtain services such as the creation of objects, verification of client security, and activation and deactivation of object instances from the ORB via an Object Adaptor. More than one object adaptor may be available since the wide range of divergent policies in these (and other) areas necessitates the potential for multiple object adaptors. However, a Basic Object Adaptor is identified that provides "conventional" services expected to be used by many objects.

The ORB Interface provides those functions that are the same for all ORB and object implementations. These functions are available to both client and target objects. The operations available via the ORB Interface are not operations on objects, and are limited to a number of support and utility routines.

7.4.4.2 Messages

Three types of request messages are possible: one-way requests, where the client does not wait for completion of the request, nor does it intend to accept results; synchronous requests, where the client waits for completion of the request before continuing activities; and deferred synchronous requests, where the client does not wait for completion of the request, but does intend to accept the results later.

Each request has the following components:

- A handle identifying the object at which the request is directed. The format of an object handle is dependent on the language binding used, but each ORB must provide the same language mapping to an object handle for a particular programming language.
- The name of the intended operation on the object.
- The set of arguments for the operation. Arguments may be input only, output only, and input-output, as defined by the object providing the service.
- Optionally, context information about the client that may affect some aspect of performance of the service.
- The identity of a structure in which to return exception information.

The execution of the operation in response to a request may optionally result in a non-void value being returned to the client. Operations may also be defined that return no value (void).

7.4.4.3 Summary of CORBA

CORBA differs significantly from the other messaging systems described in this chapter. Among the many differences are:

- CORBA represents a specification for a messaging system rather than an implementation. Implementations of ORBs and of CORBA-compliant applications are becoming available.
- CORBA is designed to operate in heterogeneous and distributed environments. The other messaging systems are primarily designed to operate with tools executing on a single platform type.
- CORBA does not identify an equivalent capability to SoftBench Encapsulator. However, it is likely that individual implementations will provide tools to facilitate the incorporation of tools into CORBA-based environments.
- Like ToolTalk, CORBA describes an object-oriented capability. However, CORBA appears to be primarily directed at future object-oriented architectures, whereas ToolTalk is clearly intended for use today.
- In keeping with its object-oriented emphasis, CORBA provides for increased data integration as well as control integration. The use of input and output arguments capable of communicating the data types and structures used in common programming languages adds significant flexibility for data transfer.

7.5 Discussion

It is tempting to view the three implementations and one specification of the message passing approach that we have examined as no more than four competing systems based on the same underlying principles. However, their differences can perhaps best be analyzed with reference to a conceptual framework developed by Brown, Earl, and McDermid [11]. This framework is reviewed, and FIELD, SoftBench, ToolTalk and CORBA are placed within that framework in Section 7.5.1.

7.5.1 A Conceptual Framework

Analyses of existing tools and environments have led to a number of proposals describing a spectrum of levels of integration within a CASE environment. Each proposal can be considered a conceptual framework for analyzing aspects of particular CASE environment standards or products.

Brown, Earl, and McDermid identified five levels of tool integration: carrier, lexical, syntactic, semantic, and method [11]. Carrier integration implies integration via the consistent formats of the basic medium (such as common character representation and file format, as in UNIX). Lexical integration involves a

7.5 Discussion

shared understanding of a sequence of lexical symbols (such as starting each command with a "."). Syntactic integration involves the sharing of rules for forming data structures (such as the use of a common parse tree by a compiler and debugger). Semantic integration involves an understanding of both the semantics of a data structure and operations on that structure (such as a common data store where the structure of data and the operations on it are stored in the repository and available to tools). Method integration implies a shared concept of the way in which the tools will be used to support a process. While the five levels of the Brown et al. proposal were originally intended to be interpreted within the context of data sharing between tools in a CASE environments,[5] it is also possible to apply the five levels to the message passing approach, as illustrated in Table 4. In this approach it is the *messages* that form the primary means of communication between tools and, hence, the information content of the messages must be considered in analyzing different approaches to integration.

TABLE 4 Five Levels of Message Passing

Integration Level	Characteristics
Carrier	Messages are uninterpreted text strings. It is the responsibility of tools to agree on the interpretation of the message.
Lexical	Tools maintain a common understanding of the data items (tokens) contained in text strings. The tools and the message server can parse text strings representing messages.
Syntactic	Tools share a common understanding of the syntax for the tokens in the message string. Not only can tools identify tokens in a message string, but they now also have an agreed format for those tokens.
Semantic	Tools share a common understanding of the meaning of the tokens in a message string. Not only do tools agree on the identification of tokens, but they also share an interpretation of actions and events.

[5.] They provide a framework for discussing tool integration, *not* an architecture for implementing tool integration in a CASE environment.

Integration Level	Characteristics
Method	Tools share common knowledge about the software development process in which the tools are participating. Tools have much more context in which to interpret messages, since they share an understanding of the preceding operations and events and subsequent activities.

Based on this analysis of the various levels of integration in the message passing approach, we can assess the systems we have examined with regard to this classification:

- FIELD is an academic prototype system, with the goal of being a flexible, adaptable system for experimentation. As a result, messages are essentially uninterpreted strings of text, with additional, external agreement between tools necessary to interpret messages. The implementation of Msg, the message server, has a protocol for identifying the tokens of a message built in. This places FIELD in the carrier level of this classification in concept, but the lexical level in practice.

- SoftBench is a commercial product with the aims of both standardizing an approach to tool integration with the SoftBench product, and making integration of tools as straightforward as possible. Hence, SoftBench has included rules about the structure of a message in terms of the tokens and their ordering. In addition, the notion of a tool protocol has been introduced. This allows collections of tools to agree on a common set of services to allow users of those services to be independent of which actual tool implements the services at any particular time. This raises SoftBench to syntactic level integration, as the information communicated between tools is essentially through "typed messages."

- ToolTalk attempts to encode much more information in the messages it sends than either FIELD or SoftBench. It describes its messages as "object-oriented" because the ToolTalk service supports many message protocol styles, messages can be addressed to groups of tools, and message protocols can be inherited through a hierarchy relating objects in the ToolTalk service. We can see ToolTalk as an attempt at semantic level integration, based on the fact that knowledge of the message components themselves is shared between tools through inheritance.

- CORBA provides a deeper level of semantic integration, as tools can dynamically access information about the objects and operations available to them by querying the Interface Repository.

7.5 Discussion

In summary, we see that the four systems of the message passing approach discussed in this chapter can be distinguished by their differing approaches toward the information conveyed among tools in the messages transmitted. In fact, the implementations show a progression from lexical to syntactic to semantic levels of tool integration according to the Brown et al. classification.

It is interesting to speculate how the "next step" in this progression might take place — toward method level integration. In the context of the message passing approach discussed in this chapter, method level integration can be interpreted as the encoding of policy or process information within the message passing mechanisms themselves. In practice, Garlan suggests this may mean that, in addition to tool protocols, policy protocols could be defined for a group of tools describing the permitted interactions among tools, which sequences of messages encode a particular policy action, and so on [34]. For example, in considering configuration management (CM) services within a CASE environment, a tool protocol may consist of a standard set of CM operations such as "check-in-version," "check-out-version," and "merge-versions." A number of individual CM tools may conform to this CM tool protocol by implementing those operations. A CM policy protocol, however, would encode particular uses of the CM tool protocol operations to support a particular CM process. Handling change requests, for instance, may be encoded as a CM policy by ensuring that a check-in-version operation is always preceded by a quality assurance (QA) approval. Such a CM policy enforces a particular use of the CM tool protocol. Further investigation of method level integration within the message passing approach to integration is ongoing [10].

7.5.2 Practical Issues

There are a number of important practical issues that affect the acceptance of the message passing approach, including extensibility, ease of encapsulation, and standard message protocols. Sections 7.5.2.1 - 7.5.2.3 discuss these issues.

7.5.2.1 Extensibility

One of the major strengths of the message passing approach to integration appears to be its flexibility with regard to tool interactions. In particular, the use of the protocol concept as seen in the BMS leads to an easily extensible environment. For example, tools in execution do not need to be aware of exactly which other tools are running — they simply broadcast notification messages through the message server, or request a service from any tool in a particular tool class. Even if there is no tool of that class currently executing, the message server has enough information to be able to start up such a tool and forward the request (through maintaining an internal database of tools and classes).

Such extensibility is highly desirable in any system interested in event-based operation. The message passing approach appears to provide an ideal mechanism to support such a technique.

7.5.2.2 Ease of Encapsulation

One problem that must be addressed by any CASE environment is the integration of existing third-party tools. Most of these tools were not designed and implemented with the CASE environment in mind, nor is the source code available to be able to amend them. The approach adopted by SoftBench and FIELD involves encapsulation. It is claimed for SoftBench that:

> *Simple tool encapsulations can be described in two to five pages of code, which can be written in less than a morning's work [40].*

Clearly, further qualification of this statement is required to understand the work involved in tool encapsulation, but a typical encapsulation involves writing code to control four aspects of the tool — Input/Output streams, BMS messages, Operating System events, and X Window System events. Each of these aspects can be more or less complex depending on the tool to be encapsulated and the constraints on the desired results (e.g., attempting to produce a consistent graphical user interface across a set of tools).

The two major components of encapsulation in BMS, developing a graphical user interface and generating a message interface, are relatively independent. However, both may potentially involve significant amounts of effort, and may require a deep understanding of the tool to be encapsulated to achieve a reasonable result. More work is certainly needed to establish the ease and effectiveness of this form of encapsulation within a message passing mechanism. It is relatively straightforward to imagine the use of encapsulation for simple data producer/consumer tools such as simple UNIX utilities. However, for complex tools that have sophisticated interactive processing, or that assume an "egocentric" approach to integration and have been designed with little emphasis on open access to their internal services, it is much less obvious how useful this approach would be. Indeed, the SoftBench descriptions clearly state that encapsulation is intended for capturing the UNIX input and output actions of simple tools. There is a need for more work to establish a set of tool architecture classifications that relate to the ease (or otherwise) with which tools from each class can be integrated through an encapsulation approach.

Independent experiments with encapsulating tools with SoftBench [15] have shown that for tools with relatively simple command line interfaces, the Encapsulator provides a rapid way to produce a "point-and-click" interface for the tool. It is much more difficult, however, to design an appropriate message inter-

7.5 Discussion

face for a tool, as it requires knowledge of both the other tools in the CASE environment and a well-defined operational scenario in which the tool will operate.

7.5.2.3 Standard Message Protocols

The need for defining a common set of message protocols has been described earlier in this chapter. There, we made the argument that syntactic and semantic levels of agreement between tools enhanced the quality of information that was transferred, and facilitated higher levels of integration. This argument can be made for tools from a single vendor within a message passing system, for tools from multiple vendors within a message passing system, and for tools from multiple vendors using multiple message passing systems. In particular, as message passing systems will be offered by a number of major suppliers,[6] there is interest in ensuring that standards are developed that will allow third-party tools to operate on different message passing systems, and to allow those message passing systems to communicate. There have been three initiatives aimed at addressing this situation: CASE Communique, the CASE Interoperability Alliance, and ANSI X3H6.

While these three initiatives are clearly in their infancy, the results of the work of these groups have the potential to aid tool writers in providing a set of messages to guide their implementation and tool users to allow greater choice over tools used in an environment. A further aim of these initiatives is to influence the direction of future development of message passing products. This should ensure that future versions of such products are more in tune with the needs of tool writers and tool users.

CASE Communique. A group led by HP, IBM, Informix, and CDC has held a number of meetings with the aim of developing standards for CASE tool communication based on HP's SoftBench product [30]. This group, known as "CASE Communique," has recognized that if a common set of messages could be defined for each class of CASE tool, then tools within a SoftBench environment would be more interchangeable within each class. The CASE Communique members work in teams on message sets for a number of different classes of tools including CM, design, documentation, and testing.

[6.] HP and Sun offerings have been described in this chapter. Both IBM and Digital have control integration products. In 1990, Digital licensed FIELD and have improved and extended it under the name of FUSE. IBM recently licensed SoftBench technology from HP, and ported it to their RISC System/6000 under the name CASE environment WorkBench/6000.

The CASE Interoperability Alliance. Digital, Silicon Graphics, and SunSoft have formed a working group to produce a proposal for a set of message standards that describe semantic (not syntactic) sets of messages for message passing systems. The aim has been to provide a number of message sets for particular application areas and scenarios, with the encouragement to other vendors to help in refining those message sets and in proposing other such sets.

ANSI X3H6. The American National Standards Institute (ANSI) has a working group involved in the definition of standards for CASE tool integration under the title of "X3H6: CASE Tool Integration Models." One of the tasks this group has undertaken is to act as the forum for harmonizing the work of CASE Communique and CASE Interoperability Alliance. The aim is to define a single set of messages that can be used by both groups. This work was begun with a document describing a common view of an architecture of a message passing system. Proposals for a common set of messages based on this architecture are planned in the 1994 time scale.

7.5.3 On the Horizon

A number of other important initiatives in this area are currently underway. As the work carried out in these initiatives matures, it is likely that it will have a major impact on the control-oriented integration marketplace.

7.5.3.1 The Common Open Software Environment (COSE)

In 1993, a consortium of UNIX system and software vendors, including HP, IBM, Sun Microsystems, Novell, Santa Cruz Operations, and Unix System Laboratories (USL), was formed with the intention of producing a common application programming interface (API) for UNIX systems. The scope of the COSE effort includes work on a common desktop environment (CDE), graphics, multimedia, networking, object technology, systems management, naming conventions, and data management. The formation of this consortium is widely regarded as a reaction to a growing threat to the fractious UNIX marketplace from Microsoft's Windows NT system.

The COSE group has completed the first version of a specification for a CDE to run on multiple UNIX system workstations.[7] This specification has been submitted to X/Open as a means for open comment on the document and has received wide support within the UNIX community.

[7.] The specification has also been supported by Digital Equipment Corporation and many other UNIX hardware and software vendors.

A major part of the CDE specification is a message passing system that is based on Sun's ToolTalk. The higher-level interface to the messaging services incorporates features from Hewlett-Packard's Encapsulator. A number of demonstrations have taken place showing that such an approach is feasible.

The implications of the COSE agreement are that HP, Sun, IBM, and others are moving toward a common set of interfaces that (if fully realized) will allow tools to be written to work on multiple UNIX platforms. The wide participation of UNIX system and software vendors raises the possibility of industry consensus on the resultant specification. Hence, this agreement has the potential for greatly simplifying the message passing system market place.

7.5.3.2 OLE and Competitors

Microsoft's Object Linking and Embedding (OLE) capability (available with Windows NT) provides the current capability for users to embed objects created by one application within data produced by another application. For example, a table produced by a spreadsheet tool can be embedded within a document produced by a word processing application. With OLE, clicking on the table will launch the spreadsheet tool to edit the table.

OLE provides a client-server model of computing; in the previous example the document serves as the client while the spreadsheet tool acts as a server application. However, OLE focuses on communication and data sharing between applications on a single desktop.

OLE has spurred competitors to band together to produce an alternative to the Microsoft technology. Novell, Borland, Apple, WordPerfect, IBM, and other organizations have formed a coalition to enhance and market Apple's OpenDoc technology. The resulting OpenDoc system is designed to provide services similar to OLE in a distributed environment. In addition, OpenDoc is intended to provide object inheritance and versioning capabilities beyond those available in OLE. Beta releases of OpenDoc are scheduled to appear during 1994. However, Microsoft intends to provide similar capabilities in future versions of its operating system.

7.6 Summary

In this chapter we have examined the message passing approach to tool integration as exemplified by the FIELD, SoftBench, ToolTalk, and CORBA frameworks. Both FIELD and SoftBench have been very successful in practice — FIELD as a research vehicle that has stimulated a great deal of interest, and SoftBench as a product that is said to have sales of more than 25,000 seats. As the most recent product of the three, it remains to be seen how widely accepted the ToolTalk service will be within the large Sun user community. However, a number of issues and questions of the message passing approach have been raised. In particular, how much this approach is appropriate for *project* (as opposed to *programming*) support is a matter for debate and further investigation. Similarly, it is unclear whether the necessary syntactic and semantic agreements among tool vendors are yet in place to allow meaningful interaction among different tools.

While a number of open issues and shortcomings of the approach have been identified, there is clearly evidence to support further investigation of the message passing approach as the basis for providing a CASE environment architecture that is more open to the addition of new tools. In particular, the simplicity and flexibility that the approach provides appear to facilitate experimentation with different levels of integration among tools. As a result, it may well provide the ideal platform for experimenting in some of the most crucial aspects of CASE environment technology, including:

- *Tool integration.* An examination of different semantic levels of tool integration in a CASE environment, how they can be supported in the same architecture, the relationships between the levels, and the benefits and drawbacks of integrating tools at different levels.
- *Process versus data versus user interface integration.* An analysis of how independent (or otherwise) tool integration in each of these dimensions is in practice.
- *Open tool interfaces.* An opportunity to learn about encapsulation of existing tools into a CASE environment to provide knowledge about the ease of providing access to third-party tools and the amount of work involved in such integration, and to determine the characteristics required of tools to ensure integration in a CASE environment is both practical and efficient.

We have also pointed toward possible future directions for the work on the message passing approach by describing the latest moves toward standardization of requests between object-based message systems and message protocols in the SoftBench product and through the application of the Brown et al. classification of tool integration levels in a CASE environment. Current approaches to control integration in a CASE environment, in particular experimentation leading to support for *method level* concepts, are an interesting avenue for further work.

CHAPTER 8
The Role of Process in Integrated CASE Environments

8.1 Introduction

Early work on CASE environment integration concentrated on the mechanistic aspects of integration between tools. The process context in which those integrated tools would be used was less of a concern. In recent years, however, the process aspect of integration has grown in importance in the eyes of most members of the software community. The role of process, and hence of process integration, is now generally regarded as critical. Such issues as determining the impact of process on the choice of tools to be integrated, how those integrations should be implemented, and how a CASE environment will be used in the overall life of an enterprise are now increasingly seen as being of paramount importance. As an example, while one could assert that a particular analysis tool should be integrated with a documentation tool, this is of little real value. A more meaningful assertion is that the analysis tool must make use of documentation services to generate documentation in some standard life-cycle model form (e.g., DoD-STD-2167 document sets).

The three-level model of integration proposed in this book reflects this interest in process. In our three-level model, process integration is orthogonal to mechanism-level integration and service-level integration. In this view, we see that integration is not just an amalgamation of related tools, but is the combination of several integrating mechanisms, used over some set of services (as implemented by tools) to achieve some specific process objective. Put another way, we view software processes as defining a design context, i.e., a set of integration requirements. When implemented, they can be expressed as a coordinated set of environment services, i.e., unified through a combination of control, data, and presentation mechanisms.

In this chapter, we explore the broad subject of process integration in more detail. We first consider several divergent views on the nature of process integration itself, and particularly the question of process in the context of "process improvement." We then examine the relationships between process integration and CASE tools and environments. We next look at some idealized examples of how processes and tools interact, and some issues raised by these examples. Finally, we summarize the key points of this chapter and speculate on future directions for process integration.

8.2 Understanding the Nature of Process Integration

The very notion of what process integration actually denotes is an area of some confusion. We survey several viewpoints that highlight the different notions of process integration. These views fall into the following categories: a "dimensional" view of process integration; a "relationship" view of process integration; process integration in the context of the user of the process; process integration in the context of software process improvement; and our own view, exemplified by the three-level model of integration. We examine each of these views in turn.

8.2.1 Process Integration as a Dimension

Together with his division of integration into three basic dimensions (i.e., data, control, and presentation), Wasserman also proposed a tool-centric view of process integration [77]. In this perspective, process integration is the weaving together of tools into coherent support for a software engineering process. This definition highlights the fact that collections of tools must be composed in a coherent fashion to cooperate in supporting a process.

Cagan goes somewhat further [19] by considering several process dimensions: model integration (specifically, CM models of product structure); life-cycle integration; and task integration. Cagan refers to task integration as "process integration." However, his use of the term specifically focuses on task specification and automation, and not on broader software process issues such as lifecycle issues.

8.2.2 Process Integration as a Relationship

A different view, proposed by Thomas and Nejmeh, concentrates on the many different kinds of *relationships* among environment components [75]. In particular, the major relationships of concern are between two tools, between a tool and the platform on which it operates, and between a tool and the process being enacted. This definition identifies three properties of a process that are of interest:

- the degree to which tools combine to support the performance of a single process step,
- the degree to which tools agree on the events needed to support a particular process (where an event is a condition that arises during a process step that may result in the execution of an associated action), and
- the degree to which relevant tools cooperate to enforce some constraint that arises as a result of the process.

The significant distinction between this view and Wasserman's is that Thomas and Nejmeh focus on the *degree* to which integration is present; Wasserman focuses more on the condition of the integration itself.

8.2.3 Process Integration in the Context of the User

These views, while expanding our understanding of process integration, do not address one key issue, namely, that the goal of process integration will vary depending on the *user* of the process. For instance, software developers may tend to prefer a process that maximizes individual freedom (because software development is often viewed as a creative activity); managers may instead prefer that the process facilitate and enforce the tracking of project activities.

These preferences are clearly divergent. One is non-intrusive, and seeks to remove or reduce tedious activities; the other is potentially very intrusive, and may focus on uniform behavior from several individuals. This issue (i.e., who is the user of the process) is addressed in a definition proposed by Feiler [28] that concentrates on the size of the user community requiring integrated support. This view suggests that individual, team, project, and organizational aspects of the software process require different types of integration. CASE environments must allow for variation in terms of process support depending on differing user roles, and these variations must remain flexible, yet co-exist and cooperate.

CASE tool interaction must be geared toward supporting these different user communities and the different paradigms of interaction required during a project.

Considering both the user and the scope of the process provides a useful perspective in understanding how process integration involves the relationships between different CASE tool functions. Building on the set of models developed by Perry and Kaiser [57] we can use a social metaphor to illustrate different communities of interest, and to highlight their differences:

- Individuals are primarily interested in support for their day-to-day tasks and the tools that support those tasks. There is seldom need to be concerned with the details of tool interaction and communication; this can normally be handcrafted on a pair-wise basis as necessary.
- Families are small groups of developers who share a common philosophy and approach. Many agreements and conventions among tools are so well internalized that they need not be explicitly defined and controlled. Integrated interaction is possible with minimal explicit external control from the CASE environment.
- Cities are larger collections of families and individuals with more complex patterns of interaction. Enforced cooperation is necessary to ensure that communication and sharing can take place. Agreements that exist informally within a family of tools can no longer be assumed among families of tools. This leads to an architecture of loosely coupled collections of tightly integrated tools.
- States are an extension of the city in which collections of cities must be managed. To manage a state there must be rules and constraints that are consistent across a number of cities. While each city is necessarily unique, there are important points of intersection which it makes sense to standardize to facilitate reuse, cooperation, and sharing among the cities. Commonality across a number of CASE environments supporting multiple projects or multiple organizations is necessary to implement the state model.

The original paper by Perry and Kaiser speculates that most of the work in environments until the late 1980s was concentrated on the individual and family models, with a few examples of the city model beginning to appear (such as ISTAR and InFuse). Attempts during the early 1990s, many of which are discussed in Section 8.3.2, have been dominated by implementations of the city model. The state model has been the subject of a number of research and development programs such as Arcadia and STARS.

8.2.4 Process Integration and Software Process Improvement

A very different perspective on process integration is seen in the concept of "process improvement." In fact, much of the current interest in process has derived from work done over the past several years in this area [37][54][43]. Central to the notion of software process improvement as proposed by Humphrey [37] is the need for clear definition, consistent execution, and continual monitoring of an organization's software development process. This is expressed in the form of a Capability Maturity Model (CMM) that highlights the process maturity of an organization. There are five levels defined in this model:

- *Initial.* The current predominant state in which an organization has in place few procedures for control, monitoring, or assessment of the processes being carried out.
- *Repeatable.* The processes being enacted are sufficiently understood that they can be repeated from one project to the next.
- *Defined.* Descriptions of an organization's processes exist. These can be used as the basis for improved understanding of the tasks carried out.
- *Managed.* Comprehensive measurement and analysis of the processes are in place.
- *Optimizing.* Continual process improvement is now possible based on the statistics gained from well-defined processes.

The CMM does not focus on process integration in the same sense as Feiler, Wasserman, and other authors. Instead, the CMM sees process as pervasive for all aspects of software development activities, and integration of the process is inherent by its very nature.

One key question faced by the CMM is the role CASE tools play in improving the software process. One general assumption of the CMM is that CASE tools will tend to be more useful in the more advanced levels than in the early ones. Humphrey suggests that adopting CASE tools is very risky prior to the point where an organization has developed a defined process framework in which to address the risk [36]. The development of this process framework (including the establishment of a process group) is considered a key action required to advance from the Repeatable to the Defined level of the CMM (from Level Two to Level Three).

8.2.5 Process Integration and the Three-Level Model

Our view of process integration borrows certain aspects of each of these views but is not entirely consistent with any of them. We have already described the three-level model of integration, where service, mechanisms, and process participate. In our view, each of these levels interacts in a fundamental way with the other two. Thus, understanding the relationships between services and the integration of tools that provide those services must take place in the context of a set of process constraints. Conversely, understanding the process must somehow be related to the abstract services, and thereby to the actual tools in the CASE environment, since these tools will shape and constrain that process. Finally, both of these levels of integration must be implemented by some mechanisms, which in turn will guide the manner of the overall integration of the environment.

This view, while somewhat at variance with the other notions of process integration, essentially builds on them. For instance, we share Thomas and Nejmeh's notion that integration is a relationship, although we see the relationship as broader and more complex. Similarly, we concur with the CMM view that process is pervasive, but we maintain that services and tools have parity with process. Because we regard the three levels of our model as necessarily interconnected, we differ from the CMM view that tends to isolate CASE tools from efforts at process improvement. It is our belief that service, mechanism, and process issues must be addressed in any process improvement strategy.

8.3 Process Integration and CASE Tools and Environments

We now consider how process integration actually relates to CASE tools and environments. To do so, we first distinguish between process automation and process support. Next we examine the characteristics of process-centered tools and environments. We then discuss the relationships between CASE tools, process maturity, and process improvement.

8.3.1 Process Automation and Process Support

Attempts to introduce process automation are motivated by the need to improve the consistency, quality, and productivity of software development. Among the many ways in which tool support can assist in software development are by:

- automating menial and/or repetitive tasks,
- enforcing consistency in support of process and methods,
- supporting analysis and understanding of programs and data,
- supporting the management of the software process, and
- maintaining a history of the software activity via versions and configurations.

8.3 Process Integration and CASE Tools and Environments

This list suggests that there are actually two different process-related needs: *process automation* and *process support*. In the former case, manual tasks are automated to ensure consistency and repeatability. In the latter case, human tasks are facilitated by better support services.

Process automation appears to have been most successful in attempting to encode a small, relatively well-understood portion of the software development process, or in automating processes that are recognized to be particularly tedious or troublesome for engineers. Process support, in the form of CASE tools that provide it, are relatively immature. Several products are now appearing (e.g., Process Weaver, Synervision) that may prove valuable in this area.

While process automation and process support are conceptually separable, they are in practice often closely interrelated. Thus, while the following sections focus on CASE tools and environments from the latter point of view, i.e., from the way that they provide process support, they are also implicitly concerned with the extent to which that support is automated.

8.3.2 Characteristics of Process-Centered Tools and Environments

Any CASE tool or CASE environment can be considered "process-centered" in the sense that the tool or environment's primary role is to support (some part of) some process. Various CASE tools or environments show significant differences from each other in two basic features:

- The extent to which the process being supported is explicitly defined. This feature affects the visibility and control available on that process.
- The ease with which the process being supported by the CASE tool or environment can be changed. These changes may be minor (such as the tailoring of a small detail in part of the process) or extensive (such as the replacement of one process with a different one).

Thus, the extent to which a CASE tool or CASE environment actually *is* process-centered will largely be related to the way in which it offers support for both these features. In examining a tool or an environment, therefore, one needs to question the ways in which these features are offered. For example, in the case of explicit process definition, it may be necessary to ascertain the notation that was used to express the process, or to discover which services are offered by the CASE tool or environment to define or query the process, and so on. In the case of process flexibility, similar questions might concern the range of changes to the process that are possible and the ease with which changes can be specified.

While an individual tool may offer some degree of process support, a number of attempts have been made to produce extensive CASE environments with a strong emphasis on explicit process support. These environments are sometimes called "process-centered CASE environments" to distinguish them from environments composed of loosely connected tools with little or no explicit definition or visibility of the processes being supported.

Attempts to build such CASE environments have been particularly common in the defense-related community and are represented by environment efforts such as STARS [44] and SLCSE [69]. However, commercial efforts also exist, and are represented by environments such as ISTAR [26] and EAST [5]. Some of these efforts (such as SLCSE) are designed to support a single, well-defined process, while others (such as ISTAR) provide mechanisms capable of encoding a variety of processes.

A number of defense-related attempts to build process-centered CASE environments are ongoing, and no definitive statements can yet be made about their ultimate success. However, it is fair to say that no known attempts at developing process-centered CASE environments have resulted in commercially viable systems. Suchman suggests that similar attempts at process automation in the domain of office automation have also not been particularly successful [70]. Suchman attributes this to a flawed premise: that workers follow defined procedures. Rather, it is suggested that an adaptation of defined procedures, based on situational needs, is the norm.

8.3.3 Relationships Between CASE Tools, Process Maturity, and Process Automation

The relationships between process improvement (as exemplified by the CMM), the use of CASE tools, and automated process support is an interesting one. We have already noted Humphrey's comments concerning CASE tools and process improvement; he gave a clear warning that the use of CASE tools and environments is likely to do more harm than good before a process framework is in place. Some organizations and individuals, adopting a rigid interpretation of Humphrey's work, have suggested that CASE tool support is inappropriate before CMM Level Three is attained.[1] In contrast, many CASE tool vendors encourage the belief that the use of CASE tools at every level is essential to manage process improvement in a cost-effective manner, and that more technology is required on the road to process improvement.

---

[1] Humphrey's own writings are somewhat ambiguous, in one case suggesting that even organizations at or near (*i.e.*, *below*) Level Two may benefit from CASE tool usage in some circumstances [38].

8.3 Process Integration and CASE Tools and Environments

It is likely that both views have some truth. For instance, in an organization with chaotic behavior and non-repeatable processes, the introduction of sophisticated CASE tools is unlikely to bring about improvement and may even make the organization's behavior worse. However, it is also true that in some situations an organization need not wait to attain Level Three before it begins to take advantage of the power and utility of CASE tools.

As an example, we consider the CMM at Level Two. The operational basis of the CMM is a set of key process areas that identify the principal topics of interest at each maturity level. In each of these key process areas, there is a set of key practices that can be used as the basis for satisfying the goals defined for that process area.

At Level Two, the key process areas are:
- Software configuration management.
- Software quality assurance.
- Software subcontract management.
- Software project tracking and oversight.
- Software project planning.
- Requirements management.

An examination of the literature from numerous CASE tool vendors reveals that many existing tools might be of value in supporting these key practices. For example, a number of configuration management tool vendors specifically focus on support for the configuration management key practices defined at Level Two. While the value of such CASE tools might not be fully realized until an organization reaches Level Three, it is very likely that use of automated configuration management support would be beneficial to an organization at Level Two, and perhaps even at Level One.

What is important to realize, however, is that while the CASE tools may support a key process area, they cannot be a substitute for a detailed understanding of an organization's approach in that area. The CASE tools may be helpful, or even essential, in managing the data and inter-relationships typical of a large, complex software development project. However, CASE tools alone are not sufficient for the task.

8.4 Examples of Process and CASE Tool Interactions

We now consider some idealized examples of how process and CASE tools interact. These examples are intended to illustrate the complex issues that affect how a defined process, the tools needed to implement it, and the integrating mechanisms that underlie both of these are all necessary factors in creating an integrated CASE environment. There are four examples: coordinating tools across different life-cycle phases, coordinating tools within a single life-cycle step, overlapping tool capabilities, and life-cycle documentation.

8.4.1 Coordinating Tools Across Different Life-Cycle Phases

One popular way to describe an overall software process is by way of a *life-cycle model*. Descriptions of software life cycles abound, and alternative models differ about whether the life cycle is iterative, whether several phases can be active simultaneously, etc. However, all share some common concepts, notably, the idea of life-cycle phases and the progression of a process through these phases. A large or extensive software life cycle is typically composed of many phases. Tools may or may not be common across these phases, but some of the tools' data are almost certainly so. From the point of view of an integrated process, it is clearly advantageous that some notion of consistent and coordinated use of the data exists. Such coordination affects CASE environment integration for a number of reasons, including the following:

- One facet of CASE environment integration is the control of global changes to data, i.e., controlling *what* changes can be made, *why* they should be made, *when* the changes should be made and *who* should make the changes.
- Tools featuring private repositories need to work within a global change control regime for effective global change control to be put into practice, yet tools frequently provide their own services and mechanisms for controlling change.

Coordination of CASE tools in the life-cycle context can be simplified if the problem is viewed in a kind of data-flow framework. For example, we can assume a CASE environment that is supported by several distinct CASE tools, each specialized to a specific life-cycle phase (e.g., requirements tool, design tool, coding tool, testing tool), and each having its own tool-specific repository services. This is justifiable since many CASE tools are closely related to activities performed in specific life-cycle steps, and have proprietary data storage formats.

Figure 21 illustrates how different life-cycle models might affect different CASE environment integration strategies. In a strict waterfall life cycle, precon-

8.4 Examples of Process and CASE Tool Interactions

ditions tend to be static, and traceability is relatively straightforward. One implication of this is that traceability links can be made (relatively) immutable since iteration does not exist. In a spiral life-cycle model, however, iteration exists. Preconditions are more flexible, and traceability links must be dynamically changeable. This fact places requirements on the choice of tools as well as on their mode of integration.

FIGURE 21 Life-Cycle Implications for Tool Integration.

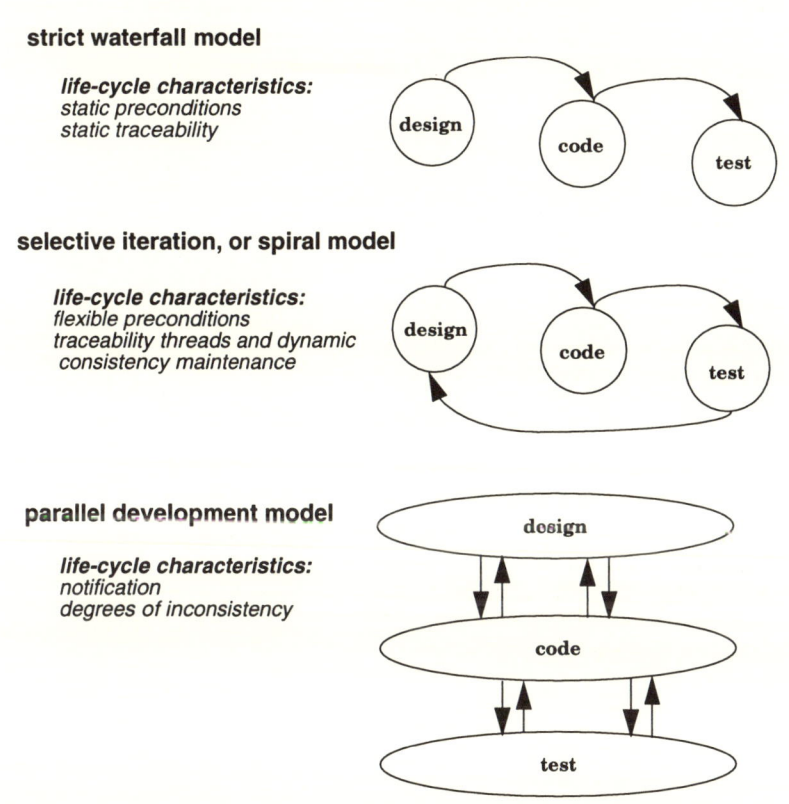

Finally, the parallel development model, which offers the greatest developmental flexibility, also places the greatest constraints on the tools and their integration. This life-cycle model implies that there are degrees of incompleteness in each phase (inherent in the notion of activity), and also demands requirements such as the possible need to notify tools and users where logically shared (or derived) information is under modification.

These examples serve to illustrate the types of issues related to the software life cycle that have an effect on the integration of CASE tools. Even in a simple example such as this, there are significant interactions between CASE tool integration and the software process.

8.4.2 Coordinating Tools Within a Single Life-Cycle Step

By their nature, processes *within* life-cycle steps are likely to be more interactive, more collaborative, and more complex in terms of number, kind, and frequency of process-related events and data. Further, support for activities within life-cycle steps often falls into the realm of individual CASE tools. Thus, many of the issues related to tool integration in this context are highly dependent upon the idiosyncracies of individual tools.

CASE tools are not developed by vendors without some preconceived notions of software process. In most cases, there is no strict separation of CASE tool functions and process constraints that can, and should, be separate from tool functions. For example, it is not uncommon for CASE tools to provide rudimentary CM services to support multiple users. These tool-specific CM services imply constraints on how group members can coordinate. Worse, these CASE tool-specific constraints may conflict with the constraints imposed by other CASE tools, or with the broader software processes specified by an organization intent upon a conscientious process improvement program.

One way to express these difficulties is to view two CASE tools simultaneously from the viewpoint of the three-level model. Figure 22 illustrates this view by showing some characteristics of integration among the different levels of Sun's Network Software Environment (NSE, a CM system) and PROCASE's SMARTSystem (a C programming development tool). Figure 22 illustrates how the peculiarities of each system at each level of integration must be reconciled to achieve satisfactory integration.

8.4 Examples of Process and CASE Tool Interactions

FIGURE 22 Integration of Different Tools Within a Single Process Step.

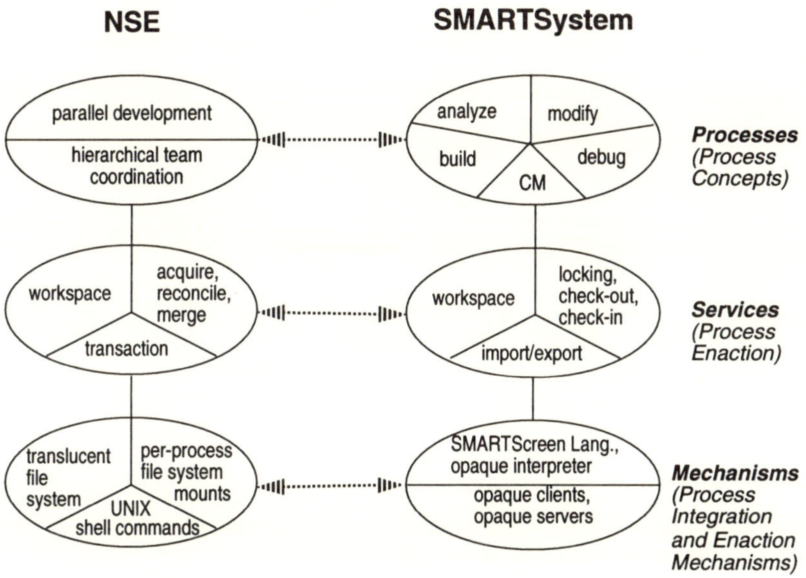

```
         NSE                        SMARTSystem

   ┌─────────────────┐         ┌─────────────────┐
   │ parallel development │     │  analyze │ modify │     Processes
   │─────────────────│  ···)   │──────────│        │     (Process
   │  hierarchical team │       │   build  │ debug  │     Concepts)
   │   coordination   │         │        CM        │
   └─────────────────┘         └─────────────────┘

   ┌─────────────────┐         ┌─────────────────┐
   │         │ acquire,│       │          │ locking, │
   │workspace│ reconcile,│ ···) │ workspace│ check-out,│   Services
   │         │ merge   │       │          │ check-in │    (Process
   │─────────────────│         │─────────────────│     Enaction)
   │   transaction   │         │  import/export  │
   └─────────────────┘         └─────────────────┘

   ┌─────────────────┐         ┌─────────────────┐
   │translucent│per-process│   │ SMARTScreen Lang.,│
   │file       │file system│   │  opaque interpreter│  Mechanisms
   │system     │  mounts  │ ···│──────────────────│  (Process
   │     UNIX         │         │  opaque clients, │  Integration
   │  shell commands  │         │  opaque servers  │  and Enaction
   └─────────────────┘         └─────────────────┘   Mechanisms)
```

8.4.3 Overlapping Tool Capabilities

The examples discussed above were based on a simple assumption, namely, that each life-cycle phase is equated with a single tool. If we remove this simplistic assumption about tools and life-cycle phases, the issues become still more complex. In Figure 23, several tools are depicted that could reasonably be available in a CASE environment. One important point to note is the overlap among various *kinds* of tools. In some cases the overlap is intentional and benign. For example, a design tool such as *Software through Pictures (StP)* can be thought to overlap coding tools to the extent to which StP can be used to generate module interface specifications. In a case such as this, CASE tools might overlap but provide services that amplify the effect of the tools. In other cases, the overlap can be useless (if not destructive). For example, it is not at all clear that there are any benefits to be gained from using two competing design notations and tools simultaneously (e.g., *AGE (Asa+Geode)* and *StP*).[2]

---

[2] Note that Figure 23 does not include references to CM tools, which could span all life-cycle phases and overlap with services provided by several of the CASE tools depicted.

FIGURE 23 Overlap Among CASE Tools Across Life-Cycle Steps.

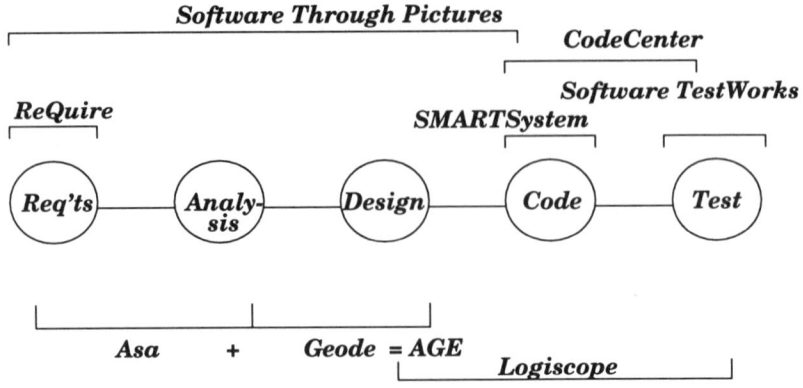

8.4.4 Life-Cycle Documentation

For almost any process as a whole, an item of particular significance is the generation and maintenance of documentation produced as a consequence of life-cycle requirements. As most developers of large-scale U.S. DoD software systems can testify, life-cycle standards such as DoD-STD-2167 require the production and maintenance of various kinds of documentation as a means of controlling and managing the software life cycle. Some kinds of documentation directly affect the kinds of CASE environment services used and, perhaps, how the services are used. For example, the requirement to maintain *unit development folders* to document every change to *software configuration items* will greatly affect the configuration management tools used and their optimal integration with the rest of the CASE environment. Other kinds of documentation may also be required that reflect traceability across various phases of the life cycle, e.g., tracing requirements to test cases.

The key problem, that of traceability, is particularly troublesome in current-generation CASE environments because of the characteristics of many CASE tool architectures that make data sharing among tools difficult. Obvious problems such as a tool's use of private, tool-specific repositories are amplified by different data models, data formats, and non-standard semantics in use among tools provided by different tool vendors. Environments such as SLCSE and Boeing's Advanced Software Environment [41] attempt to overcome these difficulties by mapping tool-specific data to a global data model representing life-cycle artifacts. Other approaches, reflected in systems such as IBM's AD/Cycle [48], attempt to bypass the need for external agents to perform tool-to-repository data mapping by specifying a standard data model to which vendor tools are intended to comply a priori.

The SLCSE and AD/Cycle approach clearly involve great expense and effort. For the purposes of practical third-party CASE tool integration, a more reasonable near-term approach is to understand and document the life-cycle data required, the relationships between those data and various CASE tools, and the procedures (manual, semi-automatic, and automatic) for generating those data.

8.5 Summary

As we have seen, process integration can be viewed from a variety of perspectives. Each of these perspectives adds to our discussion of process integration, but none completely captures the breadth and importance of process integration and its relationships to integration services and mechanisms. For example, Wasserman's perspective of process integration as a orthogonal dimension to data and control integration adds much to the discussion by focusing on the importance of process integration, but it does not address the central role of process as a driving force for choices between integration mechanisms and approaches. Viewing process integration as a set of relationships between tools (Thomas and Nejmeh) provides greater detail in how individual tools can interact to support a process, but does not address the larger picture of how multiples of tools are best organized to provide the greatest degree of support for users with multiple needs and roles. Finally, Humphrey's view of tools as secondary to process does not address the role that automation plays in determining what a reasonable process is.

The three-level model proposed in this book elevates the role of process integration to an equivalent position with services and mechanisms. In effect, this model attempts to take the middle ground between the mechanistic approaches to integration that have predominated in the CASE community, and the process-centric approach championed by Humphrey.

We suggest that neither a process-centric nor a mechanism-centric approach is adequate for constructing a CASE environment. Decisions concerning the process to be adopted within an organization should be made in the context of potential CASE support. Similarly, decisions concerning appropriate services and mechanisms should be made with consideration for the process to be supported.

We further suggest that progress in the area of integrated CASE environment support for software process will not be uniform. Process integration will likely be first achieved in support of small, well understood activities within the software life cycle, and only much later across the full life cycle. Thus, the probable future for process integration is bound up with our notion of a Federated Environment; i.e., just as tool integration will likely evolve as loose integrations of tightly integrated sets of tools, we predict that processes will be integrated in both loose and tight ways within these loose/tight federations of tools.

We also see some promise in the development of process modeling and enactment tools such as Process Weaver and Synervision. While these technologies have not yet matured, they do provide insight into ways to visualize the software process, as well as mechanisms to bind together multiple tightly integrated toolsets to form loose federations. However, we see a particular need for integration of process tools with control and data mechanisms such that the roles of the various mechanisms in implementing and maintaining the state of the supported process are clearly defined. Finally, we hope that as process tools mature, new and more intuitive ways of visualizing and encoding processes will be developed.

Part III: Practical Experiences with CASE Integration

The previous sections of this book discussed theoretical approaches to CASE integration, and integration technologies. In Part III, we report on our practical experiences in the area of CASE integration, including the use of some of the technologies introduced in the earlier sections.

First, experiments with CASE integration carried out at the Software Engineering Institute are described, and lessons learned from those experiments are identified. We view these experiments as a crucial and ongoing effort to identify how commercially available tools and framework products can be integrated in support of an organization's software activities.

Second, we discuss how various examples of a particular integration technology (in this case, message passing systems) can be used interchangeably in an integrated CASE environment. Such flexibility is particularly important in an area of unstable and rapidly developing technology.

Third, we focus on the issues involved in the integration of configuration management systems with other CASE tools in a CASE environment because doing so illustrates a number of issues that must be addressed in CASE tool integration.

Part III consists of the following chapters:

9. Experiments in Environment Integration

10. Replacing the Message Service in a CASE Integration Framework

11. Integration of CASE Tools with CM Systems: Lessons Learned

CHAPTER 9
Experiments in Environment Integration

9.1 Introduction

In assembling a CASE environment from a collection of commercial off-the-shelf (COTS) tools, tool users must find ways to connect the tools such that they provide adequate support for their particular software development approach. This task takes place in the context of limited knowledge of the tools, limited access to the source or internal structures of the tools, limited resources with which to perform and maintain the tool connections, and evolving understanding of the needs of the tool users. This places severe restrictions on what can be attempted in terms of tool interconnection.

Environment framework technologies (e.g., ECMA PCTE, ATIS, BMS, ToolTalk, or CORBA) claim to provide a set of common integration services that aid in the tool integration process. There have been numerous discussions about the value, maturity, and complexity of these framework technologies. Such discussions are characterized by three points: general agreement that framework technology per se is a valuable goal to pursue; moderate disagreement as to whether the current level of framework technology is a sufficient basis for production quality CASE environments; and considerable disagreement about which of the current technologies are the most likely to mature and succeed.

Notable about these discussions, however, is that there has *not* been extensive use of the technologies in question. This stems from several sources: their expense, their unfamiliarity and complexity to current tool users, and a widespread concern about their immaturity. This lack of use is perhaps understandable, but it has had the additional effect that partisans of one or another technology have made assertions based on little factual information about the relative merits of the technology in question.

To expand our own expertise in tool integration and framework technologies, and to answer the question, "What tool integrations are possible for third-party tool users given the current state of COTS tools and integration technology?" we performed a set of experiments involving the integration of a collection of common COTS tools with environment framework technologies in support of a typical development scenario. Our selection of these tools and technologies was based on common availability and application to the development scenario(s) of interest. Another approach to selecting tools would be to first examine the characteristics of the tools that tend to make them more or less integrable [50].

A major aim of this experimentation was to investigate the capabilities of various classes of integration technology, determine the practicality of their use, and analyze how such technology may be used in combination in the support of typical software development processes. Of particular interest was the problem of employing multiple framework components in the same CASE environment. We believe that the use of multiple framework components is inevitable due to:

- the problems of legacy tools and environments that must coexist with any new technologies,
- the need to combine framework technologies to compound their different strengths and to overcome their respective weaknesses, and
- the instability of the CASE environment marketplace and the evolutionary nature of the technology.

This chapter discusses a set of experiments integrating tools with the Emeraude Portable Common Tool Environment 1.5 (PCTE)[1] and BMS framework technologies.

9.2 The Integration Experiments

To gain initial familiarity with PCTE and BMS integration technologies and to represent the sort of third-party integration that is possible for commercial and government tool users, we defined an initial integration activity (that is, for the first experiment) constrained by a number of "ground rules." These ground rules included:

- The tool versions chosen were not to be constructed so as to take advantage of framework capabilities. We believe this reflects the reality of the present tool marketplace, with non-integrated existing tools and relatively unproven framework capabilities.
- No modifications could be made to source code of a COTS tool, even if source were available. It is our contention that only the largest organizations are able (often reluctantly) to accept the configuration and maintenance costs associated with modifying COTS tool source code. This ground rule does not preclude the use of the extensive tailoring facilities offered by many tools. In fact, such tailoring (often by updating start-up files, or building custom user interfaces) was encouraged as a way of taking maximum advantage of tool capabilities.
- The integration was to be driven by a simple process scenario. The process scenario would aid us in two ways: it would reflect a type of integration that organizations commonly want, and it would provide a blueprint for integration decisions.
- The integration experiment was to represent a relatively low to moderate investment in resources beyond those already allocated for purchase of the various tools. In our experience, a large-scale tool integration effort at an organizational level can quickly become prohibitively expensive and complex. The approach here was to attempt a less extensive level of integration that may be possible at a project level.

---

[1]. In our experiments, we used Emeraude PCTE 1.5 V12. Unless indicated otherwise, references to PCTE within this chapter pertain to this specific implementation. This implementation supports a version of the PCTE interface specification that differs considerably from that endorsed by the European Computer Manufacturers Association (ECMA). However, we believe that many of the lessons learned from our experiments with Emeraude PCTE 1.5 V12 are applicable to future ECMA PCTE implementations.

- Tool-provided capabilities for developing the system were to be used wherever possible. Thus, for example, the SoftBench Encapsulator tool was used to build a browser capability for the PCTE database.

In the first experiment, we were interested in the possibilities of a "loose" integration of the control integration capabilities of BMS with the data integration capabilities of PCTE. In keeping with a third-party strategy, a loose integration would require no changes to the source code of either framework, and would be accomplished using integration capabilities provided by PCTE and BMS as much as possible. In the initial experiment, we developed a simple, single-purpose scenario that represents the code and test cycle that is common to development and maintenance activities:

- The starting point of the scenario requires that the source code is under configuration management (CM) control.
- A change to the source is to be made.
- The source module is checked out from CM.
- The source is imported into the coding tool for modifications.
- The coding tool termination is trapped and initiates source check-in to CM.
- Check-in initiates compiling and linking.
- Completion of the compile/link initiates the activities of the testing tool.
- The test data and results are checked into CM.
- Completion of testing initiates the metrics tool.
- The metric data are checked into the CM tool.

On completion of the first experiment, a second was planned to provide further insight into the operation of framework technologies, particularly on how such technologies can work together in a "hybrid" CASE environment.

A hybrid CASE environment will likely incorporate a variety of tools with different operating environments. Some are likely to be UNIX tools, while others are likely to be more closely integrated with control and data frameworks. To experiment with creating tools ported to a framework and to simulate a hybrid environment, framework-specific tools were implemented.

Our initial efforts with building an experimental environment had served to reinforce our understanding of the importance of centering environment design on a well-defined understanding of organizational expectations and human activities. From this perspective the goal of integration is to produce an environment that supports the needs and expectations of environment users. The environment must operate within the context of the various constraints and limitations of those users. These factors provide the basis on which a CASE environment can be assembled — they guide the integration decisions that are made and can be used to validate the results of implementing those decisions.

As a result, we believe successful integration efforts are likely to be those that view construction of a CASE environment as a *design activity*. The construction of a CASE environment through design requires careful consideration of organizational and individual needs, as well as reasoned selections among various alternatives.

A major component of the context within which the design of a CASE environment takes place is a detailed understanding of the process, or scenario, that the CASE environment will support. We therefore began our second integration experiment by producing a more detailed scenario (relative to the previous experiment) describing a particular process and modeling the scenario using multiple notations.

9.2.1 Modeling the Scenario

The notations we used to model the scenario were textual description, IDEF0, structured implementation description, and ProNet (detailed below). The use of multiple notations permitted us to compare the effectiveness of each different notation, a useful exercise in itself. It also provided insight into the process scenario, since each notation has subtle differences that often affect the level of detail that can be expressed.

The textual description provides a general description of the process. It is roughly chronological ("First A happens, then B happens. If condition C arises, someone does A again...") and is neither formal nor hierarchical.

IDEF0 is a modification of the Structured Design and Analysis Technique (SADT) described in [46]. It consists of a series of rectangles and arrows. The rectangles correspond to process steps, and the arrows to data flows that form either output, input, or control to other process steps. IDEF0 diagrams are hierarchical, and a rectangle in one diagram is decomposed to produce several rectangles at lower levels. The IDEF0 notation of the scenario captured the scenario from an implementation-independent perspective.

The structured implementation description captured the details of the implementation. The form of this description separates individual process steps, isolates the actions that comprise each step, and lists inputs and outputs, assumptions about pre- and post-conditions for each process step, and also records design decisions made during implementation. This description includes particular items specific to PCTE and BMS. This description is sequential, not hierarchical. As a simple organizing principle, we decided that when the description of any process step exceeds an arbitrary length (a single page), the process step is broken into subprocesses and each is described separately.

Finally, a description using the ProNet notation was produced. ProNet is an experimental notation developed at the SEI [22]. Its primary application is in the representation of processes, and it has previously been successfully applied to the definition of a large configuration management system [68]. The approach of ProNet is to model activities that form the basic tasks within a process. Activities are linked via their entry and exit conditions and products produced. Also, ProNet represents the agents that enact the activities within particular roles. Finally, data stores are used to represent persistent objects such as documents and other products.

The textual description and the first and second level IDEF0 models are described in more detail in subsequent paragraphs. The complete set of models can be found in Brown et al. [8].

9.2.1.1 Textual Description

The scenario takes place in the context of an existing software product that is supported by an integrated development environment. At the time the scenario takes place, the product already exists in one version, and a change request triggers the creation of a new version of the product.

A change request against a version of the product is generated by a Change Control Board (CCB). (The operation of the CCB itself is outside the scope of the scenario.) The change request is read to determine information on the required change that is to be made, as well as other pertinent information (e.g, a tracking number, the name of the developer responsible). Working versions of all files (source code, tests, etc.) that will be revised to create the new product version are created. New requirements are allocated to the appropriate person: requirements on the new code to the developer; requirements on new testing to the QA personnel. The old source code is edited in accordance with new requirements indicated in the change request. The revised files are then compiled. After determining that the code has been correctly modified, the developer will indicate that the revised code is ready for QA testing.

Testing includes whatever formal testing is required by the change request. If new tests are required, they are created and performed; if coverage testing is required, the testing is performed appropriately. The result of testing is either an indication that the new revision has passed testing or that the code needs further revision. When testing has successfully completed, static analysis is done on the

9.2 The Integration Experiments

source code. After static analysis is complete, all components of the new version of the product (source files, makefile, object code, tests) are stabilized as a new version of the product.

9.2.1.2 IDEF0 Description

IDEF0 uses a graphical notation to decompose a process. By convention, the highest level of the process is shown as a single step. Figure 24 shows the top-level IDEF0 model for the process scenario.

FIGURE 24 Top-Level IDEF0 Diagram.

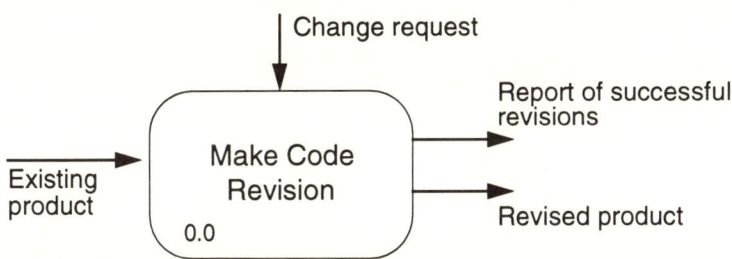

A key feature of IDEF0 is the separation of input and control arrows. Input arrows (which enter from the side) indicate that data coming into a process step will undergo some transformation during the step; an example is code that is modified. Control arrows (which enter from the top) indicate data that govern a transformation, but that are not themselves transformed. An example is a set of requirements that control a code modification.

At all levels other than the highest one, IDEF0 requires that any arrow that enters or leaves the page be traceable to the next higher or lower level. Thus, at the next level, shown in Figure 25, the input arrow from the first level appears, as does the single control arrow and the two output arrows. This figure shows that the single rectangle from the first level (Make Code Revision) has been decomposed into four steps: Begin Code Revision, Implement Code Change, Implement Test Procedures, and Finalize Code Change. Succeeding levels of decomposition break these steps into lower-level descriptions.

FIGURE 25 Second-Level IDEF0 Diagram.

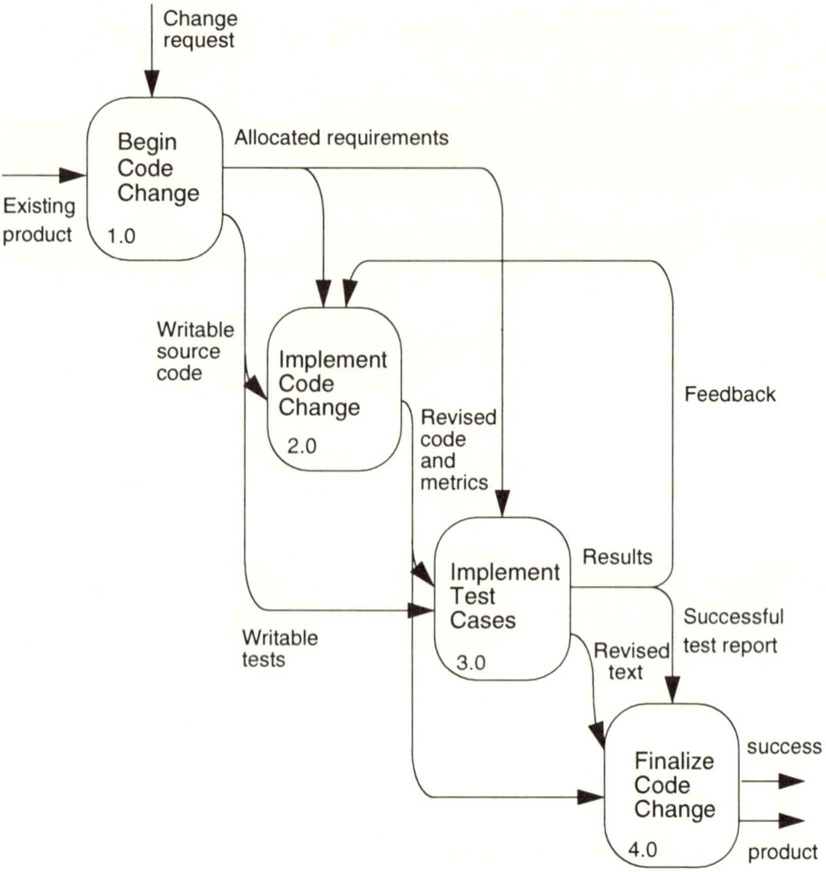

9.2.2 Tools

The tools used in these experiments were selected for their fit into the scenario(s), the degree of process support afforded, and opportunities provided by the tools to integrate more tightly with frameworks (porting and custom implementation). The specific tools incorporated into the experiments are described below.

9.2 The Integration Experiments 159

Tools used in the first experiment only included:

- A custom-built CM tool making use of existing versioning functions built into the PCTE system. Operations of the tool were driven via BMS request messages to check-in/check-out a particular object from or to the UNIX file system and PCTE.
- PROCASE SMARTSystem was chosen to provide code management and development capabilities. The SMARTSystem tool was treated as a "black box." That is, a source file was imported into the system, and a (potentially) modified version was exported back to a UNIX file. A BMS encapsulation was built for SMARTSystem to provide a message interface making use of existing command line functionality.

Tools common to both experiments included:

- Development/coding tools of the HP SoftBench framework were used heavily in both experiments. This toolset includes a Development Manager (DM) tool, a Program Builder (BUILD) tool, a Program Editor (EDIT) tool, and a Configuration Management (CM) tool interface. These tools are all tightly integrated (via BMS) within SoftBench.
- In the first experiment, Software TestWorks tools were encapsulated and messages were developed to generate test cases and execute tests. Test success or failure was communicated via a BMS notification message. In the second experiment, the tools were integrated via the SoftBench BUILD facility to incorporate code coverage analysis into the testing phase. To do this, the source code under test had to be instrumented and recompiled. We felt that this process was best left to the BUILD utility (via "makefile" additions to invoke the source code instrumenter, compile the instrumented source, and link the intermediate objects). As this portion of the "testing" was to be under BUILD control, it seemed a relatively easy (and appropriate) extension to add makefile rules to also generate test cases, execute test cases, and collect test statistics (i.e., execution results and coverage analysis). This removed the requirement of porting the testing tools to the PCTE framework. Additionally, no new BMS messages had to be defined or modified as they are already defined by SoftBench and the BUILD utility.
- In the first experiment, existing public domain utilities providing McCabe, Halstead, and KDSI metrics were encapsulated. The encapsulation was driven via BMS requests for application of one of the specific metrics. Completion of the metrics operation was broadcast via a BMS notification message. In addition, the existing SoftBench static analysis tool ("softstatic") was used to gather additional metrics data. Only the public domain Metrics Tool that provided KDSI metrics was used in the second experiment. However, to learn more about the C language interface to Emeraude PCTE 1.5,

we ported this UNIX-based tool to the PCTE framework. The KDSI Metrics Tool source code was modified to store the metrics results (lines of code, number of blank lines, number of comment lines, and number of comments) as individual attributes on the OMS object containing the C source code. In addition, the tool was modified to support BMS messages.

Tools used in the second experiment only included:

- A custom Change Request Parser was developed that is conversant in the vocabularies of both PCTE and BMS. The Change Request Parser transfers change request information stored in an ASCII file into the PCTE OMS to be stored as part of the new version. The raw change request is stored as the contents of the "change_request" object as well as parsed into its components, each of which is stored in an attribute on the change_request object. The Change Request Parser is activated by a BMS message that states the path to the change_request object, the schema to be used, and the location of the change request in the file system. On completion, the Change Request Parser sends a PASS or FAIL reply message. Information maintained for a change request includes a tracking number; names and e-mail addresses for the Change Control Board approving the change and the responsible developer and quality assurance personnel; the priority of the change; and data about the testing to be performed on the modified software. Testing information includes a flag indicating whether new tests are required, as well as a specification (as a percentage) of the level of code coverage that is required in testing.
- The SCCS configuration management system was used. The existing SoftBench interface to SCCS was used to provide CM control over files after they had been exported from the PCTE OMS. The use of SCCS to provide CM control in the user's workspace and PCTE to provide similar control in the project OMS set up a two-level configuration management structure. The import/export of the source code and makefiles to and from the two CM levels was initiated through the use of BMS messages (Figure 26).

9.2 The Integration Experiments

FIGURE 26 Two-Level Configuration Management.

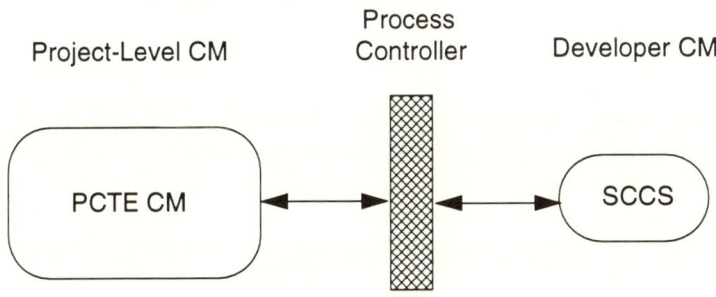

9.2.3 Frameworks

Framework mechanisms were chosen to provide both data and control integration capabilities (PCTE and BMS, respectively). We were interested both in the manner in which the individual mechanisms supported integration of tools in the context of a well-defined process, as well as how they could be used in concert. A Process Controller was developed in part to relate the capabilities of the data and control-oriented approaches. For this reason, it is considered here as part of the framework.

The HP Encapsulator tool integration facility of the HP SoftBench environment was used to produce an Object Management System (OMS) browser for the PCTE OMS and to provide graphical user interfaces and message interfaces for existing tools. In the first experiment, the SoftBench Encapsulator Definition Language (EDL) was chosen for our encapsulations. In the second experiment, encapsulations were created using the C language interface to the Encapsulator tool.

Encapsulations providing a graphical user interface were built for tools employing standard input/output and command line interfaces. In addition, an encapsulation was built for the PROCASE SMARTSystem (in the first experiment) to provide a message interface making use of command line functionality, but with no Encapsulator-defined graphical user interface.

9.2.3.1 PCTE

In the first experiment, Emeraude's PCTE 1.5 was used primarily to define a repository in which to store tool artifacts, and to provide configuration and version control over those artifacts. Tools were not rewritten to take advantage of PCTE services, nor was the structure of a tool's internal data modified or mapped onto PCTE. The data files from individual tools were stored directly as the contents of PCTE file objects. When a tool was to be started, a copy of the data in the PCTE file object was made available to the tool. When the processing of the tool was complete, a new PCTE object was created along with the appropriate links to other objects.

To avoid forcing the encapsulation code to be aware of the object type and name in the PCTE OMS, a mapping scheme was developed that allowed the encapsulation code to derive the necessary PCTE OMS information based on a standard file-naming convention. This resulted in a message interface to the PCTE encapsulation that supported the same message types as the SCCS and RCS encapsulations. Thus, the CM service could be implemented either by the SoftBench SCCS encapsulation or our PCTE CM encapsulation simply by changing a single entry in a start-up file for the experiment. This approach illustrates the potential advantages of a common message standard within a service domain.

A particularly significant capability of the PCTE data framework that we wished to exercise more completely in the second experiment (than in the initial experiment) is the capability to define data objects, attributes of those objects, and relationships to other objects. These types of attributes and relationships are defined in a schema definition set (SDS). The SDS serves as a mechanism by which the relationships among the data generated by a collection of tools can be defined.

Based on the scenario described earlier, an SDS for this experiment was designed to maintain information about a number of aspects of the "product" under development. Data types represented in the SDS included information about the change request that initiates the scenario, the source and object files for code, test data and test results, a series of attributes that reflects current process status, and a log of process steps and access to objects and attributes.

A significant change from the earlier experiment was the use of the PCTE OMS to maintain information about the state of each data object. Process information was stored as a set of attributes. The more significant process attributes include:

- *is_stable*, indicating whether the version was a "stable" or working version.
- *is_compiled*, indicating whether the developer had compiled a source file.
- *is_tested*, indicating whether testing had been completed.
- *is_modified*, indicating whether a component had been changed.
- *is_analyzed*, indicating whether a component had been analyzed.
- *currently_exported*, indicating whether somebody was using the version.
- *regression_tests_passed*, indicating whether recession testing was complete.
- *new_tests_passed*, indicating whether new testing was complete.

9.2.3.2 BMS

In the experiments, integrated communication takes place via BMS messages. Tools were integrated with BMS by registering interest in messages of various types. Typically, a "Request" message was sent to indicate that processing of the tool should begin. On completion of its task, a tool would inform the requesting tool of its activities via a "Notify" message. Similar Request and Notify messages were used to send mail, gather metrics data, execute tests, and operate the SoftBench Development Manager and development tools.

Lacking the capability to modify BMS itself, we wanted to determine whether the standard BMS product could be of use with PCTE frameworks to provide control integration. Especially important would be the capability for this control integration mechanism to cross the boundary between the UNIX world of files, pipes and UNIX processes, and the PCTE world of objects, relationships, and message queues so that UNIX-based tools could communicate with PCTE-based tools.

To enable UNIX- and PCTE-based tools to be co-resident in the same environment (in the second experiment), it was necessary to establish agreements or protocols that controlled their collective use. For example, the context portion of a BMS message normally communicates the UNIX host, directory, and filename that a tool is to act on. We adopted the convention that the directory and filename components of the context portion of a BMS message represent the path to a PCTE object. This enabled us to add a message interface to the PCTE-based Metrics Tool that is identical to the interface for the UNIX-based tool. Such agreements are an essential component and critical design decision when using multiple framework technologies.

Information in the PCTE OMS was accessed by providing an encapsulated BMS interface to the required PCTE interfaces. In this manner, the exporting and importing of objects between the PCTE OMS and UNIX file system, along with the storage and retrieval of information from objects and attributes, could be directed. Thus, for example, the Change Request Parser executed by reading a UNIX file and storing information in appropriate attributes on receipt of a BMS request message.

9.2.3.3 Process Controller

The Process Controller was developed as the "backbone" of the environment to provide a means of guiding and coordinating activities in support of the chosen development scenario. The Process Controller can be thought of as an automated or centralized process "director" residing on top of a collection of user- and process-related environment services. Without the Process Controller or a similar capability, the individual tools in the environment would have to be rewritten to incorporate scenario and process attributes.

The Process Controller is a central component of the experiment because it alone has knowledge of all aspects of the process scenario, the relationships of the integrated tools, and the product data. It serves to guide, enforce, and monitor the process, as well as to report on the status of the process. It is the Process Controller that directs and initiates the sending of BMS messages to start tools in the appropriate sequence.

In the first experiment, the Process Controller was an EDL-based encapsulation. The experiment scenario was "hard coded" inside the Process Controller, acting much like a serialized shell script. The successful completion of one step of the scenario (as indicated by a BMS notification message from an encapsulated tool) would initiate the next step (via a BMS request message from the process controller to an encapsulated tool). The Process Controller also maintained the state of the scenario via interaction with the CM tool. Prior to initiating each step of the scenario, the Process Controller requested check-out of required objects. As each step was completed, the process controller would request check-in of any resulting objects.

In the second experiment, the Process Controller was constructed in a modular fashion using the C language and the Emeraude PCTE 1.5 and HP Encapsulator libraries. The Encapsulator libraries provided for control integration via BMS messages and a Motif-style graphical user interface (GUI), whereas the PCTE libraries provided access to data services.

The Process Controller was originally conceived as a single capability, but was subsequently modified to reflect two distinct layers: environment services and process enactment. The environment services layer defines a set of primitive actions in the environment. For example, services are defined to check out a version, perform testing, and send mail. The process enactment layer serves to bind together the environment services into a sequence of activities reflecting the required process. It also enforces process-specific rules constraining transitions between process steps, and initiates the sending of mail messages to interested parties.

The flow between process steps in the Process Controller occurs in two manners: event-driven and automatic. An event-driven transition is caused by the selection of a menu item by a user to activate or complete a process step. An automatic transition occurs upon completion of a process step that inevitably (according to the encoded process) must be followed by a specific activity. Both transition methods are desirable in a development environment. Event-driven

9.2 The Integration Experiments

transitions are useful when the user is to be given control over activities, generally in less constraining process steps. Automatic transitions are useful when strict process enforcement is required or when activities that require no user intervention are to occur (such as the recording of process data for future verification).

To initiate the scenario execution in the second experiment, a script is executed that starts all of the PCTE-based tools. This is to ensure that all these tools are available when they are needed since they cannot be started via BMS messages in the UNIX-PCTE context (a limitation of the particular implementations we were using). This was not a problem in the initial experiment, as SoftBench could automatically start the appropriate tools (via the Execution Manager) in the UNIX-only context.

The menu items on the Process Controller GUI are updated to show only currently allowable actions, thus limiting the choice of actions that can be taken as the user proceeds through the process steps. In the second experiment, the user sets the context of the session by selecting the desired product and version from scrollable lists when the Process Controller is started. The determination of what choices are to be presented to the user is then made by scanning attributes within the PCTE OMS that encode the state of the process. Figure 27 shows this Process Controller user interface.

FIGURE 27 Process Controller User Interface.

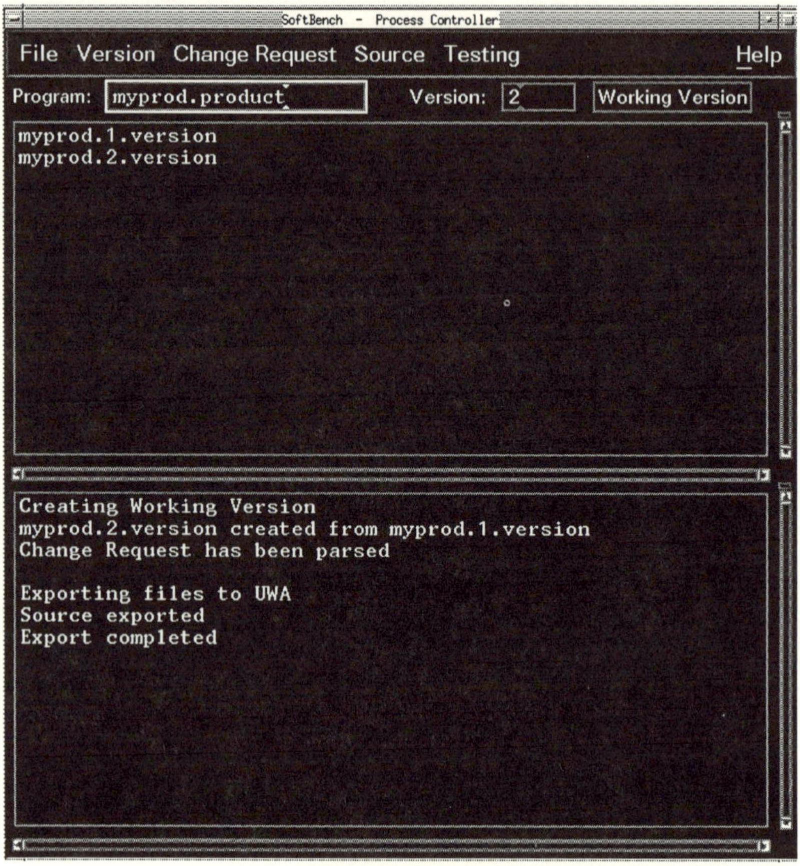

In contrast to the first experiment, all process status information here is maintained completely within the OMS; none is maintained within the Process Controller. However, the Process Controller does provide an interface to browse the status of development. Figure 28 provides status output after a new version has been created but before actual code modifications have begun.

9.2 The Integration Experiments

FIGURE 28 Development Status Before Code Modification.

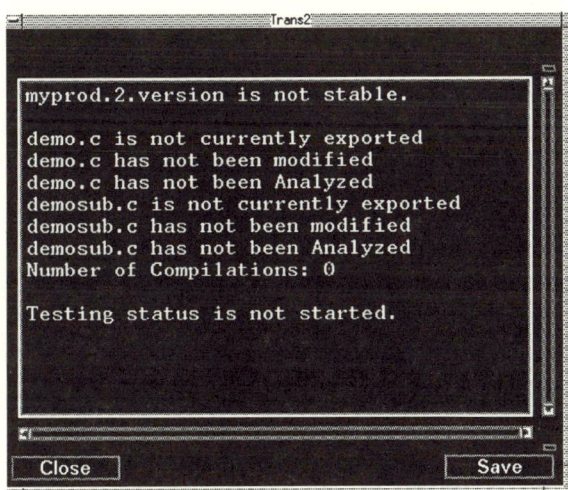

As the scenario is executed, the PCTE OMS is updated with new status information. Figure 29 provides status output after code modifications, testing, and analysis are complete for the new version.

FIGURE 29 Development Status After Modification, Testing, and Analysis.

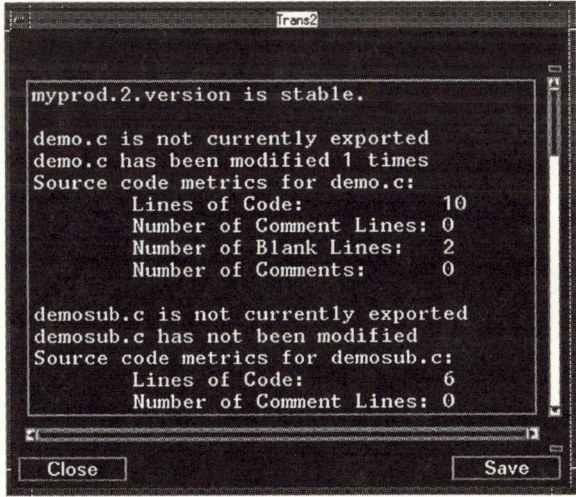

9.2.4 Lessons Learned from the Experiments

While the experiments discussed in this chapter provided interesting insights into the potential of integration frameworks, those insights must be evaluated within the constraints placed on the work. These constraints include:

- No implementation of ECMA PCTE was available. Integration activities were carried out using Emeraude PCTE 1.5. While the two PCTE variants are conceptually similar, differences do exist between the two technologies. It is our intention to identify relevant differences by porting our experimental environment to ECMA PCTE when an implementation becomes available to us.

- The process scenarios we chose to enact do not reflect the complete software life cycle. Specifically, no attempt was made to include front-end tools (such as analysis and design tools) or to address Mil-Std documentation requirements. However, we do believe that the chosen scenarios reflect a realistic process, oriented toward code maintenance.

- The scope of investigation into issues such as suitability for programming in the large and robustness of the framework products was limited by our resource constraints. Experimentation and development activities beyond the means available to us are necessary before such issues can be fully addressed.

These experiments were intended to provide insight *based on actual use* into whether the current level of framework technology is helpful in building process-centered software environments. Of particular interest was the potential for coexistence of control-oriented (BMS) and data-oriented (PCTE) technologies in producing an integrated process-centered environment. Subsequent to the completion of these experiments, a PCTE supplier announced the intention of integrating its forthcoming ECMA PCTE capability with the ToolTalk control-oriented capability available on Sun Microsystems platforms. Potentially, these experiments can suggest ways in which such integrated capabilities can work together, and illustrate their limitations and weaknesses.

The conclusions we have derived from our experiments fall into three areas: framework support, process support, and tool support. These areas are addressed below.

9.2.4.1 Framework Support

9.2.4.1.1 PCTE

Emeraude PCTE 1.5 functioned effectively in our experiments, providing particularly useful support in the areas of data relationships, persistent storage of process state, and versioning/configuration management. UNIX tools were integrated effectively into the experimental environments by providing a capability to import/export data between UNIX and the PCTE OMS, or by direct porting of the tools. PCTE relationships were defined between data from various tools.

In the initial experiment, PCTE served as a data storage mechanism only (to store versions of objects), with the custom-designed CM tool providing a bridge between PCTE and UNIX for checking data in and out of the PCTE OMS. All data storage in the PCTE OMS was coarse-grained, using the contents of PCTE objects to store file-sized data.

While few PCTE facilities were used in our first experiment, the use of PCTE to maintain and relate tool data did provide a measure of traceability between the data (source, object, metrics, and test data) and the potential for defining new tools to access the shared data. While this capability was useful, we found that we could substitute a traditional CM/versioning system (SCCS) for PCTE with few ill effects to the experiment. Clearly, PCTE was underused in the initial experiment.

In the subsequent experiment, the PCTE database, and in particular attributes associated with objects, served as the persistent storage mechanism for the state of the enacted process. Information about the state of the process was therefore always available for query. Not only does this approach provide a natural relationship of process state with the artifacts of development, but it also leads to a potential for the development of useful process browsing tools. Browsing tools could allow the user to gather such information as the coding assignments of engineers, the testing status of each source component, and the status of specific change requests. We view this capability to be particularly important for project managers.

However, based on this work and preliminary work with the new generation of process management tools such as Process Weaver [29], it is apparent that a potential tension exists between process management tools and object management systems and messaging systems. Both approaches incorporate the capability to maintain process state, as well as to enact the process. However, current generation process management tools do not provide a capability for data integration.

From our perspective, the object management system (whether based on PCTE or other technology) is the more appropriate locale for process state information. This allows state information to be stored directly with the associated artifact (e.g., source files, documents) and provides the opportunity to build browsing tools accessing this information. Therefore, the value added due to process management tools appears to be primarily in the area of process visualization where, for example, Process Weaver provides for a petri net model of the process being enacted.

Our experience and the experience of others [6] suggests that the PCTE schema will often be closely tied to the process to be supported. This in turn suggests that there may be opportunities to develop process management tools that are custom-crafted to work with PCTE environments. Ideally, these tools would allow graphical representation of the activity flow representing a process, the associated PCTE schema, and the relationships between the process and the schema. Such a tool could simplify both the definition and modification of process-centered environments built around PCTE.

9.2.4.1.2 BMS

A primary finding of our work is that the commercial BMS product (which is not specifically developed to run on a PCTE framework) can be a useful mechanism to integrate UNIX, BMS, and PCTE tools into a single, process-centered environment. The BMS provided us with a basic messaging substrate that simplified the sequencing of tools in support of the process scenario. From our perspective, the messaging interface provided by BMS was at a higher level, and therefore easier to use than the low-level communication services provided by Emeraude PCTE 1.5 (and also ECMA PCTE).

However, managing the diverse mechanisms for starting processes in Emeraude PCTE 1.5, BMS, and UNIX was particularly troublesome. We were unable to find a way to start Emeraude PCTE 1.5 processes via BMS messages (BMS was running in the UNIX environment, not as a PCTE process). We view this as a particularly important capability since it is likely that initial environments will contain a mix of PCTE and UNIX resident tools, much like our experimental environment.

We also found that the use of messaging standards is critical to achieving the goal of a control-oriented, federated environment to allow multiple, equivalent implementations of a tool or service to be interchanged in the environment. The approach to enabling such flexibility is to reach an agreement in any one service area on the exact syntax and semantics of the messages that are sent and received for that service. By conforming to predefined SoftBench version management message types, for example, we were able to exchange SCCS with the PCTE-based CM tool in the first experiment.

Finally, it should be noted that while we used BMS in these experiments, the results also apply to other equivalent message-passing systems. This is illustrated in detail in the following chapter, which describes a subsequent experiment that was performed to incorporate the Sun ToolTalk and DEC FUSE message servers into our experiment framework in place of BMS.

9.2.4.2 Process Management Support

In our experiments, the only component that bridged the gap between BMS and PCTE is the Process Controller. While constructing the Process Controller was not difficult once the basics of PCTE and BMS were mastered, the process to encode within the Process Controller became the most significant issue raised by these experiments. For example, the integrated environment developed in the first experiment was highly inflexible, and users were forced to follow the carefully scripted scenario in lock step. Deviation from the script was prohibited to preserve the integrity of data. While this mode of operation may be entirely appropriate in some circumstances, it is too restrictive in general.

It became clear that we do not yet understand the types of process integration that are appropriate for various organizations and individuals. Within even this simple experiment, we were forced to make a number of decisions concerning whether to implement process support (which guides a worker), process control (which enforces certain activities), or process monitoring (recording the state of given activities). The distinction among these approaches to process support is quite obvious to developers, who commonly react negatively to what they perceive as over-intrusive process control and monitoring. It is also obvious to project managers, who frequently favor the more controlled approaches to insure that project engineers adhere to a specified process.

Even among ourselves, the nature of process enactment led to lively debate. Management advocates were in favor of maintaining a count of the number of compiles attempted against a particular software component, while software developers viewed such monitoring as a clumsy attempt to control the manner in which they performed their responsibilities. Eventually, the monitoring of compiles was incorporated into the second experiment, but developers began discussing ways to circumvent the monitoring function!

In spite of the disagreements concerning the level of process support that was appropriate, we reached an unexpected conclusion that a "hybrid" environment, consisting of only a few PCTE-knowledgeable tools cooperating with other, non-PCTE tools, can provide a significant degree of process integration. The implication of this finding is that the "shallow" integrations (sometimes called encapsulations) of COTS tools with PCTE that are likely to appear first may be useful when combined with a few carefully chosen, "deep" tool integrations. As we have stressed throughout this book, the key to their effective use lies in the appropriate selection of process fragments that would benefit from automated support. Without a clear and precise understanding of the process being supported, this integration will be haphazard at best.

9.2.4.3 Tools

We found that PCTE encapsulation of an existing tool (representing tool data as the contents of PCTE objects, and importing/exporting tool data between UNIX and PCTE) provided a modest, but useful, degree of integration for tools that are not PCTE-based. However, with this approach, the engineer is constrained by the design decisions made by the original tool architects. Significant limitations can derive from the fact that the file structure used by the tool to store data cannot be modified and therefore must be modeled directly as one or more PCTE objects.

In our experiments, we identified several cases where the granularity of data and notifications provided by a tool were not ideal for the needs of a CASE environment. For example, while we were able to trap a message from the SoftBench BUILD utility indicating that a compilation had occurred, we could not discern which component had been compiled (the granularity of the notification was not sufficient). Such information would be necessary to keep complete and accurate statistics of software compilations. Lacking this information, we were forced to make assumptions about a compilation.

In addition, it was sometimes difficult to interpret the messages returned from specific tools. For example, one tool may return a status indicating that the tool was successful when the tool does not fail with an error (even though the tool could not complete the expected processing). However, another tool may use "success" to mean that the tool executed to completion and accomplished the intended actions. This variation in meaning on occasion forced us to look for alternative methods of determining what had actually happened. Unfortunately, the alternatives were frequently awkward.

Fortunately, we found it relatively easy to build simple PCTE tools or to convert simple UNIX tools (for which source was available) to PCTE. The primary change necessary in converting a tool was to modify file-based input and output to the storing and retrieving of object contents and the setting and retrieving of attributes. A public domain static analysis tool was converted to PCTE in this manner, and a change request tool was custom-built to make extensive use of PCTE objects and attributes.

9.2 The Integration Experiments 173

We derived two benefits in storing data values as individual attributes on objects rather than in a related object: data could be closely tied to the object with which they were associated; and data could be stored in fine granularity requiring no additional parsing. However, since the goals of our experiments and the tools ported or implemented for PCTE were quite simple, no attempt was needed or made to structure the tools to take advantage of the many other capabilities of PCTE. In addition, the schema modifications necessary to support these tools were trivial.

It is clear that porting a more complex tool like a structured analysis and design tool would require extensive schema design work to model the complex data relationships both within the tool, and to external data objects. In addition, a more complex tool would likely use more PCTE services and be composed of multiple PCTE processes. It is also likely that the porting of a UNIX tool to ECMA PCTE would be slightly more difficult than a similar port to Emeraude PCTE 1.5, since ECMA PCTE interfaces diverge more from UNIX than those of Emeraude PCTE 1.5. The burden imposed by these changes to prevailing tool structure is unclear.

In contrast to the expectations of some framework supporters, we were unable to design a tool that we considered to be "general purpose" (i.e., one that could be used in a wide variety of environments, but that could still provide the level of process support desired). While designing the Change Request Parser, we were faced with a trade-off between producing a general-purpose tool that was loosely connected to the experimental process and producing a special-purpose tool with strong process support characteristics. In an attempt to produce a tool that is less dependent on a particular process and schema (and in theory more general purpose), the working schema is passed to the Change Request Parser as an input parameter to the tool. However, to provide the level of integrated support that is desired, the attributes managed by the Change Request Parser are closely wedded to the specific process scenario and the associated schema. As a result, it is likely that the tool would only be of use in alternate situations where the associated process and schema are highly similar to the experimental process and schema.

In summary, based on our experiences of writing a simple PCTE tool, it appears that writing for a PCTE platform (as opposed to a UNIX platform) does not significantly increase the difficulty of producing the tool. However, decisions with respect to the process supported and schema used by the tool are inevitably built into the tool itself. This may reduce the portability of the tool across different PCTE-based environments.

9.3 Summary

A surprising degree of process support was provided by a few tools tightly integrated with the framework products. Chief among these tools was the Process Controller, which provided a smooth process interface bridging the gap between the various frameworks.

We can summarize the results of our experiments as follows:

- It appears to be possible for third-party tool users to construct simple, integrated CASE environments using existing tools and framework technologies.
- The coexistence of data- and control-oriented frameworks, even when these frameworks are not integrated, can be extremely useful in developing process-centered environments.
- While non-integrated framework support is useful, integrated data- and control-oriented frameworks could help to solve problems of object naming and process start-up, and enhance the capabilities of both framework components.
- Hybrid environments that include PCTE-resident and UNIX-resident components can provide a practical and useful degree of integration. The few PCTE-resident tools in our experiment provided significant process support in conjunction with the OMS. However, this approach places significant constraints on the Process Controller software, which must be conversant in multiple worlds.
- Porting of individual, simple tools to a PCTE framework is not complex. The degree of difficulty for more complex tools is unclear.
- The process information resident in the structure of the PCTE schema and the contents of its objects and attributes can be used to guide a process scenario.
- While tool and framework technology are beginning to provide a mechanism for process integration, our understanding of the types of process integration that are appropriate for users is not well developed.

In conclusion, these experiments have suggested a number of areas where additional research is needed. Primary among these is a need to investigate the appropriate types of process support and process-centered environments for various individuals, groups, and organizations. Work on our experimental environment suggests that the process needs of individuals, groups, and organizations differ, and successful process-centered CASE environments must address these varying needs.

9.3 Summary

A second research area involves addressing the many issues that remain concerning framework technology. Issues to be addressed include: technical issues, since framework technology is new and unproven; market issues, since no single framework technology has been universally accepted by users, and the increasingly blurred distinction between workstations and personal computers may bring new vendors into play; and adoption issues, since unbiased comparisons of various framework technologies are generally not available, and strategies for adopting frameworks are largely untried.

A third potential area of research involves determining a way in which migration from the current heterogenous toolsets to future framework-based environments may occur. This problem is of particular importance to organizations employing multiple subcontractors to build very large systems. Many such organizations are now pondering how to incorporate current tools and development artifacts into framework-based environments. It is likely that the structure of the framework-based environments under development will influence the difficulty of this process.

CHAPTER 10
Replacing the Message Service in a CASE Integration Framework

10.1 Introduction

In the experiment scenario described in the previous chapter, control integration was accomplished through inter-tool communication via messages. In this approach, tools interact by passing messages (through a message system) requesting services of each other and notifying each other of their actions. This eliminates the need to duplicate functionality among tools, and the need to coordinate and operate via a shared tool database. Many influential vendors have considered this approach as a basis for control integration in CASE environment applications. To this end, Hewlett-Packard, Sun Microsystems, IBM, Unix Systems Laboratories (USL), The Santa Cruz Operation (SCO), and Univel formed the Common Open Software Environment (COSE) alliance.

Hewlett-Packard already uses the "control integration via messaging" approach in its SoftBench framework product. Therefore, the original experiment used the message passing capabilities of SoftBench (particularly, the SoftBench

Encapsulator and Broadcast Message Server (BMS)) as the primary means of tool-activity synchronization in the scenario.

While analyzing the results of the initial set of experiments, we determined that the use of BMS as the message passing component of the experiment framework could (at least in principle) be replaced by an equivalent product such as Sun's ToolTalk or Digital's FUSE. This is significant in that one of the premises of the work of the SEI CASE Environments Project, and of the experiments in particular, is that different implementations of similar services can be easily interchanged to provide a degree of interoperability. The ability to interchange control-oriented integration framework mechanisms is an important part of that premise.

While it would have been possible to hypothesize about the feasibility of the message service replacement by comparing and contrasting the services and their inherent functionality, it was decided to demonstrate better the practicality of the operation by example. An extension to the experiment was undertaken then, not to see if the message service replacement was theoretically possible, but to examine the process of actually performing (or attempting to perform) the replacement. An additional consideration of this experiment was to see if it was realistically possible to determine if one message service was "more applicable" to a specific framework or scenario than the other.

The initial set of experiments concentrated on the examination of messaging systems as the basis of control integration within a development framework. It was proposed that message server replacement, even with the stipulation that it be (for all practical purposes) transparent to the framework or scenario, was ultimately achievable. With this experiment, it was also proposed that although these different message services provide different functional capabilities in support of control integration, the choice of message service is basically application independent.

This chapter is presented as an introduction to the task of determining whether an integration framework that is message passing-based would be better purchased for use in a CASE environment, or built using existing message service components. The chapter outlines the types of activities that precede development of a specific message-based integration framework (i.e., one that emulates the SoftBench Encapsulator), the considerations involved in choosing a specific messaging interface for a set of tools, and the effort involved in adapting that message interface to the framework.

This chapter also discusses the background to the message server replacement experiment, the development of an Encapsulator emulation for use with

ToolTalk, the addition of the ToolTalk interface to the emulation framework, the execution of the original experiment scenario under the emulation, and the task of replacement of the message service in the emulation framework. It concludes with a presentation of the lessons learned, a summary of the experiment, and consideration of possible areas for follow-on work and experimentation.

10.2 Background

According to the original experiment scenario, the tools used provide support for a typical software maintenance function. The scenario was structured around coding, metrics, testing, message server, and CM tools, along with a process control tool to manage execution of the scenario. The scenario was initially implemented around BMS as the integration framework, with PCTE as the CM data repository. To use the capabilities of PCTE, a simple file transfer mechanism was developed between PCTE and the UNIX file system. Figure 30 identifies the tools and framework components of the scenario.

FIGURE 30 Tool and Framework Structure.

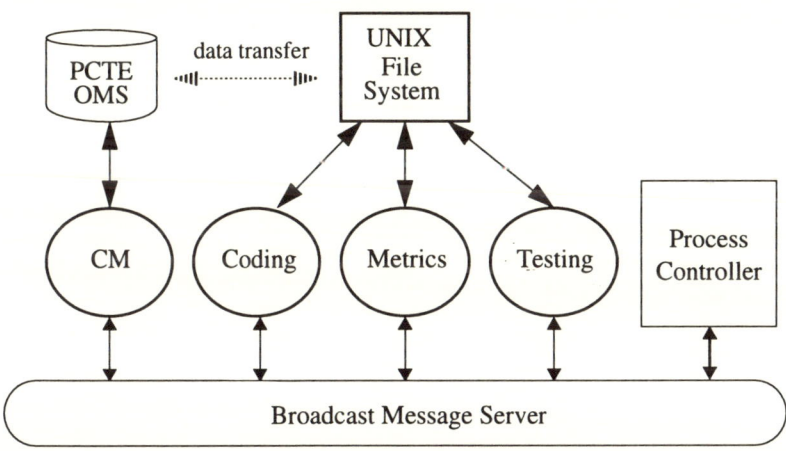

In this experiment, it was decided that ToolTalk would be used as the alternate message service as it was readily available (ToolTalk is included as part of Sun OpenWindows Version 3.0). The preferred approach was to modify the Soft-Bench Encapsulator to use ToolTalk instead of BMS, but the SoftBench source code was unavailable. It was decided instead that some portion of SoftBench would be "reinvented" to support the experiment. It was also noted that the Soft-

Bench utilities of the Encapsulator would have to be replaced by other technologies. ToolTalk does not provide the support for user interface generation available via SoftBench's Encapsulator. ToolTalk also does not provide ready-made integrations to tools such as editors, compilers, and SCCS. These features were used heavily in the integration experiments.

Due to resource limitations, it was decided that only the C language interface functions of SoftBench Encapsulator would be emulated for use with ToolTalk. This would help keep the experiment focused on the integration mechanisms and eliminate the need to restructure or redesign the process scenario. It also allowed the experiment to use the same Encapsulator source code "scripts" without requiring development of a script interpreter (as in Encapsulator). Again, the intent was to make the emulation and message service replacements completely transparent to the original experiment scenario. This emulation approach is illustrated in Figure 31.

FIGURE 31 Message Service Interface Structure.

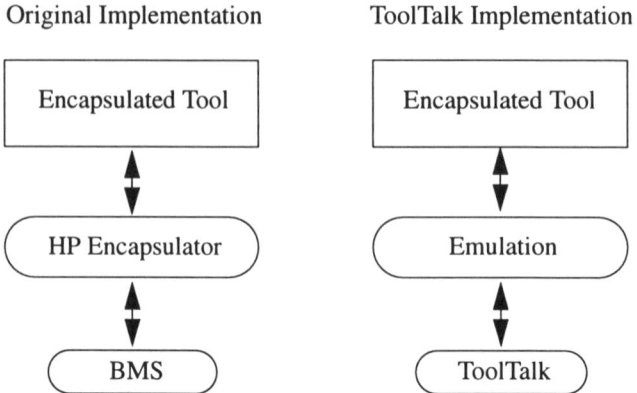

It should be noted here that this experiment was not intended as an evaluation of ToolTalk, nor as a lesson in "redevelopment" of SoftBench. As such, it was not necessary to use all of the features of ToolTalk (e.g., object-oriented messaging, static message patterns), although the experiment did attempt to provide the (rough) equivalent of Encapsulator/BMS to the original process scenario. It should also be noted that while the experiment employed framework components that are equivalent to those being integrated by the COSE alliance (i.e., SoftBench and ToolTalk), the experiment was intended to be generic in purpose, and the lessons learned from the experiment are no less valid.

10.3 Getting Started

10.3.1 Experiments with Encapsulator and BMS

In preparation for development of a framework to emulate Encapsulator/BMS, more specific information was needed concerning the functioning of Encapsulated applications and of BMS. Therefore, the emulation was based not only on information provided in the *SoftBench Encapsulator: Programmer's Guide* and *SoftBench Encapsulator: Programmer's Reference* manuals from Hewlett-Packard, but on observed performance of the Encapsulator (version A.02) as well.

Several experiments were performed to determine the appropriate functions of the Encapsulated subprocess under control, the syntax and resulting format for context specifications, and the proper matching and handling of BMS messages. In addition, many other "throw away" experiments were developed on an "as needed" basis to determine the appropriate actions of the emulation under specific conditions that could arise in use (e.g., Encapsulator responses to unexpected NULL pointers, BMS handling of specific message pattern wildcards, or the format of message identifiers).

Later in the development of the emulation, experiments into the workings of the user interface were performed. Again, it was intended here to provide a reasonable approximation of the Encapsulator user interface, not to identically reproduce it. However, some experimentation was necessary to determine appropriate actions based on specification of user "events," user responses to interface selections, etc.

10.3.2 Writing the Emulation Code

Development time encompassed coding of all the C language bindings (library routines) per those defined in the Encapsulator, including emulation of the subprocess control functions. All of the library routines were implemented, even though the experimental scenario written for Encapsulator did not make use of all the functions available. The reasoning here was that any extensions or changes to the Encapsulator version of the scenario could be readily reflected in the emulation version.

The library routines were developed in three phases. First, the utility and subprocess routines were written to provide the "framework" for the remainder of the emulation. This included support for the basic Encapsulator data types ("string," "boolean," "event," and "integer"), and utilities to accept and handle "Application" and "System" events. Next, the message server interface and context-specific routines were written, as these were the basis of the experiment.

This included all of the support necessary for "Message" events. Finally, the user interface routines were written, including support for "User" events, and the associated "object" and "attribute" data types.

The code was initially written with a "debug" interface so that functions could be verified as they were implemented, without requiring the message server and Motif user interface services. In addition, the message server interface code was developed so that specific interfaces to other message services could be (theoretically) easily added at a later date. After development of the basic portions of the emulation was completed, a Motif interface (for "User" events) was added partially as an exercise in completing the framework, but primarily so that the scenario could be run identically as it was when using Encapsulator.

Due to a single-user/single-system limitation imposed in the original experiment scenario, and to the time constraints of the experiment, no remote host-processing capabilities were incorporated into the emulation. Also, some user interface-specific attributes of Encapsulator (e.g., background/foreground colors, edit source type) were not implemented as they were not used in the scenario and, again, were deemed to be beyond the scope of the experiment. However, some other attributes that were not used in the scenario (e.g., object mapping, row/column size designation) were supported as they were easily derived from the addition of the Motif user interface.

10.3.3 Developing "Support Utilities"

Since the emulation consisted of only a small portion of the SoftBench framework, some consideration had to be made as to the extent that other facilities of SoftBench would have to be incorporated to support the emulation. While many of the tools provided with SoftBench would not be needed or could be substituted for, two facilities were thought to be important enough to be included as part of the emulation.

SoftBench provides a message monitor/send facility that is useful primarily for debug purposes. Such a tool was also incorporated into the experiment extension to facilitate testing of the interface to the message system. Although Sun includes the source for a ToolTalk message monitoring tool as a demo within the OpenWindows installation hierarchy, it was not functionally equivalent to the tool desired (e.g., the demo tool does not allow specification or display of message data arguments), and the user interfaces and message monitoring output were not compatible. As the demo tool was written for the "XView" windowing interface, it seemed easier to develop a tool specifically for the X Window System and Motif interfaces (and built upon the emulation framework) than to modify the tool supplied by Sun to fit the needs of the experiment.

SoftBench also contains an Execution Manager component that provides the ability to start a tool upon demand from another tool via a message request through BMS. ToolTalk provides a similar "auto-start" facility via static message pattern definition (i.e., matching message types are predefined). However, due to the dynamic messaging model of the emulation (see Section 10.4.2), the experiment could not make use of the ToolTalk facility. Therefore, a tool server utility was developed for use in the experiment to provide equivalent functionality to that of SoftBench (although tangential to the scenario).

10.4 Adding the ToolTalk Interface

10.4.1 Learning How to Use ToolTalk

Programming with the ToolTalk message interface was basically a self-taught undertaking. This was accomplished primarily via reference to the documents *ToolTalk 1.0 Programmer's Guide* and *Application Integration with ToolTalk — A Tutorial*, both of which are provided by Sun Microsystems. The tutorial provided a basic example that was used as a starting point for interface code development. The goal at this stage of the experiment was to add a straightforward interface to ToolTalk without any "bells and whistles." At this point, some basic experiments were conducted with ToolTalk (via the Application Programming Interface (API)) to determine the most appropriate messaging model for use in the emulation.

10.4.2 Emulating BMS with ToolTalk

To be compatible with the previously developed integration scenario, the experiment attempted to emulate the messaging actions of BMS via ToolTalk. An overview of these two message services and their corresponding message formats was presented in Chapter 7.

While attempting to emulate BMS with ToolTalk, several limiting factors were discovered relating to message delivery (see Figure 32). All BMS messages ("request," "notify," or "failure") are handled on a "one-to-many" basis. That is, BMS makes any message equally available to any interested tool for as many message events (i.e. message patterns) that are matched. On the other hand, ToolTalk limits tool access by the message class ("request" or "notice"), and further by handler response to request messages ("reply," "reject," or "fail").

ToolTalk request messages are sent to one handler at a time until the request has been satisfied (either positively or negatively). A specific request message will not be sent to a handler more than once, regardless of the number of message patterns that it matches for that handler. In contrast, ToolTalk notification messages are sent to all tools, and may be sent to the same tool multiple times depending on the specifics of the registered message patterns.

FIGURE 32 BMS and ToolTalk Message Delivery.

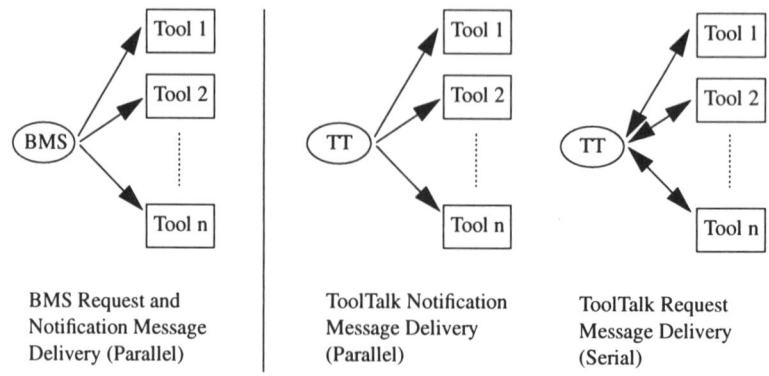

BMS Request and Notification Message Delivery (Parallel)

ToolTalk Notification Message Delivery (Parallel)

ToolTalk Request Message Delivery (Serial)

To make all ToolTalk messages available to all interested tools (exactly once), to allow the tool server utility to "hold" messages for tools that it was starting, and to accommodate wildcard message classes, a simple model was used wherein all messages were sent as requests, and each message handler would release each message to the next interested tool by rejecting the message after it had examined and processed it. The model was later extended to include notification messages and used a single "exact" message pattern for each user-specified notify/failure message event (to eliminate multiple message delivery).

In addition, since the message pattern-matching capabilities of BMS and ToolTalk are not identical, and the intent was to emulate the BMS characteristics, some of the finer-grained pattern matching function (most specifically relating to context and "wildcard" considerations) was performed by the emulation as opposed to ToolTalk. This was done by having the emulation dynamically define a minimal pattern for message send/receive consisting of (basically) a generic identifier for the toolset. When sending a message, the context attributes (e.g., host, directory, file) were attached as the first n data elements of the message pattern (where n was constant), followed by any additional user-defined data elements. After receiving a message that met the ToolTalk pattern-matching requirements (i.e., the generic tool identifier), the emulation would examine the data elements to further determine a contextual pattern match. The emulation would simply reject any message that did not meet the expanded

10.4 Adding the ToolTalk Interface

match characteristics. This did not seem to have an adverse performance impact on the emulation.

It should be noted here that the ToolTalk message patterns could have been (and ultimately were) expanded to limit message reception based on the specific message context. However, even with the more exact receiver pattern match, the emulation still had to examine the context attributes of the message to determine which internal message event(s) had been matched, and to perform the appropriate "callback" processing. ToolTalk pattern callbacks could not be used for this purpose, as they would not provide the same function as BMS for multiple message patterns that matched on the same request message (due to the "single request message delivery per handler" attribute of ToolTalk).

One other consideration when developing the emulation was the issue of "unhandled" messages. This can be due to a ToolTalk selected handler "blocking" message events, not having yet entered the event loop (via a "start" or "restart" command), or simply being otherwise busy (and therefore unable to handle the message). Since ToolTalk delivers request messages in a serialized fashion, a handler can block other handlers from receiving a message until it unblocks and/or handles the message (or exits). While the documentation would indicate that ToolTalk might conceivably time out in this situation and offer the message to another handler, limited experimentation did not identify the timeout interval. There did not seem to be any way to work around this limitation in the emulation, although it did not present itself as a problem in the experiment scenario.

10.4.3 Adding ToolTalk to the Emulation Framework

Once the emulation framework was developed and the ToolTalk experimentation was completed, the addition of ToolTalk to the emulation as the message server was, in itself, actually quite easy. Addition of the ToolTalk interface added less than 100 lines of code to the emulation (for comparison, there were about 5,000 lines of code in the entire emulation). The ToolTalk interface code developed included support for:

- initialization of the interface to the ToolTalk message server,
- message pattern creation, registration, and deletion/destruction,
- message creation and transmittal,
- message acknowledgment and acceptance (based on context),
- message data argument extraction, and
- controlled disconnection from the ToolTalk message server.

10.5 Running the Experiment Scenario

10.5.1 Modifying the EDL Scripts

The scenario was originally coded for the SoftBench Encapsulator in Encapsulator Definition Language (EDL). EDL is similar in syntax to C, so each of the EDL-based encapsulations used in the scenario was (easily) rewritten in C. Some changes had to be made specifically to turn the EDL scripts into working C programs (e.g., creating a "main" routine, calling an initialization routine), but no more than would have been required to modify the scripts to run with the Encapsulator C language interface (provided with SoftBench).

10.5.2 Physical Placement of Tools and Support Software

One of the first difficulties encountered with running the scenario was the problem of having different software tools physically located on different machines. ToolTalk is included as part of the Sun OpenWindows Version 3.0 (or greater) installation and only runs on SunOS version 4.1.x, a combination of which was running on only one machine in the network supporting the experiment. Meanwhile, PCTE, the coding tools, and the testing tools were licensed only on a different machine. As it turned out, the version of OpenWindows on the "license" machine could be upgraded without having to reinstall the entire system (possibly requiring updated versions of some or all of the COTS tools used in the scenario). Although such configuration problems were eluded in the experiment, it does point out a potential problem in the general case.

10.5.3 Limitations of the Emulation

As previously mentioned, the issue of replacing (SoftBench-supplied) support utilities was considered before attempting to fully implement the emulation. The scenario made use of the SoftBench "softeditsrv" and "softbuild" tools as a visual editor and compiler, respectively. As it was deemed to be beyond the scope of the experiment to provide an interface to these specific tools, simple "encapsulations" were developed to the X11 "xedit" (in place of "softeditsrv") and UNIX "cc" (in place of "softbuild") utilities. Identical message interfaces (at least to the extent of that required in the scenario) were incorporated into these encapsulations so that no changes to the scenario were required.

In addition, the server process could not be used in the scenario due to a (since fixed) problem encountered in ToolTalk with respect to the mode in which it was used within the emulation (i.e., rejected messages were not being delivered to other matching handlers). Therefore, all of the processes involved in the scenario had to be started in advance and would then wait for message "instructions." This removed the "on demand" process-starting capability of the scenario (available with SoftBench). It did not, however, change the scenario itself nor did it require any changes to the tool encapsulations (other than to remain installed throughout the duration of the scenario).

10.6 Replacing ToolTalk in the Emulation Framework

As indicated previously, the emulation was written so as to make it possible to replace the interface to ToolTalk with that of another message service. When access to Digital's FUSE became available, an extension to the message service replacement experiment was subsequently conducted.

10.6.1 FUSE

In FUSE, the message server is accessed through a set of programming facilities called FUSE EnCASE. Like BMS, messages received by FUSE are distributed to all tools in the session that have registered interest in those messages.

FUSE EnCASE employs a Tool Integration Language (TIL) to specify the attributes of the messages that a tool sends and receives, and stores that information in a schema file for use by the message server. The language has the following components:

- *Class.* The name of the tool.
- *Attributes.* A specification of the tool for use by the FUSE EnCASE Control Panel and the FUSE message server; contains such information as the tool label, the tool pathname, and the tool grouping characteristics ("local" or "global" scope of message exchange).
- *Messages.* A list of names and response, parameter, and return-value types for each message type that the tool can send and receive.
- *States.* A specification of the tool state name, and the types of messages (both predefined FUSE message types and those from the "Messages" list) that can be sent and received by the tool in each state.

10.6.2 Use of FUSE in the Emulation Framework

It turned out to be very easy to add the FUSE interface to the emulation, as the callable interface and associated documentation are quite straightforward. For purposes of the experiment, the documentation used was the *DEC FUSE Reference Manual* and *DEC FUSE EnCASE Manual* (based on FUSE version 1.2) from Digital.

A simple model was chosen for use with FUSE that used a single message type consisting of a simple character string parameter (the BMS-type message pattern). Much of the original debug interface code of the emulation doubled as "support" code for the FUSE interface, or was modified slightly to also serve as such. Only about 20 lines of C language code were written specifically to provide the actual emulation interface to FUSE/EnCASE.

The only problem encountered in the FUSE version of the emulation was similar to that of the "unhandled messages" problem encountered with ToolTalk. In the case of FUSE, though, messages sent while message events were not being handled were simply lost, and no coding work-around could be determined. The only tool involved in the scenario that this affected was the CM tool, which blocks messages during initialization. This process was simply prestarted and allowed to initialize in advance of running the scenario.

10.7 Lessons Learned

10.7.1 Time Requirements

The task took approximately three staff months to complete, which included the time needed to learn some of the more "esoteric" features of the Encapsulator/BMS, and the time to learn how to program with ToolTalk and with the Xt Intrinsics package of Motif. While the amount of effort required to complete the emulation had been fairly accurately predicted, more time was expended experimenting with SoftBench/BMS than was expected, while less time was expended learning the ToolTalk interface than was expected.

Also, while the Motif-based user interface of the emulation "approximates" that of Encapsulator, it was not fully debugged as part of the emulation effort, and some simplifying changes were made to the mode of operation. These changes were user-related, none of which affected the actual scenario.

10.7.2 GUI Screen Builder

Access to a GUI screen builder would have made creation of the user interface for the emulation much easier. However, as this was a secondary part of the emulation, it was decided that a "limited" amount of time would be spent learning enough of the X Window System and Motif programming interfaces required to support the emulation instead of purchasing such a tool. As such, a "build versus buy" decision was made here.

10.7.3 Programming Requirements

The amount of coding required to support the experiment, given the time involved, required a reasonable level of proficiency in C (or C++, or whatever language would ultimately be chosen). In addition, the time frame for completion of the experiment required a fairly steep learning curve for familiarization with X Window System and Motif interface programming specifics. In contrast, development of the ToolTalk interface code was fairly straightforward once the task of learning the ToolTalk interface was completed.

10.7.4 Documentation Limitations

While the task of incorporating ToolTalk into the emulation would have been impossible without the documentation provided, the documentation did prove to be on a level less than would have been desired. There was a fair amount of information presented relating to ToolTalk from a conceptual standpoint as well as at the "overview" level for programming considerations. However, the programming examples provided were limited, and the mechanics of operation were presented without enough practical application information (e.g., little mention of default settings, little discussion or explanation of message or pattern attributes and settings other than those that are required).

10.7.5 Applicability of ToolTalk

In this experiment, the capabilities and usage of ToolTalk were limited by the constraints of the framework into which it was being added (i.e., the Encapsulator/BMS emulation). Throughout both experimentation and documentation review, it seemed that it would have been easier (and more efficient) to fit ToolTalk into a general application framework instead of having to emulate a specific one (SoftBench/BMS). In addition, the former case would have allowed for better use of the capabilities of ToolTalk by designing the framework and message interface specifically for that purpose. Many of the decisions made in the development of the interface to ToolTalk were dictated solely by the attempt to make ToolTalk emulate the function of BMS.

10.8 Summary

As indicated in the introduction, there were basically two premises being tested within this experiment: that the message service replacement could be reasonably performed, and that the choice of message servers was mostly independent of the application for which it provided the control integration mechanism.

The experiment showed that replacement of the message service in a controlled experiment framework is quite possible. As outlined in the chapter, however, such an undertaking does have preconditions to success. A substantial amount of groundwork had to be performed to begin the message service replacement portion of the task. Also, in the experiment situation there was more interest in the capability and applicability aspects than in the specific level of effort expended or in the "product worthiness" of the end result.

These factors all contribute to the consideration of the level of priority that an organization must place on development time versus cost of purchase (i.e., the decision of build versus buy). A product like SoftBench is relatively expensive, but requires little in the way of engineering resources to be fully used. On the other hand, while ToolTalk is "free" (as part of SunOS), it requires a significant investment in development of an integration framework and associated support tools.

In addition, as discussed in Section 10.7, it was discovered that replacement of the message service is not entirely independent of the framework or application. While there would seem to be less of a dependency when initially defining or selecting a service specifically for an application, there are compatibility issues to be considered (and handled) when attempting to replace the service in an existing framework where messaging characteristics (e.g., types, formats, or handling) are already defined. Without messaging standards, it would appear that "plug-and-play" message service components would be impossible.

One final consideration is that when an organization decides to build its own framework (or modify a purchased one), it assumes all responsibility for future extensions or compatibility considerations (e.g., adding support tools, resolving problems, incorporating new versions of tools or framework components). On the other hand, the organization also maintains control of the integration and can make changes as it sees fit to tailor the system to its needs.

While the experiment proved that message service replacement in the framework could be done, there are other aspects of the experiment that could be examined. These include:

- *Incorporate object-oriented capabilities provided by ToolTalk into the emulation.* It would be interesting to see how the support framework (and the experiment scenario) might be changed with the addition of object-oriented messaging. In the "process-oriented" messaging model used in the experiment, messages are directed to process(es) for handling. In an "object-oriented" messaging model, messages are directed to objects (data) instead of

10.8 Summary

processes. In this model, ToolTalk determines the handler process based on preregistered object-process addressing rules.

- *Investigate adding other support tools with ToolTalk interface to the scenario.* As the scenario changes, it might be interesting to see if new tools could also be added to the emulation version. In addition, it might be interesting to see if any new COTS tools that employ a ToolTalk message interface could be integrated into the scenario (or possibly integrated via the emulation).

- *Add interface to another message server.* It would be interesting to incorporate another message service interface (e.g., one based on CORBA) into the emulation. This type of experiment should again be fairly straightforward as the emulation framework has already been completed, and the interface insertion points have already been identified. What is left is to emulate BMS according to the capabilities of the alternate message service. Along these lines, it would be interesting to obtain the SoftBench BMS interface library itself for use by the emulation.

CHAPTER 11
Integration of CASE Tools with CM Systems: Lessons Learned

11.1 Introduction

The problem of CASE tool integration has several concerns that overlap with those of configuration management (CM), so much so that a discussion of one topic is often difficult to separate from a discussion of the other. To illustrate, we note that when choosing a solution to a problem in configuration management, we often must make choices that involve understanding process requirements, examining the services available (and their semantics), and analyzing implementation constraints. We also note that these activities are done simultaneously with making design trade-off decisions related to the integration of these process, service, and mechanism concepts. These factors are *applicable* to CM, but are not *particular* to CM: most of these same issues underlie any set of decisions one makes about combining a set of CASE tools into an integrated environment.

However, CM and its relationship to CASE tool integration in general poses a unique set of problems. This is most apparent when we realize that CM is sometimes considered as a service (or set of services) provided by the environment or its framework, sometimes as a service provided by a separate stand-alone tool, and sometimes as an integral aspect of each individual CASE tool. These competing views lead to overlaps in functionality and responsibility between individual tools and the environment's (or framework's) CM capabilities. For instance:

- A fundamental issue for CM is data redundancy. This results when different tools store the same data in separate repositories. Correspondingly, different data models may make data sharing (a fundamental issue for tool integration) difficult.
- Version management (VM) and CM services provided by individual tools are frequently linked with private tool data model and data management services. These VM and CM services are not always delegable — sometimes these services are an intricate part of tool function (e.g., for multi-user support and build).
- The VM and CM services provided by individual tools may imply or enforce vendor-specific VM/CM policies, as opposed to the CM policies of the environment.

This short list of potential overlaps by no means exhausts the topic. The difficulties of coordinating and sharing data among egocentric tools and the introduction of multiple tool repositories make it difficult to answer such simple CM questions as:

- Who is changing this configuration item?
- How many changes have been made to this configuration item?
- How do we reestablish consistency among these configuration items?
- How do we retrieve and restore a particular version of the configuration (e.g., design, code, and test items)?

In short, the non-locality and redundancy of data among multiple tool repositories may make it essential that a sound CM strategy be in place to manage the products produced by tools. Part of this strategy must involve the integration of the tools with CM services. A CASE environment that incorporates CM services and policies will address not only the mechanistic aspects of integration (e.g., managing redundant data across heterogeneous tool repositories) but also the process aspects of the integration (e.g., change control policies dictated by the organization).

This chapter reports on the lessons learned from a series of experiments that took place with particular CM systems to examine the integration issues of CASE environments containing multiple CM solutions. The particular CM systems used were a representative sample of those available at the time. The aim of the experiments was not to criticize those systems per se, but to make general statements about the classes of technology they represent.

In the remainder of this chapter we identify and discuss some key concepts underlying the relationship between CASE tool integration and CM. We then examine some of the essential issues of CM and their interaction with the essential issues of tool integration. Finally, we examine several example scenarios of CM tools and systems in the context of how they might function in an integrated CASE environment.

11.2 Key Concepts Related to CM and CASE Tool Integration

Incorporating configuration management with a set of integrated CASE tools takes place in the context of the three levels of integration (process, services, and mechanisms) discussed in earlier chapters. As an illustration, we imagine a CASE tool that provides its own repository and workspace services. In a hypothetical integration of this tool with a CM system that also provides some support for managing developer workspaces, an obvious issue that must be addressed is: when and under what circumstances should data held locally in the CASE tool's repository be exported to the CM workspace and vice versa? A number of possibilities exist. For example, it is possible to export the changes:

- as they are made,
- at the end of each user session,
- at designated times (e.g., weekly dumps),
- at designated events (e.g., major or minor releases), or
- only at the end of a life-cycle phase, e.g., coding phase.

There are important implications from the choice made. For example, if the changes are exported as they are made, then the CASE tool and the CM system are consistent for the majority of the time. However, the overhead involved in propagating the changes may be very high. In a working context in which relatively few people will wish to access the latest design changes, this overhead may be unwarranted. On the other hand, exporting changes at the end of life-cycle phases will mean that the CASE tool and CM system may be inconsistent for long periods of time. If many other tools are using the data recorded in the CM system, then problems of out-of-date information may arise.

As with any solution that pertains to CASE tool integration, the selection of any one (or more) of these alternatives can be seen in the light of an underlying process, in terms of the services on which it depends, or on the mechanisms that implement those services. Hence, choices about the hypothetical integration described above will be dependent upon the existing CM process policies and constraints, the logical services provided by the tool and the CM system, and on the intrinsic implementation characteristics of both. We examine these concepts in turn.

11.2.1 Process Concepts

At a process level there are a number of interesting and problematic issues to be addressed in integrating CASE tools and CM systems. These issues arise due to the different views of CM that different communities hold, and the range of support required by those communities. We highlight two major considerations in the integration of CASE tools with CM systems that are strongly affected by process-level issues: support for different user communities, and support for different life-cycle approaches.

In considering the different user roles that must be supported by a CASE environment, a useful approach in discussing integration of CASE tools with CM systems is to differentiate among CM systems by classifying them according to the communities they support. One useful partition distinguishes three different communities [23]:

- *Corporate CM.* Support for an organization as a whole, recognizing the need for corporate policies and approaches that provide consistency of support across all products produced by the organization.
- *Project CM.* Support for a single project, providing a common approach to all phases of support for a single product.
- *Developer CM.* Support for individuals in their daily tasks of development and maintenance of one or more product pieces.

Based on this partition, an organization may define CM practices (possibly supported by different CM systems) for each of these levels. Integration of CM processes is required to determine when, for example, configuration items at the developer level are promoted to the rest of the project, and which configuration items are considered sufficiently important to be offered at a corporate level. In terms of their automated support, division of CM responsibilities such as this gives rise to concern about the integration of various CM systems with each other, e.g., how the metrics gathered by project CM systems are made available to corporate CM systems.

11.2 Key Concepts Related to CM and CASE Tool Integration

A different, and far more complex, problem is seen when we examine the different life-cycle processes that a CM system may support. The view of the life cycle that an individual, project, or corporation adopts will have a significant influence on the CM policies and practices that must be supported.

It is useful to consider the relationship between CM and the software life cycle in terms of at least two kinds of relationships: the relation of CM to the process as a whole, and the relation of CM to activities that occur within the context of specific life-cycle phases. In the former case, the integration addresses global process constraints; in the latter case, the integration addresses the more interactive tool-level aspects involving the coordination of tools across different life-cycle steps.

As an example, we can consider the coordination of tools across different life-cycle steps. Many issues must be addressed, including:

- *Change control.* Controlling *what* changes can be made, *why* they should be made, *when* the changes should be made, and *who* should make the changes.
- *Data synchronization.* Tools featuring private repositories need to work within a global CM control regime for effective global change control to be put into practice, yet tools frequently provide their own services and mechanisms for controlling change.

Therefore, as the needs and perspectives of different CASE environment users can vary widely, the CM support they require must be sufficiently flexible to provide that range of support. The result is that CASE environments frequently use a number of different CM systems that support each of the different communities. These CM systems may offer unique blends of CM functionality, with emphasis on different CM requirements. Complex and sophisticated approaches to the synchronization of these CM systems is often required to ensure that they are consistent with each other, and with the CASE tools with which they must interact.

11.2.2 Service Concepts

CM is a common discipline across many software development projects. As a result, a wide variety of research and commercial CM products is available to support many aspects of the CM discipline. This has led to a relatively mature understanding of the essential elements of CM services in comparison with other service domains. The work of Katz [42], Feiler [27], and Dart [23] is representative of the state of maturity of CM concepts. Thus, a tool integrator is in a reasonably strong position to characterize the elements of CM services that will contribute to the integration of CASE tools with CM systems.

The importance of the services view of CM is evident when the concept of *service profiling* is introduced. Profiling in this context refers to an analysis of services from a particular perspective. Here we choose to highlight two perspectives that produce useful profiles: profiling across CM user communities, and profiling within a CM user community.

Figure 33 illustrates a profile of three different CM systems (Change and Confirguration Control Environment (CCC) and NSE, which are commercial products; and NetherWorld, which is an internal U.S. government CM system) and a CASE programming support tools with a significant CM component (SMARTSystem). The figure is not meant to convey the results of a concrete analysis, but rather to convey the different foci of CM support offered by the different systems, and the potential effect those different foci have on their selection and integration.

FIGURE 33 Profiling CM Systems by CM User Category.

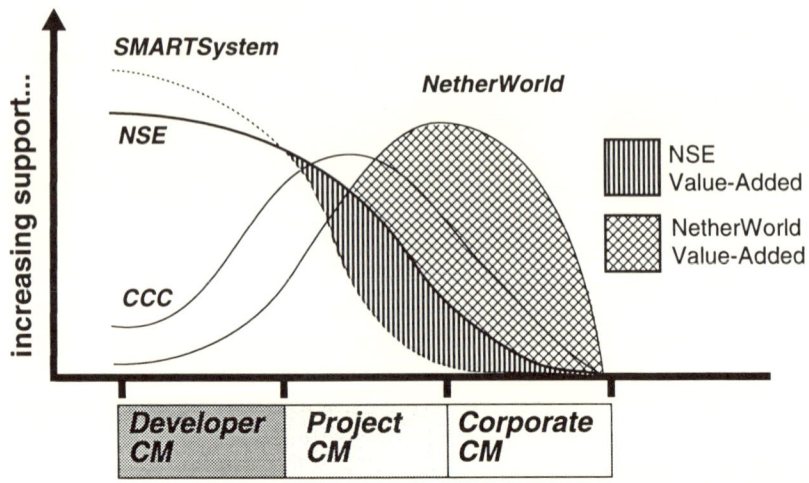

Analysis of Figure 33 can be the basis for a number of important decisions with respect to integration of CM systems. For example, both SMARTSystem and NSE show similar profiles for developer, project, and corporate CM. A reasonable question to ask is whether there would be a practical cost/benefit ratio to justify an integration effort involving these two products given this similarity of service support. Conversely, functions provided by NetherWorld complement those provided by SMARTSystem, so intuitively there would be ample scope for enhancing an environment composed of these systems by integrating them.

11.2 Key Concepts Related to CM and CASE Tool Integration

Unfortunately, such an analysis is too simplistic. Besides being unsatisfactory on a strictly quantifiable basis, the cost/benefit analysis alluded to above must consider the semantic and mechanistic compatibility of SMARTSystem with NSE versus SMARTSystem with NetherWorld. In Figure 33, for example, one could also speculate that NSE services harmonize better with SMARTSystem than do NetherWorld's. As such, both the cost and effect of a SMARTSystem integration with NSE might be more satisfying and practical than an integration of SMARTSystem with NetherWorld. Thus, while such an intuitive profiling technique might be useful for coarse "anatomical" comparisons of tools, a comparison at a finer level of services granularity is necessary.

This more detailed level of analysis can take place given the profiles of CM systems within each user community. In Figure 34, for example, a subset of the CM requirements discussed in Nejmeh [50] that may be considered as supportive of developer CM defines a perspective for profiling NSE and the CM component of SMARTSystem. This profile depicts the level of support for various developer CM services on a scale of *no* support, *medium* support, and *high* support (with the circumference defining high support).

FIGURE 34 Profiles Within the Developer CM User Category.

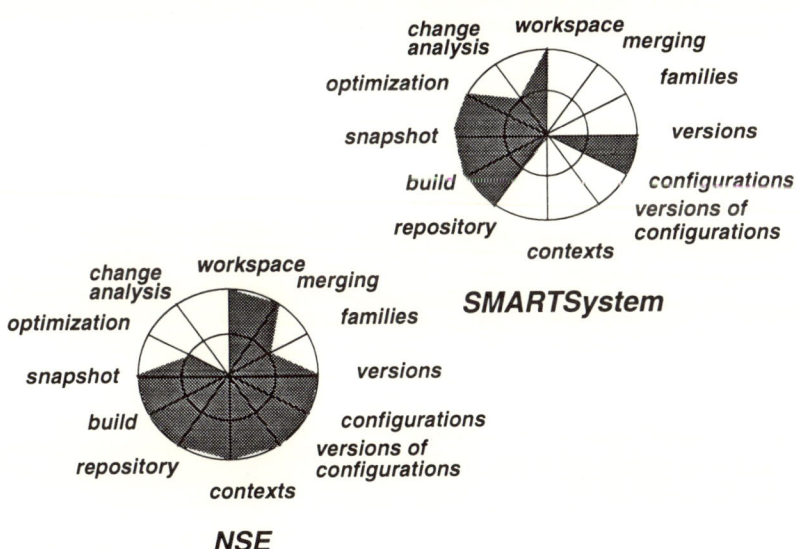

The three-tiered ranking is useful not only for identifying areas of overlapping support, but also in (loosely) quantifying a level of support that may be used in later determining how to allocate responsibility for services across tools. For example, SMARTSystem has stronger support for build optimization than does NSE. This might indicate that SMARTSystem should manage the build-related activities of developer CM. Conversely, NSE would be in a position to describe versions of configurations, which is something SMARTSystem does not support at all.

While this analysis of support within a CM user community provides useful information, a more detailed analysis of overlapping services can be performed. Such an analysis is necessary because:

- The services are too broad (as currently defined) to form a basis for making detailed integration design decisions. At least one further level of detail would be required to facilitate these decisions.
- The services are not standardized, and so different vendor implementations may impose different semantics on the services. For example, two CM systems providing a transaction service does not provide sufficient information for many decisions to be made (further details concerning recovery approach, levels of nesting permitted, and so on).

11.2.3 Mechanism Concepts

In the preceding discussion of services, the notion of services profiling was described as ultimately resulting in a comparative view of two (or more) systems. The objective of such comparisons was to expose commonality and variance among the services provided and the semantics associated with these services. Such an analysis must also take place at the mechanism level to allow systems to be compared at the level of *how* they implement the various services they provide.

A number of mechanism-level factors have a significant effect on the design of integrated CM systems and CASE tools. From our experiments, we have found it useful to think in terms of two major categories of mechanism factors that contribute to an integrated solution: CASE tool architectures and CM architectures. These categories are discussed in more detail below.

11.2.3.1 CASE Tool Architectures

The idea of describing characteristics of CASE tools that make them integrable (or unintegrable) has been explored by Nejmeh [50]. Nejmeh's approach is to describe these characteristics as attributes of the tool as a whole, e.g., use of standards such as window system and licensing schemes, and sensitivity to environment characteristics such as location independence of tool binaries and data.

11.2 Key Concepts Related to CM and CASE Tool Integration

We have found it useful to consider two additional dimensions of tool characteristics: a tool's architecture with respect to data management and its low-level process structure.

- *Data management architectures.* Where a tool stores data (if at all), how it accesses data, and what kinds of data it manages are all likely to impinge on the practicality of various CASE tool and CM system solutions. We can identify four classes of tools with respect to data management architectures: filter tools, which process data independent of the data's location; deriver tools, which transform data from one format to another; data dictionary tools, which structure and manage the target data from transformations they perform; and database tools, which extend data dictionary tools with support for the source of the transformations.
- *Operating system process architectures.* The operating system (OS) process architecture of tools can play a significant role in establishing and maintaining communication among different tools. While tools can be constructed that make use of an arbitrary number of processes connected in arbitrary ways, four main kinds of OS process architectures can be identified that can affect CASE integration with CM: transient tools, in which the duration of tool execution is tied to the completion of a discrete task; persistent tools, which remain active servers for repeated invocation; parent/child tools, in which the parent tool is persistent but "forks" or "spawns" transient tools that are tied to particular activities; and client/server tools, in which the server acts as a persistent tool while the client is typically a transient tool that makes use of the services provided by the server.

11.2.3.2 CM Architectures

The architecture of the CM system itself may have an effect on the integration approach that is taken. We can distinguish between two CM architectures:

- *CM tools.* CM tools are separate, stand-alone programs that are executed explicitly by some agent (a user or another computer program). It is reasonable to view CASE tool integration with CM tools as a special case of tool-to-tool integration [74].
- *CM systems.* CM systems are components that are pervasive throughout the environment, perhaps implemented as part of the basic environment framework itself. It is reasonable to view CASE tool integration with CM systems as a special case of tool-to-framework integration [74].

The significance of integrating tools with CM tools versus CM systems hinges upon the balance between the benefits (e.g., simplicity) of integration provided by pervasive, transparent VM and CM services weighed against the possibly subtle implementation dependencies (such as per-process context) in the way these services are provided.

11.3 CASE Tool Integration Scenarios Involving CM

The previous section described concepts of CM and their relation to CASE tool integration. In this section these concepts are illustrated through a series of integration scenarios. Identification of these scenarios resulted from an experimental integration of PROCASE's SMARTSystem with Sun's NSE.

The main focus of the experiment was placed on developer CM, wherein the significant role of workspaces in CASE integration with CM was highlighted. Workspaces support individual developers and teams of developers by providing support for two opposing but complementary concepts:

- *Insulation* insures a stable context in which individuals can perform builds and tests. Without insulation, changes introduced by other developers would force continuous integration and complicate the process of introducing and testing isolated functionality.
- *Communication* refers to the way changes are coordinated between workspaces. Communication provides a means of notifying users and tools of some important event, or change in status within a workspace, and a means of propagating changes to other workspaces.

These common threads are woven into each of the scenarios presented. To simplify the discussion, we limit the services involved in the integration scenarios to simple CM services (e.g., check-out/check-in, workspaces, and locking) and limit the mechanism dimension to deriver and data dictionary tools. We then focus on the implications on software process raised by integrating these tool architectures and simple CM services. The first scenario is a simple one. Complexity is added in succeeding scenarios.

11.3.1 Scenario 1: Deriver Tool and Check-Out/Check-In

This scenario is that of a simple deriver tool integrated with a simple check-out- and check-in-based CM tool.

This scenario is illustrated in Figure 35, and introduces some of the terminology used in the succeeding examples:

- *Source data*. The input to a derivation process.
- *Derived data*. The output of a derivation process.

11.3 CASE Tool Integration Scenarios Involving CM

- *Unmanaged work area.* A collection of source and derived objects under user management, located arbitrarily in the file system or object management system of a CASE environment.
- *Managed repository.* A data repository under CM administrative control.

FIGURE 35 Deriver and Check Out/In.

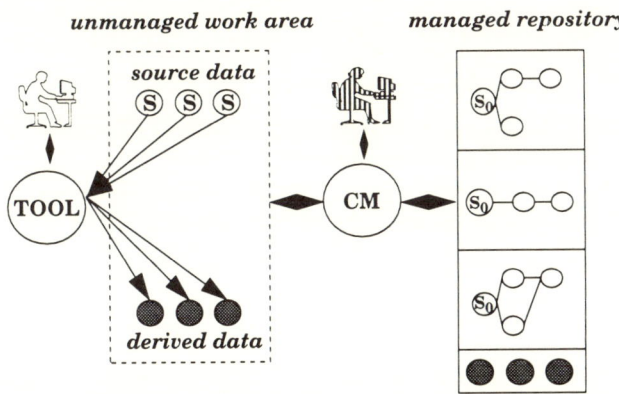

The simplicity of this scenario is deceptive. The issues raised in integrating deriver tools with check-out/check-in CM tools characterize many state-of-the-practice software development environments. Most seasoned project leaders will recognize some (if not all) of the following issues illustrated in Figure 35:

- Data are exported from the CM system into an unmanaged (from the CM perspective) part of the file system, described as an *unmanaged work area*. The lack of CM control over the developer work area means that developer support is limited (substantially) to locking and change synchronization.
- There may need to be different project roles associated with the export and import of data between the repository and the unmanaged work area. Since the work area is unmanaged, this project role may need to determine where and to whom the sources were checked out, and perform quality-control functions when objects are checked in to the repository.
- There is a question about whether derived objects (such as executable binary files) should be managed along with the source in the repository. The answer may depend upon the implementation capabilities of the CM tool, such as whether binary data can be managed in the repository, and whether versions of binary data can be managed.
- If several unmanaged work areas are active simultaneously, the CM system can guarantee mutual exclusion on source file edit operations, but can not guarantee consistency of changes made in separate work areas. Such addi-

tional semantic constraints as found in Ploedereder and Fergany [58] would need to be added as additional CM services. As a consequence, the repository may become unstable during developer check-in phases.

There are, of course, many more issues that can be raised in this simple scenario. Most of these issues still apply where more complex CASE tools are integrated with CM. However, complex CASE tools also introduce new sets of issues.

11.3.2 Scenario 2: Data Dictionary Tool and Check-Out/Check-In

Data dictionary tools introduce data management services for highly structured derived data. A number of possibilities exist for integrating a data dictionary tool with other tools in an environment. Several scenarios (versioned dictionary, private dictionary, shared dictionary) that highlight these issues are discussed below.

11.3.2.1 CM-Managed Data Dictionary

One consideration in integrating data dictionary tools with CM systems is whether the data dictionary is managed by the CM system or by a CASE tool. Figure 36 illustrates the CM-managed dictionary by indicating that although source files are manipulated in unmanaged work areas, the consequences of these changes affect the data dictionary within the CM repository. Although this integration scenario has the potential for reducing the costs of maintaining data dictionaries (disk space and re-creation time), a number of troubling issues arise. Most notably, if multiple work areas are active simultaneously, and if one workspace has read-only copies of objects being modified in another workspace (and vice versa), the dictionary from one work area will "undo" the changes made from the other work area. The underlying problem is the sharing of data dictionary items that are derived from the source data, but not the sharing of the source objects themselves. The result is instability of developer work areas.

FIGURE 36 CM-Managed Data Dictionary.

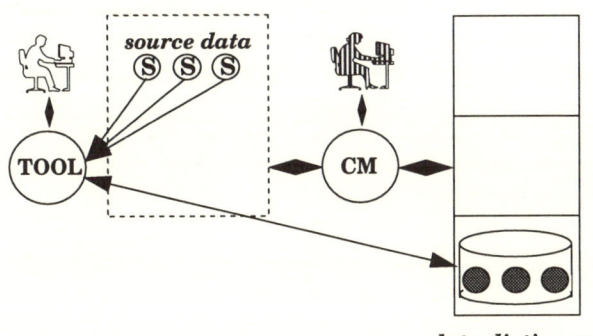

data dictionary

For reasons such as this, it may be impractical to rely on the CM system to maintain a single copy of a data dictionary. Although it may be advisable to associate a data dictionary with a repository, i.e., as a derived object that reflects the latest (or some other designated) version in the source repository, in practice a closer relationship of dictionaries with developer work areas is required. Three alternatives, private and shared dictionaries and multiple repositories, are discussed.

11.3.2.2 Work Area-Managed Data Dictionary: Private Data Dictionary

An approach to alleviating one problem raised in Figure 36, work area instability, is to associate the data dictionary more closely with the source files. This would produce an integration scheme as illustrated in Figure 35 with derived files existing in both the work area and in the repository. The scenario in Figure 37 goes a little further[1] by illustrating two active workspaces, each with different copies of the data dictionary.

In this scenario, the repository is used to synchronize access to the shared resources (in this case, the source files) so that the local copies of the derived files (the data dictionary) will be consistent. A number of issues arise with this scenario:

---

[1]. The extra user role for repository management has been omitted from the remaining figures for clarity.

- Copies of the data dictionary can proliferate, introducing significant resource consumption (compute cycles and disk storage).
- The use of locking in the repository guarantees consistency of data dictionaries with respect to source files in the same work area, not with source files in different work areas. Ultimately, a separate merge operation must be performed on the data dictionary, i.e., to combine the source files from the separate workspaces into a single data dictionary. This can be done within the repository or within a designated work area. This extra overhead can be considerable and needs to be weighed against the benefits of work area stability.
- Related to this last point is the interaction of repository locking semantics with the difficulty of performing a data dictionary merge operation. In Figure 37, objects on two branches of a version hierarchy are being modified. In this scenario, the two source objects will need to be merged. This merge is a separate, but related, merge operation to the merge that needs to be done on the data dictionary. In some situations it may be necessary to merge the data dictionaries as a by-product, or instrument, of merging the source objects. Again, this can be a costly operation. Note that locking the entire version hierarchy for an object may simplify, but not bypass, the need for a separate data dictionary merge.

FIGURE 37 Private Data Dictionaries.

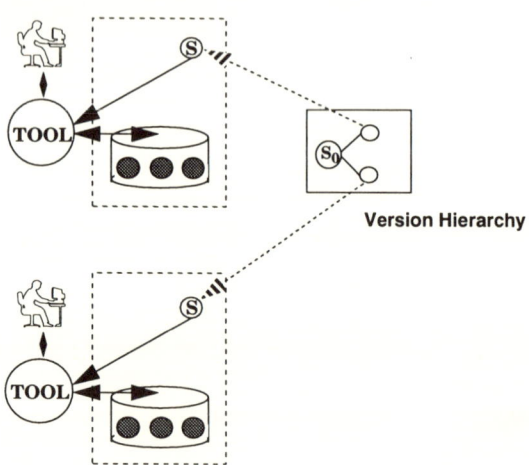

In the above scenario, the greater convenience of work area stability is offset by the costs of dictionary maintenance. In the next scenario, the need for dictionary merging is bypassed by having developers share dictionaries.

11.3.2.3 Work Area-Managed Data Dictionary: Shared Data Dictionary

Dictionary sharing is one way to avoid duplication of dictionaries and to enhance coordination of developers. However, the model illustrated in Figure 38, Figure 39, and Figure 40 and discussed below requires that some policies be established to coordinate multiple users sharing one derived object. The following scenario leads toward the notion of CM-managed *workspaces* as a means for achieving the same effect.

FIGURE 38 Shared Data Dictionaries — 1.

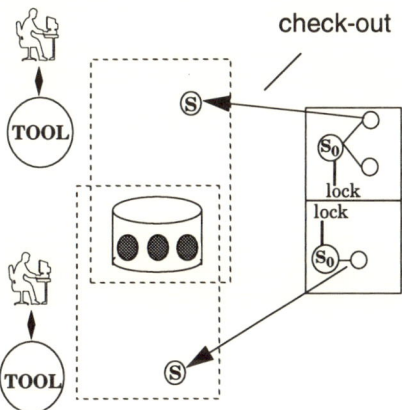

Figure 38 illustrates the start of the scenario, whereby two developers each manage private copies of source, while sharing a single data dictionary. This is similar to the scenario depicted in Figure 36, except that consistency management policies are part of the work area policies managed by the developer (and not by the CM system or administrator). Note that this scenario implies that multiple data dictionaries can be created.

To avoid the problem of updates by one user being overwritten by another as described in Figure 36, we must arrange that the read-only copy of each developer's sources is kept consistent with respect to the version of this source under modification in another work area. Various operating systems and object management systems will have different mechanisms for doing this; in UNIX it can be done through file *links*. The use of UNIX links is illustrated in Figure 39, where the shaded source objects are virtual objects, i.e., are linked to the real source objects.

The use of links in this way in effect merges the two developer work areas into one logical work area. Clearly, one consequence is that while the dictionary may be guaranteed to be consistent, the work areas as a whole are not stable. Thus, the developers will not have a stable, predictable development environment in which to work.

FIGURE 39 Shared Data Dictionaries — 2.

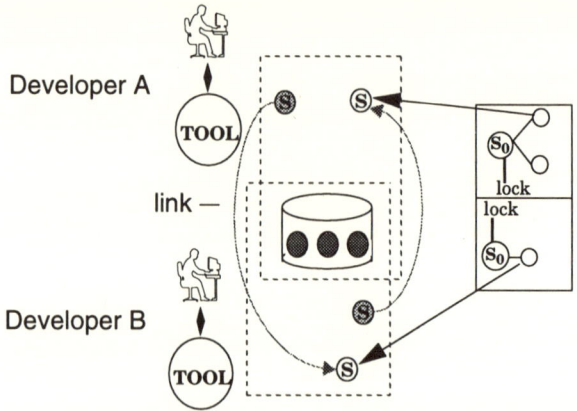

Further complications can ensue through continued use of these shared work areas, as illustrated in Figure 40. In Figure 40, Developer B has completed the modifications to the source and has "checked in" the object to the repository. Note the creation of a new version of the object in the repository (highlighted as a blackened circle). At a later date, a third developer, Developer C, needs to modify the source recently checked in by Developer B.

11.3 CASE Tool Integration Scenarios Involving CM

FIGURE 40 Shared Data Dictionaries — 3.

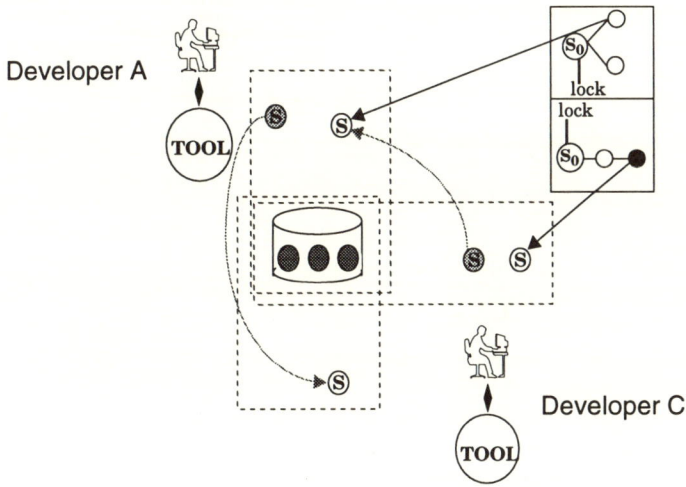

Unfortunately, the lack of integration between the CM repository and the informally managed work areas causes a problem. Developer C finds the desired source unlocked, and so copies it to a local work area. Even if Developer C is alert enough to correctly link the needed auxiliary source from Developer A's work area, Developer A's auxiliary sources are now linked to the wrong object. From Developer A's perspective, it would have been better for Developer B to remove the old copy of the checked-in file to create a "dangling link" in Developer A's work area. This might at least cause an overt error rather than an insidious source of data dictionary inconsistency.

This last illustration is contrived, of course, and any of several reasonable work area management conventions or policies would have sufficed to avoid such problems. For example:

- Check-in operations result in a broadcast message to users of the checked-in object (as an auxiliary, or linked, object). The links can be reestablished to refer to the repository versions.
- Check-out operations result in a broadcast message to potential users of the checked-out object so that new links can be established.
- "Link-chains" can be established by linking the last checked-in object to the newly checked-out object. Thus, in Figure 40, Developer B's old object would be deleted and replaced by a link to Developer C's newly checked-out object.

Each of these alternatives has benefits and pitfalls. However, the point behind this extended and somewhat low-level discussion is that greater coordination among users — which is needed to reduce the cost of managing large derived objects such as data dictionaries — requires a degree of care in work area management to avoid excessive reprocessing of the data dictionary, excessive secondary storage costs, and costly errors caused by inconsistent data dictionaries or inconsistent views of data dictionaries.

11.3.2.4 Multiple Repositories

The problems discussed in the previous scenario resulted from the intricate machinery introduced to maintain consistency among multiple copies of source items across private work areas. An alternative approach is to have developers share the same work areas. This requires some form of synchronization, or locking, of source objects in the shared work area. One way to do this is to associate a local repository with each work area. In the following discussions, the term *workspace* is used to mean a work area with an associated repository.

If the work area's repository is used to manage complete configurations (i.e., is used for more than locking), a collection of workspaces can be combined into hierarchies of configurations. Each work area can then be thought of as a scope in which changes can be made. In combination with scope, the use of links versus copying objects to "nested" workspaces can provide different degrees of visibility, stability, and sharing among workspaces.

Such a scenario is illustrated in Figure 41, which shows two child workspaces supporting different types of workspace insulation. Further, in this scenario each workspace can have associated with it different repository policies. For example, workspaces higher in a hierarchy may have stricter access privileges that reflect the effect of the wider scope of changes made near the top of a hierarchy.

It is interesting to consider that many of the advanced CM features provided by NSE [51] can be simulated readily using the techniques just described. Naturally, as the previous sections have illustrated, there will be issues raised by any integration scheme for CASE tools and CM systems, especially those that imply data duplication and/or require manual intervention.

11.3 CASE Tool Integration Scenarios Involving CM

FIGURE 41 Multiple Nested Workspaces.

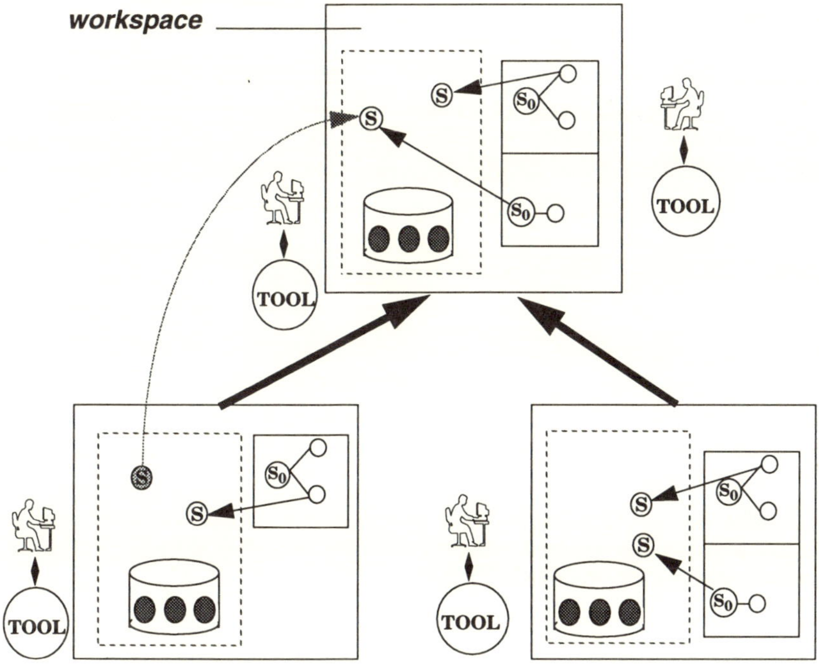

11.3.2.5 Single Repository, Multiple Partitions

One problem inherent in the multiple-repository approach just outlined is the non-locality of information on a configuration, or sets of versions of configurations, that defines the current status of a project. This is especially true if the creation of workspaces is under the control of developers and not the configuration manager.

Instead of physically associating a unique repository with each work area, another approach is to partition a single repository into versions of configurations, with each work area being associated with one of these partitions. This relationship between a central CM repository and developer work areas is a key component of CM-managed developer workspaces. However, implementation constraints imposed by widely available version management systems such as RCS and SCCS may make such partitioning impractical without a concerted implementation effort to extend the primitive VM capabilities. CM systems such as SoftTool's CCC [18] and integration frameworks such as PCTE [4] do provide the foundations upon which managed workspaces can be more directly constructed.

11.3.3 Summary of Scenarios

The scenarios discussed in this section were necessarily simplified. They did not take into consideration many of the real-world software process constraints, or implementation peculiarities of the host system, CM system, or tool. Nonetheless, a number of intricate design implications were observed when combining even these simple tools and simple CM services. The main points to note are that:

- There is no one "right" way to integrate CASE tools with CM systems. Rather, there are different costs and benefits associated with each approach.
- Effective integration of CASE tools with CM systems requires that attention be given to issues of developer work area management.
- The benefits of developer isolation (e.g., work area stability) need to be balanced against the costs of maintaining separate expensive derived objects such as Ada program libraries.
- Sophisticated CM services can be modeled on, or constructed from, primitive services such as check-out/check-in. The use of conventions and manual processes can be effective in this respect.

11.4 Summary

When integrating any set of CASE tools, there are many complex issues that must be addressed. Some of these issues are very detailed in nature and have subtle effects on the operation of the environment. We have focused attention on a single subproblem, CM support in a CASE environment, to illustrate the decisions that are typically faced and the effects of those decisions.

In the context of CASE tool integration, the problems of CM can be thought of as a special case of tool-to-tool or tool-to-framework integration. The three-level model of integration — processes, services, and mechanisms — provides a context for identifying the factors that will contribute to a successful integration strategy:

- The process level introduces many factors that need to be addressed. Besides those process factors that are peculiar to CM (e.g., change control policies), other more generic process issues must also be considered, including integration with life-cycle models and steps within the life-cycle model, process-modeling notation, and process evolution. Finally, most tools imply their

11.4 Summary

own process constraints that must be considered when integrating tools with software processes.

- The service level introduces a logical layer between process and mechanism, and is a means for tool integrators to focus on *what* needs to be integrated instead of *how* to do the integration. The work of Feiler [27] and Dart [23] is particularly useful in identifying CM services that need to be integrated among CASE tools and dedicated CM systems. Services for other engineering domains (e.g., design, test, requirements) are not as well established.
- The mechanism level characterizes the factors that affect the implementation of an integration solution. Mechanism characteristics of CASE tool architectures, CM architectures, and tool/CM integration architectures were discussed in the context of the integration of CASE tools and CM systems.

The relationships among processes, services, and mechanisms can be complex. One consequence of this complexity is that there is no "right" way to integrate CASE with CM. Instead, CASE tool and CM system integration must be viewed as a design problem with various trade-off decisions that must be made.

Part IV: A Review of the Current State of CASE Tool Integration

In Part IV, we first review the current state of CASE tool integration as determined by extensive contact with organizations that have attempted to build and use integrated toolsets and environments. A large focus is placed on the experiences of organizations trying to build practical integrations with commonly available technology. We conclude this book with a summary of our approach to constructing CASE environments, and provide suggestions concerning how progress can be made in the field.

Part IV consists of the following chapters:

12. CASE Environments in Practice

13. Summary and Conclusions

CHAPTER 12

CASE Environments in Practice

12.1 Introduction

While there have been automated tools to support software engineers from the earliest days of computer programming, it was the concept of an IPSE developed in the late 1970s and early 1980s that directly focused attention on the central role played by integration in a support environment. The Stoneman report [16] defining the architecture of an Ada programming support environment (APSE) has proven to be a seminal work on environments, influencing a range of research and activities that have attempted to develop an integrated environment supporting all aspects of software development.

However, in the 15 years since the Stoneman report, it can be argued that no commercially successful full life-cycle CASE environment has been developed. There are many reasons for this lack of success. Perhaps the most obvious is that CASE environment technology has proven to be far more complex than initially anticipated. Additional reasons may include the rapid technological changes in workstations, client-server technology, open systems, and rapid growth in the numbers of commercial CASE tools and integration technology. As discussed in earlier chapters, these trends have led to a more recent movement away from efforts to develop full life-cycle CASE environments from scratch toward efforts to build limited collections of CASE tool solutions from combinations of commercially available tools and integrating frameworks.

It is instructive to evaluate the progress made during the 1980s and to reflect on likely directions as we head toward the year 2000. Among the questions we can ask are:

- How much progress has been made since Stoneman?
- What lessons have we learned about good and bad approaches to the development of CASE environments?
- What do we see as the key issues for the future?

12.2 Background of the Studies

Two important data points for answering these questions are the historical record and current state of previous CASE environment efforts. To gather data, we completed two studies of experts involved in building and/or using such environments. The results of these studies are the basis for this chapter.

The first of these studies [49] involved discussions with experts from a small representative sample of the early commercial and government-sponsored efforts to develop large-scale CASE environments. The main environments represented were the Ada Language System (ALS), Ada Integrated Environment (AIE), Software Life-Cycle Support Environment (SLCSE) [69], and the Boeing Automated Software Engineering (BASE) Environment. These environments were primarily developed during the early to mid-1980s, with some continuing (often in highly modified form) until the late 1980s and even beyond.

Architecturally these environments shared a number of characteristics. In particular, following the model of Stoneman, they were each organized around a central data repository that acted as the primary means of coordination between the individual tools. In addition, they tended to concentrate their support on source code editing, compiling, linking, and debugging aspects of a project as opposed to managerial aspects of development.

The second, more recent study involved discussions with experts from a small representative sample of organizations currently involved in building CASE environments [60]. In this study, in-depth discussions took place with six organizations, and less detailed discussions occurred with six more. The people we worked with were part of large, high-technology corporations primarily involved in the aerospace or communications industries.[1] Most had made significant investment in CASE tool technology prior to beginning their integration activities. They viewed their integration effort as a mechanism for enhancing CASE impact and acceptance within the organization. An overview of several of the organizations interviewed in the study is presented in Appendix A.

Furthermore, in this more recent study the architectural approach being pursued was somewhat different from the earlier study. In particular, these more recent efforts began with the use of existing CASE tool technology and were attempting to incrementally expand or combine their capabilities. This was in the hope of building upon the significant existing investment the organizations had already made in CASE tools. It was anticipated that new tools and approaches would be added to an environment in an evolutionary manner, rather than the all-or-nothing approach of the CASE environments studied earlier.

Both studies were conducted in an informal, open-ended manner. Questions designed to elicit discussion of various aspects of CASE environment integration were asked. Comments made by the questioned individual were followed up with additional questions (where appropriate) to probe and clarify interesting points.

On the basis of our informal discussions, we developed a set of lessons learned. While the lessons are clearly drawn from a small sample of the many CASE environment efforts that have taken place over the past decade or more, we believe that these lessons can reasonably be interpreted as an important illustration of how the software engineering community's understanding of CASE environment concepts has evolved over time.

12.3 Observations

The most striking observation from our studies is the migration from a lifecycle-wide, repository-based approach (which we refer to as an IPSE approach) to a CASE tool-based approach to environment integration. Whereas in the IPSE approach tools were custom-built or substantially amended to conform to interfaces specified for a central data repository, in the CASE-based approach, efforts were made to use existing COTS tools and their provided interfaces. However, beyond this most high-level and obvious transition, we abstracted five

---

[1]. As these are commercial organizations, the study was conducted on the basis that we do not identify them by name.

major activities that improve the chances of successfully developing and introducing an integrated CASE environment. These activities are:

- a concerted effort to understand and support end-user requirements for a CASE environment,
- recognition that CASE environment construction is a large-scale engineering activity in its own right,
- measured, incremental use of CASE environment framework mechanisms as a primary means of coordinating tools,
- a realistic approach to the automated support of software processes by the CASE environment, and
- substantial, planned investment in adoption activities to help ensure the successful introduction and continued use of the CASE environment.

These activities are discussed in detail below.

12.3.1 Understanding End-User Requirements

The IPSE-based efforts in our study were greatly influenced by the Stoneman requirements for Ada programing support environments [16]. In fact, at least two of these efforts began with a set of "idealized" or "timeless" requirements derived from Stoneman. Such requirements commonly stated that the environment would automate all phases of software development, provide a unified database to store all data, and provide for the enactment and control of all tasks in a project.

However, experts involved in the development of these IPSEs consistently stated that such requirements proved to be inadequate for the actual construction of an environment. They further stated that the definition of an actual environment requires more than a listing of what is considered "good" for an environment. It also requires a detailed description of the actual processes to be automated, objects to be maintained, and reports and documents to be produced.

Collected experiences from the IPSE efforts we studied provides a list of the shortcomings of idealized or timeless requirements for developing an actual integrated environment. This list includes:

- lack of operational definitions for terms and phrases such as "integration," "portable," "compatible," and "support,"
- incomplete definitions of the expected relationships between tools in terms of the data that must be shared and the synchronization that is necessary,
- insufficient support for an individual's preferences in day-to-day work (e.g., user interface appearance, customization of tasks, addition of new tools),

12.3 Observations

- insufficient support for the variations between different projects and organizations that use the same environment,
- incomplete definitions of the content, format, and possible evolution of expected products of the environment, and
- incomplete or inappropriate concepts of the typical operation of the CASE environment.

Such insufficient understanding of what was to be built often led to difficulties in implementation. This uncertainty played a role in the significant redesign of some environment efforts and the commercial failure of others.

The CASE environment integration efforts covered by the more recent study tend to be much more modest in scale than those examined in the earlier study. This is due in part to lessons learned from the mistakes of the early, wide-ranging, IPSE-based efforts, and also to the subsequent maturing of CASE tools supporting specific activities within the software process.

In most cases, the environments examined in the more recent study focus on the support of a relatively small set of activities within the software process. As a consequence, the requirements identified for these environments, while much more modest in scope, are much better defined and more achievable within a realistic time scale. The organizations involved in these efforts typically had established one of three aims for their integration activities that served to bound and focus the requirements for the environments themselves:

- Automated support for document generation. Most often discussed was the integration of a CASE analysis and design tool with a document production system. The requirements for this integration were typically focused on the documents that had to be delivered as part of a project's development activities. For DoD contractors this meant providing the capability to generate DoD-STD-2167A documents automatically from the analysis and design tool.
- Integration focused on the code generation cycle. As one of the most well-understood aspects of any software project, support for the editing, compiling, and debugging of source code programs was seen as a high priority. With many projects producing large, modular software systems over a long time scale, control for multiple versions of many source code modules was also viewed as essential.
- Wider-scale integrations. Organizations with significant investment in a variety of CASE tools required some means to more easily transfer data among those tools. A few organizations had implemented more wide-scale integrations between collections of CASE tools. However, those integrations tended

to be very focused on particular data transfer or synchronization needs, and were also at a relative coarse-grained level (e.g., transfer of large blocks of data between tools, and the ability to start and stop one tool from another).

In addition, the organizations involved in our recent study attempted to actively involve end-users in decisions concerning the type of support to be provided. Reasons given for involving end-users were to insure a close match between user needs and integrated tool capabilities, and to enhance the probability that the integrated CASE capabilities would be adopted by end-users. This contrasts with the IPSE approaches of our earlier study in which requirements were more typically defined by a relatively small group of people divorced from the current software development practices. These latter requirements were assumed to be more universally applicable.

12.3.2 CASE Environment Construction Is a Large-Scale Activity

Common across the IPSE-based efforts of our first study was the tendency to profoundly underestimate the effort required to build a large-scale environment. The chronologies of these efforts is similar: an initial, relatively modest proposal; followed by the expansion of the scope of the effort; followed by almost instant cost overruns; followed by a severe down-sizing to salvage something from the effort; and finally sometimes abandonment of the effort. This chronology can be seen most clearly in the history of the ALS and AIE government programs. However, it is also seen in commercial-sector efforts, such as Boeing BASE.

The scale and complexity of a CASE environment was one source of problems to organizations constructing a CASE environment. The specific mistakes cited by the organizations involved in our early study include:

- attempting (unsuccessfully) to advance multiple technologies simultaneously,
- poor understanding of technological trends that were affecting a radical change in the computing environment,
- lack of understanding of various design trade-offs to be made during development of the CASE environment,
- grossly underestimating the number of personnel required to design, build, test, and field a CASE environment,
- poor understanding of the technical issues involved in developing a CASE environment on the part of government overseers of the development,
- poor choice of contractors, who often had little experience in large-scale system integration activities,

12.3 Observations

- little use of prototyping to help define requirements and technological challenges,
- where prototypes were used, poor understanding of the effort required to scale up to a deployed environment from the prototype,
- insufficient planning, training, and documentation for overcoming the cultural resistance to the introduction of CASE environment technology, and
- an immature concept of the type of support required by the CASE environment user to ensure continued effective use.

The chronology and problems shared by the CASE environment efforts of our initial study are easily recognized elsewhere within the software engineering community. In fact, they represent an exceedingly common cycle for the development of large, unprecedented systems in many domains. According to the people involved in our study, many problems with these early IPSE-based efforts were caused in part by the lack of recognition that CASE environment development represented such a large, unprecedented effort.

The organizations involved in the second of our CASE environment studies appear to have recognized that full-scale CASE environment construction is a massive effort. Often this lesson was learned due to the failures of earlier efforts they funded. As a result, to avoid the massive engineering effort associated with earlier efforts, the CASE environments we examined were relatively modest in scope, relying to a large extent on focused connections between existing CASE tools.They are typically centered on a small number of commercial tools (frequently two or three) and the integration capabilities provided by those tools.

While the approach of building a CASE environment by integrating individual commercial tools does not require the same level of effort as developing a full environment from scratch, it is equally important to recognize that the integration effort remains a complex activity requiring a phased design and implementation approach. The organizations involved in our study all recognized the complexity of the problem, and were in the process of specifying and building an integrated CASE environment in a series of phases. In all cases the solution was still evolving in design, scope, and technology used.

Among the specific steps taken by organizations in our later study to avoid the problems associated with the size and complexity of CASE environments were:

- choosing a small number of well-known CASE tools as the basis for integration,
- maintaining close cooperation with CASE tool vendors, including attempts to influence vendor direction in terms of tool design,

- selecting computing hardware and support software that offered the greatest range of alternatives in terms of CASE tools and integration technology,
- carrying out a phased implementation and maintenance approach emphasizing end-user feedback,
- maintaining close cooperation with process groups within the organization to ensure that the CASE environment adequately supported the organization's defined processes (see Section 12.3.4), and
- carefully developing and implementing adoption plans to improve the chances that the CASE environment would be used (see Section 12.3.5).

It is frustrating to note, however, that the CASE environment projects examined in our second study frequently suffered from cost overruns and downscaling of expectations during the course of their work. Clearly the development of a CASE environment remains a complex activity. Organizations that appear to be the most successful recognize and expect that some setbacks are likely. The key to success appears to be well-defined procedures to control the impact of these setbacks on the environment and its users.

12.3.3 Use of CASE Environment Framework Mechanisms

The organizations in our initial study concentrated most of their attention on developing data integration mechanisms as a primary means of coordinating tools. The environment was built around a data repository that defined and provided a set of data structures that could be shared among all of the tools.

In fact, in those environments, an attempt was made to provide a complete layer of services between tools and the underlying operating system. The interface to these services provided tool portability across different platforms, as all of the tools were expected to be written to this interface and not to directly access the operating system of the host machine. Hence, new tools would either need to be specifically written to this interface, or existing tools would need to be significantly altered to use this interface.

Apparent in the environments examined in our initial study was a relatively sophisticated use of data integration, but more poorly developed capabilities for process, control, and user interface (presentation) integration. Thus, while the underlying data repository supported concepts such as versioning and traceability between (coarse-grained) data items, there were few mechanisms to support synchronization of shared events, explicit definition of processes, or development of a common visual consistency across all tools.

12.3 Observations

For example, process integration in environments such as AIE, ALS, and SLCSE was relatively ill-defined, but often revolved around somewhat rigid support for a specific development standard. Some environments did provide more explicit, flexible support for process control (e.g., the ISTAR environment). However, in these cases the underlying technology was often not well matched to process support required. Control integration (inter-tool communication and synchronization) capabilities were commonly limited to those provided by the underlying operating system with little added value. The user interface was character-oriented and unified by a common protocol or command structure for tool invocation. For example, ALS used "Ada-like" commands.

Mechanism-related comments made by people involved in our initial study included:

- While the need for tight integration between data from various tools was recognized, the difficulty of providing such capability in an efficient manner was beyond the capabilities of available database technology.
- The reliability of first-generation implementations of framework technology products was notoriously poor, making them unusable for most medium- and large-scale projects.
- The speed with which the baseline computer technology changed from character-oriented terminals and multi-user mainframes to bit-mapped, single user workstations and personal computers was not anticipated.
- Understanding of process, control, and user interface integration was not well developed, and hence poorly supported.

The CASE environments examined in the more recent study were often centered on individual tools and the mechanisms provided by those tools rather than on an integrating framework or centralized database. The approach chosen uses the interfaces provided by a tool vendor to provide specific point-to-point integrations between specific tools. The integrator of the tools either enhances an integration provided by the tool vendor (in concert with another vendor) or attempts to use the available tool interfaces to construct an integration unique to the organization's needs.

These current efforts are characterized by filters, which extract data from one tool database and make it available to another tool, and scripts, which control sequences of data extraction and tool invocation.

While two organizations were making use of commercial relational database products, only one of the organizations in our recent study was actively involved in using an integration framework product within its CASE environment. While such an approach was often cited as a goal for the future, operational use of such products was not common. Interestingly, in these database and integration framework examples the use of these products was viewed as a success. In one case it was end-user feedback on the quality and consistency of the CASE environment that was viewed as the measure of success; in the others, it was the decrease in the costs of implementation and maintenance of the integrated tools. In this regard these organizations felt that a framework-based approach to integration was potentially a large improvement over earlier, point-to-point solutions.

A possible reason for the general lack of effort to incorporate framework technology in the organizations we studied is that many tool users are currently struggling to absorb and integrate basic tool functionality. Most have not progressed to the point of even beginning to address framework products, in part because of the relative immaturity of the technology. However, a number of organizations see the long-term future of their integrated CASE solutions as a more consistent, framework-based solution, and look to products and standards such as HP SoftBench, Sun ToolTalk, CORBA, and ECMA PCTE as being likely to play a significant role.

Given our observations on the current state of the practice, it is likely to be a number of years before framework products and standards are of sufficient maturity so that organizations can readily apply them. Currently, these organizations claim to have an insufficient knowledge of the relationship between the technology and its effect on their organizational and engineering processes to be in a position to take advantage of these products and standards.

Based on our recent study, the more specific observations made concerning integrating mechanisms include:

- There was only limited use of integrating frameworks. Of the organizations interviewed that had CASE tool integrations in operational use, only one was using a message-based integration framework. Another organization was using a relational database to accumulate data from multiple tools. Two other organizations were in the process of developing integrations of tool data centered on a database, but had not achieved operational use. In all of the cases mentioned, the CASE tools used had not been substantially altered to take advantage of the integrating mechanisms.
- All organizations we talked with expressed frustration with the integration capabilities and mechanisms provided by the CASE tools they were using. Reasons given for this frustration include the inability to invoke the full range of functionality from outside the tools, awkward and incomplete access to data stored by the tools, and poorly documented interfaces to the tools.

12.3 Observations

- Visual consistency across tools was seen as important. A degree of user interface consistency is commonly implemented by extending and customizing tool menus to allow access to some of the capabilities of other tools. While this consistency was important, the difficulties involved in implementing it meant that no organization we talked with was attempting to build a single, common user interface across all tools.
- Among operational users, data sharing between tools was primarily accomplished via vendor-provided access routines to tool-resident data. As previously indicated, in our study only one instance of use of a relational database for recording all data shared between tools was identified.
- Data sharing between CASE tools was accomplished but primarily limited to coarse-grained objects. For example, a common data integration scenario involved the extraction of a complete data-flow diagram for inclusion in a document.
- All tool integrations observed allowed only unidirectional data flow from one tool to a second tool. No instances of bidirectional data flow were identified. For example, changes made to a name on a data-flow diagram in a documentation tool were not reflected in the "source" diagram in the analysis and design tool.
- Synchronization among tools was commonly enacted by developing scripts that control tool invocation. Scripts written in both a general-purpose programming language (e.g., C) and operating system command language (e.g., UNIX shell scripts) were identified. In one case, use was being made of a framework capability to provide tool synchronization (in this case Sun's ToolTalk).

Overall, the actual level of tool integration achieved in many of the organizations we interviewed is quite modest compared to our (and their) initial expectations. This general finding is somewhat surprising in light of the fact that we attempted to locate the best examples of tool integration available. The observed state of the practice in general did not support the claims made by some CASE vendors concerning the ease of tool integration. The interviewed organizations commonly found the available mechanisms to be inadequate, tight integration extremely difficult to achieve, and the time to achieve the desired gains in productivity and quality more likely to be measured in months than in days.

12.3.4 Automated Support for Software Processes

The CASE environments examined in our initial study tended to have a rigid and inflexible view of the software processes that were supported. For example, one commercial effort encoded those portions of the organization's process model primarily concerned with document structure in a set of standardized interfaces for tool invocation and in special integrating tools to produce documents and reports. The original process model was then rigidly enforced by the environment user interface.

Experience with this and similarly inflexible encodings of the process model was viewed in hindsight as a major limitation of those environments by a number of people we talked with in our study. We were told that they quickly found out that individual projects often required unique process and document support, due to individual preferences, hardware and software environments, and special requirements of a funding agency. In at least one case, user dissatisfaction was remedied by removing the rigid process encoding.

Not all CASE environments developed in the 1980s had an inflexible approach to encoding the software process. The ISTAR effort, while not commercially successful, was noteworthy in its attempt to allow the user to define the process via a series of "contract" descriptions. This aspect of the environment was widely viewed as its most important and innovative feature.

Many of the ideas on automated support for the software process have matured over the past ten years. Abstracting from the observations of our initial study of CASE environments, our study confirms a number of widely held beliefs:

- The definition of appropriate automated process support is exceedingly important to the success of a CASE environment, yet difficult to implement in practice.
- Rigid process enforcement, while often favored by many software development managers, will commonly be rejected by many software engineers due to the constraints it imposes on their work habits.
- No single process can be encoded within a CASE environment that will suit the needs of all user roles within an organization.
- One potentially viable approach to automated process support is to concentrate attention on restricted subprocesses that share widespread acceptance across an organization.

Observations from our more recent study of CASE environment efforts indicate that they have taken good advantage of an evolving understanding of the importance of software process. The organizations interviewed were aware of the need to integrate their processes with tool support. In some cases, the strength of the relationship between process definition and tool support was extremely strong; one organization considered process and tools to be inseparable and refused to even consider the value of either process or tools alone.

12.3 Observations

The majority of the organizations interviewed professed a strong process orientation within some part of the company. A number of those we interviewed had efforts directed toward process improvement programs in line with the SEI Capability Maturity Model (CMM). The strong CMM process orientation identified is not surprising due to the intimate relationship that most of the interviewed organizations had with the DoD and the SEI. However, even those organizations that had a much looser connection to the DoD and SEI were introducing comparable process assessment and improvement programs.

Still, a number of the organizations we interviewed took issue with what they perceive as a strong "process-first" focus of software process advocates. These organizations suggested that while in theory an organization can specify a process and then identify tools that support that process, in practice this approach is faulty. They found that the quality of the tool support available is often a major consideration in developing, encouraging and enforcing a process. For those organizations, knowledge of available tool support is an important input when defining a software process.

One organization suggested that as tools are integrated, the importance of a strong fit to process increases rapidly. While an organization's processes can often be modified to incorporate a single tool, an integrated CASE environment is likely to address a larger portion of those software processes. In the case of an integrated CASE environment, deviation from the existing processes may affect a larger number of individuals and subprocesses. The end result may be increased difficulty in transitioning the CASE environment technology within the organization.

The following specific observations were made in our study concerning the relationship between CASE environment technology and the processes being supported:

- A majority of the organizations interviewed acknowledged the importance of the link between tool integration and process support activities. This link was commonly supported by close cooperation between separate process and tool support groups, and by the combining of process and tools functions under a single managerial chain of command. One organization suggested that interrelated and permanent process and tool support groups were essential.
- A number of organizations interviewed expressed concern over the integration of CASE tools with CM practices and structure. To these organizations, overall consistency of CM practice was a primary concern but was particularly hard to achieve, since CASE tools frequently support a CM approach that is at variance with the approach adopted by the organization.

- All organizations interviewed were tailoring analysis and design tool integrations to fit their own process needs. No organization was using the integration exactly as it came from the vendor. As a result, all organizations felt that flexibility and tailorability are important characteristics of any CASE tool.
- All organizations interviewed were using a structured method supported by an analysis and design tool. A number of organizations were also using inspection techniques such as Fagan code inspections, and had some form of support for collating the results of those inspections.

Not surprisingly, within organizations we interviewed, integration is most often achieved within more manageable and well-understood engineering subprocesses. The most common subprocesses for which tools are integrated are the documentation processes such as the generation of design documents from the data stored in design and analysis tools. The editing/coding/debugging cycle is another common target for tool integration, using one of the numerous coding workbenches offered by vendors.

The corollary to the above observation is that for less well-defined (or more variable) portions of the life cycle, integration has proven more difficult. This appears to be true even for organizations using the most sophisticated integration technology available.

12.3.5 A Planned Approach to Adoption

While a number of the CASE environments examined in our initial study were completed in part or in whole, the people we interviewed were quick to point out that none had been effectively transitioned into widespread use. This lack of transition was attributed not only to the technical limitations of the CASE environment efforts, but also to a poor understanding of the difficulty of transitioning such new technologies to the user community. A number of people believed that the transition aspects of CASE environments were at least as substantial as the technical aspects.

This concern on the part of those interviewed reflects a growing awareness within the software engineering community as a whole of the difficulty of technology transition. The transition-related observations identified in our study confirm many of the problems of the wider software engineering community:

- The resources needed to address technology transition requirements are frequently underestimated.
- Detailed "productization" and transition plans are not constructed during project planning.

12.3 Observations

- The common approach within the DoD of mandating the use of a single technological solution across a broad spectrum of users is typically poorly conceived and unlikely to succeed.
- Projects that were encouraged to become early adopters of new technology often have little concept of the culture change required within their own organizations and receive little support for achieving this change.

In our more recent study of CASE environments, there was a clear pattern to those organizations that had achieved some measure of successful technology transition. In all those organizations, there was an accumulation of experience with CASE tool and environment technology over a number of years. Their successful use of CASE environment technology was part of their evolving use of modern CASE tools and techniques.

A striking characteristic of the successful organizations interviewed was their emphasis on "selling" their integrated CASE environment solutions to internal clients. Most had made multiple attempts to make their integrated capabilities more attractive to users by carefully modifying the integrated support provided in light of input from end-users and through other financial incentives.

In spite of these incentives, we were told that the staff on many software projects were often extremely reluctant to adopt the new technology. Frequently the reasons given for this reluctance were based on previous unsatisfactory experiences with CASE technology. Unsuccessful experiences had often left a general feeling that CASE benefits are greatly exaggerated, and the difficulties of using CASE tools successfully are greatly underestimated. Specific complaints included concern about the reliability and performance of early CASE tools, a lack of necessary training and practice time, and inadequate support to address problems with the technology as they arose.

The most successful organizations interviewed emphasized the importance of a strong support staff for early adopters of the technology. This staff was necessary to perform several distinct functions: for keeping the tools alive and well on the host operating system; for handholding new users; for problem solving with more experienced users; and for tailoring and enhancement to support new projects. One organization estimated that support services required for each project using a CASE environment was of the order of a halftime employee for the first two years that CASE environment was in use. This organization also reported that a postmortem interview was conducted with users after every major document delivery generated by their CASE environment. Problems were identified and weighted by the number of project staff hours required to work around the problem. Over an 18-month period, they reduced the work-around rates by a factor of eight.

Having the right experienced staff to carry out a support role was also viewed as important by some of the organizations we interviewed. To facilitate the interaction between users and support staff, one organization switched people back and forth between the tools support group and operational projects. This provided highly experienced tool experts for projects and infused user viewpoints into the tools group.

The experiences of a number of organizations we interviewed suggests that transition support can become a major portion of the CASE environment effort. One commercial in-house CASE environment effort now allocates approximately half of available resources to transition support, including training in the development methods supported, direct CASE environment support, tailoring, and proposal writing support. One effort that initially suffered from insufficient understanding of transition needs now focuses on providing extensive on-site expertise on CASE environment issues.

Specific observations made during our study include:

- Organizations are often extremely reluctant to adopt CASE environment capabilities due to earlier unsuccessful experiences with CASE tools and environments.
- Incentives such as new workstations, price breaks on tool acquisitions, and help with the installation and customization of tools can encourage organizations to adopt CASE environment technology.
- User feedback is essential to identify changes that will encourage CASE environment use.
- Word of mouth of successful use of CASE environments is critical to successful transition of the environment within an organization.
- Extensive and long-term "handholding" of new CASE environment users is essential.
- Resources needed for training on the CASE environment and the methods supported should not be underestimated.
- It is best to time training to be delivered just as a new feature or integrated tool capability is needed.

In spite of the many efforts to ease the transition of CASE environment technology undertaken by the organizations we interviewed, transition of the technology has been far more difficult than originally assumed. One of the most painful lessons for these experts is that even the best efforts of highly motivated and creative CASE environment advocates does not guarantee success in "selling" the capabilities of the technology.

12.4 An Example of a Transitional CASE Environment

In this section, we highlight one CASE environment, the SLCSE environment sponsored by Rome Air Force Labs, as an example of how the prevalent concept of a CASE environment was transitioned from the earlier monolithic IPSE view to a decentralized, CASE tool driven approach.

SLCSE has its roots in the period that spawned the ALS, AIE, and STARS. One of the early products of the STARS effort (produced circa 1982-1983) was a system specification for a SEE. STARS redirection led to abandoning this document, however. The U.S. Air Force, concerned about a turn away from the previously identified direction, funded a small-scale effort to define requirements and the high level design of an environment to support DoD-STD-2167A style development. The STARS system specification was taken as the starting point of the effort.

It was assumed at the time that a centralized environment would be built, with all tools developed as part of the SLCSE effort. However, the SLCSE Project was funded at a relatively low level, leading to a relatively cautious development approach and protracted schedule. This protracted schedule for SLCSE had the fortuitous side effect of preventing a premature "freezing" of technology that is apparent is other early IPSE efforts.

For example, when SLCSE was first envisioned, only the earliest, primitive CASE tools were on the market. By the time work on a prototype SLCSE environment had begun, however, CASE tools and advanced database concepts were better developed. The initial SLCSE prototype was positioned to take advantage of these.

As commercial tools began to mature, several factors converged to encourage the incorporation of these tools into SLCSE, resulting in a mixed environment consisting of some custom tools together with some commercial tools. These factors included the opportunity of building on tools already widely in use, the relatively low cost of purchasing commercial software versus both the development and maintenance costs of custom software, and the fact that the commercial software had greater functionality and user friendliness than could be easily developed from scratch. Because of these factors, several commercial tools, such as Cadre Teamwork and MacProject, were integrated into SLCSE.

The emergence of commercial tools created problems as well as opportunities for environment integration. Whereas SLCSE had been originally intended to rely on custom-built tools, it was now forced to provide a data management approach that could incorporate the new COTS tool approach. Fortunately,

SLCSE was also well positioned to take advantage of advances in database support, particularly the maturing of entity-relationship (ER) modeling. However, since true ER databases were not readily available to SLCSE designers, an ER front end to a traditional relational database was used.

SLCSE designers chose an ER data model of DoD-STD-2167A as the central data integration structure for their environment. As might be expected, the integration between individual tool databases and the SLCSE data model was incomplete. The data objects maintained in individual tool databases did not correspond ideally with the data objects defined by the SLCSE data model. A particular problem concerned the granularity of data objects necessary to support the ER data model. Most tools export only coarse-grained objects, so it was difficult to map tool data objects to the finer-grained SLCSE data model.

The SLCSE prototype addressed the problem of data granularity by creating a number of individual "filters" to extract and format data from tools for storage in the centralized database. However, SLCSE designers quickly noted potential problems with this approach, including the significant long-term burden associated with maintaining filters and dealing with the variation (and sometimes contradiction) of the CM systems in various tools and databases. The prototype SLCSE environment also incorporated a primarily one-way (to the centralized repository) flow of information, leading to potentially conflicting and inconsistent data between the individual tools and the central repository.

The decisions to incorporate developing COTS tool technology and an ER data modeling approach have proven to be fortuitous. By doing so, SLCSE migrated from its original IPSE roots to a position in keeping with current trends in technology. However, the SLCSE prototype was left with a number of vestiges of its early 1980s birth. For example, the prototype was built on the proprietary VAX/VMS platform and provided a primarily character-oriented user interface.

To account for these changes in technology and the state of the practice, PROSLCSE, a full-scale version of the earlier prototype, was envisioned. This version would replace VAX/VMS and character orientation with a more open platform and with window-based technology (Posix and the X Window System, respectively). PCTE data management capabilities also would be incorporated as a more appropriate mechanism for capturing the SLCSE ER data model. In addition, extensive transition planning was included in the contract. These changes are currently underway. However, as of this writing continued funding for this project is unclear.

12.5 CASE Environment Progress over the Past Decade

The two studies we have conducted into the state of the practice in CASE environments present us with the opportunity to reflect on the progress that has been made over the past decade. A large number of useful lessons have been learned, and the accomplishments of previous CASE environment efforts have been substantial. Below we summarize a number of main areas of progress:

- A commercial CASE tool and environment industry has been encouraged. The range and sophistication of CASE tools and environment technology have increased significantly over the past decade. Not only are there more tools available, but their quality has increased, and their purchase costs have decreased.
- Cooperation between CASE tool vendors has been encouraged. From the isolated, stand-alone CASE tools of a decade ago, CASE vendors are now much more inclined to ensure some measure of compatibility between their tools. This change in approach has been in part a consequence of the demands from users for more easily integrable CASE environment technology.
- Progress in CASE environment standardization has been made. There are many standardization efforts currently underway that have learned from the successes and failures of earlier efforts.
- Useful and interesting CASE environment prototypes were developed. In hindsight many of the initial efforts at developing CASE environments can be viewed as sophisticated prototypes that were used to elicit user requirements and to test out new technical solutions.
- A critical mass of funding and personnel has led to advances in a number of technology areas. The scope of the CASE environments field has had the effect of catalyzing work in a number of areas. Most notably the fields of database systems and object-oriented systems have made great advances in the past decade, in part due to the support of the CASE environments community.

Current CASE environment efforts are beginning to learn from these trends in the hope of providing better CASE environments in the future. However, two important barriers to the successful use of CASE environment technology within an organization remain:

- In spite of the improvements in the quality of many CASE tools and environment technology, the field as a whole is still very immature. The efficiency and performance of many CASE environment products are a substantial barrier to many organizations hoping to adopt the technology.

- Many organizations are naive in the expectations of CASE tools and environments. While CASE has been an acronym in use for a number of years, substantial use of CASE technology has only recently taken place. Many organizations require more experience with the technology before major successes are likely to take place within those organizations.

12.6 Summary

This chapter has described the insights gained from two studies into CASE environments: IPSE-based efforts of the 1980s, and CASE-based efforts of the early 1990s. One value of these studies is to illustrate the state of the practice of CASE environment integration during two periods of time. From these data, we can begin to draw conclusions concerning the evolution of the construction and application of CASE environment technology.

Of even more significant value to developers of current and future SEEs are the lessons that were learned from these two sets of efforts. Primary among these lessons is the clear message to work toward a better understanding of the requirements of a SEE. Even very recent SEE specifications tend toward being primarily composed of lists of tools to be incorporated into the SEE. While it is much harder to identify the by-products and end-products of integration, along with the usage scenarios to achieve those products, it is precisely these things that are needed to provide guidance to SEE builders.

Among the many valuable lessons we can gain from previous and current integration efforts are:

- *Gain experience with process support.* Organizations should experiment with both software processes and technology supporting process integration to determine which processes and what degree of process encoding are appropriate for an organization's future SEE.
- *Gain experience with current tools and frameworks.* It is unclear whether any available tool or environment technology will be the foundation of a SEE or will improve an organization's ability to build and maintain software. However, current technologies do provide a valuable mechanism to investigate the requirements and capabilities of SEEs. In addition to increasing understanding of tool and environment practices and benefits, experience with current technology can help us gather a baseline of productivity and quality data from which to judge future efforts, as well as instruct us in the development of suitable metrics for the field.
- *Focus on a relatively limited problem.* Experiences of previous and current integration efforts suggest that the technology is not yet in place and the

12.6 Summary

requirements are not well enough understood to develop production quality, large-scale, and full life-cycle SEEs. More successful environment efforts have focused on addressing one or a few specific problems. Environment efforts beginning in the near future would be well advised to initially limit their focus to a relatively contained problem. The limiting of focus can serve two primary needs: it can provide a constrained problem space in which to learn about integration needs and the capabilities of current tools and environments, and it can limit the immediate investment in unproven technology. As more is learned about successful integration in a problem space of limited scope, decisions to expand environment coverage can be made.

- *Focus on evolutionary prototypes.* To avoid committing to technologies before they mature, it is suggested that organizations adopt an evolutionary prototyping strategy for developing and transitioning environments. Such a strategy begins with currently available technology and aims toward incremental (rather than revolutionary) improvement in the environment capabilities of software organizations. The evolutionary strategy begins with the assumption that the initially developed environment prototypes will be flawed and unable to support the large-scale production and maintenance of software.

- *Incorporate mechanisms that maintain flexibility.* Regardless of what direction an organization takes with environment technology, it should address the likelihood of technology change over the next several years. A number of mechanisms are suggested, including: avoid requirements that specify certain technologies except where the direction of technology development is clear; avoid requirements that may limit the incorporation of future technologies; require contractors to explicitly identify areas of unstable technology and provide a plan for change; and develop standards and procedures for review and inclusion of new technology.

- *Identify appropriate strategies for transition.* The need for a sound transition strategy has been echoed by experts from both previous and current efforts. Guidelines for developing a transition strategy can be found in Oakes et al. [52].

In many respects, operational use of CASE tools and integration technology is in its early stages, and will undoubtedly see many shifts and changes through the remainder of the decade and beyond. To accelerate the maturity of operational use of integrated CASE, a greater focus on real end-user needs is required by CASE tool vendors and applied researchers. This will improve the likelihood that integrated CASE technology will be directed at the most acute problems faced by software engineers.

CHAPTER 13
Summary and Conclusions

13.1 Introduction

This book has taken the reader on a long journey through terrain that is at times difficult to negotiate. There are aspects of the integration problem that are open to interpretation, a source of heated debate, or perhaps undergoing great change in terms of people's perceptions of the problems and solutions. We hope that the reader now has a better understanding of the range of issues that must be addressed and the viewpoints that are possible when the phrase "integrated CASE environment" is used.

In this final chapter, we look back at the major points discussed earlier, and look ahead toward the future. Section 13.2 reviews the major themes that have been presented in this book. Section 13.3 highlights a number of avenues of work that provide hope for the future in this field. Section 13.4 concludes with a few final thoughts and observations.

13.2 Major Themes Discussed

The three overall themes that have been used to provide a structure to the book are the following:

- Understanding of CASE environment integration is enhanced by considering three levels at which integration occurs — end-user services, mechanism, and process levels.
- CASE environment architectures are evolving toward a hybrid approach that combines elements of framework-centered and CASE tool-centered approaches.
- The construction of an integrated CASE environment can usefully be viewed as a design activity in which design decisions are made based on a number of trade-offs that must be made.

For the purposes of recapitulation, these themes are brought together and summarized briefly below.

13.2.1 Three-Level Model of Integration

One of this book's main conceptual tools for improving understanding of the many issues connected with CASE environment integration is a three-level model that distinguishes end-user services, mechanism, and process aspects of a CASE environment.

By way of a summary of this model and its utility, we consider two tools that are integrated within a CASE environment. At the conceptual level, integration of the two CASE tools implies that the overlap, or coordination, between the functionality offered by those tools is well understood. For example, if one tool is a requirements capture tool and the other is a design and analysis tool, then the relationships between the functionality offered by those tools can be analyzed and discussed.

The process, or operational scenario, in which the tools operate acts as a context for understanding at the end-user services level how the tools interact. For example, the tools are a version management tool and a text editor, and if the process is a bug-tracking and modification-request process, that process will dictate exactly when source modules can be checked out of the version control tool, what permissions are needed on each module, who is allowed to check items into the version control tool, and so on. Hence, from a conceptual viewpoint it is a detailed knowledge of the process that provides the focus for deciding which services provided by each of the tools need to interact.

At the mechanistic level, the way in which the tools communicate to synchronize their actions or to share data will be to support the service interactions dictated by the process. The requirements imposed by this interaction will determine exactly which mechanisms to use, how the data are transferred, and so on. The particular interfaces between the tools and the platform and between the tools and any integration mechanisms used must be defined and understood.

13.2.2 Federated CASE Environments

In earlier chapters we argued that the current trend in CASE environment architectures is that the IPSE tradition and the independent CASE tool tradition are merging in the concept of a federated CASE environment. The need for one CASE tool vendor to provide tools that more easily interact with tools from other vendors has motivated the interest in framework mechanisms that can provide some of the facilities for sharing and coordination between tools. On the other hand, IPSE framework developers realize that they cannot offer idealized frameworks on which none of the currently available CASE tools can operate without major reimplementation of those tools. Hence, the move toward a federated approach to CASE environments is a pragmatic realization on behalf of both communities that they need to learn from each other to be successful.

The increase in the range and sophistication of the services provided by individual CASE tools has not been sufficient in itself to enable CASE environments to be easily assembled. These tools often have substantial overlaps in functionality, make use of competing proprietary databases for persistent storage, and do not share an understanding of the data items that are in common between them. For those CASE tools to be used in concert, the sharing of data and events between the tools requires some overall approach to integration. The current trend of federated CASE environments can best be described as "loosely integrated collections of tightly integrated tools." That is, several coalitions of CASE tools are connected via an integrating framework. A large part of this book has highlighted the conceptual and practical realities that have led to this approach.

Experiments with examples of current CASE environment technology have illustrated the feasibility of a federated approach. In particular, our experimental work with products such as Emeraude PCTE, HP SoftBench, Sun ToolTalk, and Digital FUSE has provided a number of lessons learned concerning the use and applicability of this technology.

13.2.3 Integration Is a Design Activity

In the popular trade press and some vendor literature, the claims and counterclaims concerning the integration of CASE tools can lead one to believe that solutions exist to all needs in this area. However, as this book has shown, in reality integration in a CASE environment can be viewed from many different perspectives. One view that we have promoted provides interesting insight into the task of assembling an integrated CASE environment from a collection of CASE tools. In this view, integration is a complex task involving a number of trade-offs. Each trade-off may offer a set of decisions that would be appropriate in some situations, less appropriate in other cases, and inappropriate in other situations. Like other software qualities such as robustness and portability, answers about "good" integration are neither obvious nor simple, and integration needs to be planned for and designed for throughout the life of an environment.

Consequently, for any given integration, it is important to first understand the goals of a project and the way in which these goals become articulated within a defined process. Implicit and explicit organizational and project goals are manifested in the process that is used for developing software, together with the specific needs for integration. Different goal and process combinations may have different implications for integration. For example, one project may have a goal of maximizing communication among a large number of programmers, a second may need to maintain tight configuration management control, while a third may require a common shared set of definitions of all information it manipulates. As a result of these differences in requirements, the solutions appropriate to each organization may be different. The first may focus on control integration solutions that explicitly support synchronization between CASE tools, the second may focus on the use of a configuration management system, while the third may develop a database solution that specifically encodes the organization's information model.

The technical solution selected by an organization must be tempered with the realities of the many different constraints that guide the successful adoption of that solution. Factors such as available budget, receptiveness to new technology, and migration strategy for current tools and system will all need to be considered. Thus, any attempt to introduce a CASE environment represents a realistic trade-off of desired services against technical, economic, and political reality factors. Decisions on trade-offs can be aided through explicit reference to the three-level model of use services, integration mechanisms, and process.

13.3 How Will Progress Be Made?

To help in providing a deeper understanding of CASE tool integration, and in encouraging better integrated products in the future, a wide range of work is currently taking place in many different forms. The following is a partial list that illustrates the ways in which we foresee future progress in CASE environment integration taking place. We again make use of the three-level model as a way to organize the list.

13.3.1 Services

Understanding the functionality offered by CASE tools and describing how that functionality can be made to interact usefully requires a common set of terminology and concepts that can be used as the basis for any such exercise. Efforts such as the Navy's Next Generation Computing Resources (NGCR) PSE Reference Model are an attempt to provide that basis. Using such a reference model, it is not only possible to examine different products and standards with the aim of describing them individually, but it is also possible to look at collections of those products and standards to see how they relate.

These "profiles" of standards and products are important because CASE environments will typically support many different standards and be constructed of products from different vendors. Overlap, interference, and misunderstanding among elements of these profiles are inevitable. Use of a reference model can help in providing a common basis with which to describe the interactions among the profile elements. As use of these reference models becomes more widespread, our understanding of CASE environment profiles will also greatly increase.

13.3.2 Mechanisms

The products available to support integration in a CASE environment are as yet rather immature. As discussed in previous chapters, much of this technology has been available for a relatively short period of time, and has yet to gain widespread operational use in many organizations. As this situation improves, the lessons learned from the use of these products will be invaluable.

Based on previous experience, it is also likely that existing products will evolve greatly over the coming years to meet the changing needs of end-users. For example, a wider range of point-to-point integration of tools will become available to meet different user needs. Experimentation with this technology will be vital in assessing its strengths and weaknesses.

Vendors are also currently under pressure from users of their tools to provide more open tool architectures. A consequence is that the tools are becoming more modular in design, with more accessible interfaces to each of the modules. This allows end-users to more easily access the services provided by the tools. General guidelines must be developed to instruct end-users on the most appropriate ways to make use of tools with open architectures within the context of an integrated CASE environment.

13.3.3 Processes

The last few years have seen a great deal of interest in increasing understanding of the processes by which software is developed. This interest is directed at devising models for describing software development processes, defining notations for representing those processes, and understanding how processes can be adopted and evolved within an organization.

This work is typified by the definition of a process Capability Maturity Model (CMM) [56]. In this model, the maturity of an organization is evaluated through an examination of its software development practices. The organization can be rated based on its understanding and implementation of software development processes and practices. Many organizations around the world have initiated schemes aimed at improving their "process maturity." A major focus of this approach is that development processes must be well-defined, repeatable, measurable, and eventually optimized through continual, measurable improvement.

As organizations gain more understanding of their software development processes, the importance of being able to automate (some part of) those processes can be envisioned. Indeed, the relationship between software development processes and CASE tools and environments is an interesting and important one. The view of integration in a CASE environment as a design activity is based on this relationship, taking the approach that an in-depth understanding of the processes is essential for integration to take place in a meaningful way.

Hence, interest in the CMM in particular, and in process maturity in general, is a great opportunity for CASE environment researchers. As organizations gain a deeper understanding of their processes, there is the promise that CASE environments can be assembled that directly support those processes and thus are more attuned to an organization's needs.

13.4 Final Thoughts

This book has emphasized the multifaceted nature of the CASE environment integration problem, and the roles that each of the various CASE user communities has to play. It has been the basic thesis of this book that it is essential to bring the experiences of CASE tool vendors, tool users, environment builders, and environment researchers together to obtain a more complete picture of the integration landscape. It is by developing a common understanding of the integration needs and perspectives of these different communities that real, meaningful progress will be made.

We look forward to future progress in this field, and to the continuation of this journey.

References

[1]   Atherton Technology. *Integration SoftBoard User's Guide, Integration SoftBoard Release 3.0*. Atherton Technology, Sunnyvale, CA, May 1992.

[2]   Bass, L. & Dewan, P. (Eds.) *User Interface Software*. New York: Wiley, 1993.

[3]   Bernstein, P.A. "Database System Support for Software Engineering." *Proceedings of the 9th International Conference on Software Engineering*. pp 166-179, March 1987.

[4]   Boudier, G., Gallo, T., Minot, R., & Thomas, I. "An Overview of PCTE and PCTE+." *Proceedings of ACM SIGSOFT/SIGPLAN Software Engineering Symposium on Practical Software Engineering Environments*. Boston, MA, 1988.

[5] Bourguignon, J.P. "The EAST Eureka Project: European Software Advanced Technology." In *Software Engineering Environments: Research and Practice*. Durham, U.K., April 11-14, 1989, pp 5-16, Ellis Horwood, Chichester, U.K., 1989.

[6] Bremeau, Christian & Thomas, Ian. "A Schema Design Method for ECMA PCTE." To appear in *Proceedings of PCTE'93, Paris, France*. November 1993.

[7] Brown, A.W. *Database Support for Software Engineering*. New York: Wiley, 1989.

[8] Brown, A.W., Caldwell, W.M., Carney, D.J., Christie, A.M., Morris, E.J., & Zarrella, P.F. "Use of Cooperating Integration Mechanisms in a Software Engineering Environment." Special Report, Software Engineering Institute, Carnegie Mellon University, Pittsburgh, PA, September 1993.

[9] Brown, A.W. & Carney D.J. "Towards a Disciplined Approach to the Construction and Analysis of Software Engineering Environments." *Proceedings of SEE '93*. IEEE Computer Society Press, July 1993.

[10] Brown, A.W., Dart, S.A., Feiler P.H., & Wallnau K.C. "The State of Automated Configuration Management." *Annual Technical Review*. Software Engineering Institute, Carnegie Mellon University, Pittsburgh, PA, 1991.

[11] Brown, A.W., Earl, A.N., & McDermid, J.A. *Software Engineering Environments: Automated Support for Software Engineering Environments*. McGraw-Hill: London, U.K., 1992.

[12] Brown, A.W. & Feiler, P.H. *A Project Support Environment Services Reference Model*. Technical Report CMU/SEI-92-TR-2, ADA253324, Software Engineering Institute, Carnegie Mellon University, Pittsburgh, PA, 1992.

[13] Brown, A.W. & Feiler, P.H. *An Analysis Technique for Examining Integration in a Project Support Environment*. Technical Report CMU/SEI-92-TR-3, ADA253351, Software Engineering Institute, Carnegie Mellon University, Pittsburgh, PA, 1992.

[14] Brown, A.W. & McDermid, J.A. "Learning from IPSE's Mistakes." *IEEE Software* 9(2), pp 23-28, March 1992.

References

[15] Brown, A.W., Morris, E.J., Zarrella, P.F., Long, F.W., & Caldwell, W.M. "Experiences with a Federated Environment Testbed." *Proceedings of the Fourth European Software Engineering Conference.* Garmisch-Partenkirchen, Germany, September 13-17, 1993.

[16] Buxton, J.N. *Requirements for Ada Programming Support Environments (APSEs) — Stoneman.* U.S. Department of Defense, February 1980.

[17] *CASE Interface Services Base Document.* Digital Equipment Corporation, Nashua, NH, 1990.

[18] *CCC: Change and Configuration Control Environment.* SoftTool Corporation, 340 South Kellogg Ave., Goleta, CA 93117, 1987.

[19] Cagan, M.R. *Forms of Software Tool Integration.* Technical Report IDE-TI-90-04, Interactive Development Environments, 595 Market Street, 10th Floor, San Francisco, CA 94105, 1990.

[20] Cagan, M.R. "The HP SoftBench Environment: An Architecture for a New Generation of Software Tools." *Hewlett-Packard Journal 41*(3), June 1990.

[21] Chen, Peter. *The Entity-Relationship Approach to Logical Database Design.* Q.E.D. Monograph Series No. 6, Q.E.D Information Services, Wellesley, MA, 1977.

[22] Christie, A.M. *Process-Centered Development Environments: An Exploration of Issues.* Technical Report CMU/SEI-93-TR-4, ADA26103, Software Engineering Institute, Carnegie Mellon University, Pittsburgh, PA, June 1993.

[23] Dart, S.A. "Concepts in Configuration Management Systems." *Proceedings of the Third International Conference on Software Configuration Management.* ACM, Trondheim, Norway, June 1991.

[24] Dart, S.A., Ellison, R., Feiler, P.H., & Habermann, A.N. *Software Development Environments.* Technical Report CMU/SEI-87-TR-24, ADA200542, Software Engineering Institute, Carnegie Mellon University, Pittsburgh, PA, November 1990.

[25] Dataquest. *CASE Vendors Handbook.* Prepared for the STARS Program, July 1991.

[26] Dowson, M. "ISTAR - An Integrated Project Support Environment." *SIGPLAN Notices (Proceedings of the Second ACM SIGSoft/SIGPlan Software Engineering Symposium on Practical Software Engineering Environments)*. pp 27-33, January 1987.

[27] Feiler, P.H. *Configuration Management Models in Commercial Environments*. Technical Report CMU/SEI-91-TR-7, ADA235782, Software Engineering Institute, Carnegie Mellon University, Pittsburgh, PA, March 1991.

[28] Feiler, P.H. "Position Statement at the Process-Sensitive SEE Architecture Workshop." In M.H. Penedo and W. Riddle, editors, *PSEEA Workshop Summary, ACM SIGSOFT Software Engineering Notes*, 1993.

[29] Fernstrom, C. "PROCESS WEAVER: Adding Process Support to UNIX." *Proceedings of the Second International Conference on the Software Process*. Berlin, Germany, February 1993.

[30] Fischer, H. Personal Notes from CASE Communique Meeting, October 17, 1991.

[31] Frankel, R. *Introduction to the ToolTalk Service*. Sun Microsystems Inc., Mountain View, CA, 1991.

[32] Frankel, R. *ToolTalk in Electronic Design Automation*. Sun Microsystems Inc., Mountain View, CA, 1991.

[33] Frankel, R. *The ToolTalk Service*. Sun Microsystems Inc., Mountain View, CA, 1991.

[34] Garlan, D. & Ilias, E. "Low-Cost, Adaptable Tool Integration Policies for Integrated Environments." *SIGSOFT Software Engineering Notes* *16*(6), pp 1-10, December 1990.

[35] Habermann, A.N. & Notkin, D. "Gandalf: Software Development Environments." *IEEE Transactions on Software Engineering*. pp 1117-1127, December 1986.

[36] Humphrey, W.S. "Characterizing the Software Process: A Maturity Framework." *IEEE Software*. pp 73-79, March 1988.

References

[37] Humphrey, W.S. *Managing the Software Process.* New York: Addison-Wesley, 1989.

[38] Humphrey, W.S. *CASE Planning and the Software Process.* Technical Report CMU/SEI-89-TR-26, ADA219066, Software Engineering Institute, Carnegie Mellon University, Pittsburgh, PA, May 1989.

[39] *IEEE Standard Glossary of Software Engineering Terminology.* The Institute of Electrical and Electronics Engineers Inc. (IEEE), 345 East 47th Street, New York, NY 10017, 1990, IEEE Std. 610.12-1990.

[40] Ison, R. "An Experimental Ada Programming Support Environment in the HP CASEdge Integration Framework." In F. Long, editor, *Software Engineering Environments. Lecture Notes in Computer Science 467*, pp 179-193, Springer-Verlag, Berlin, Germany, 1990.

[41] Jolley, T.M. & Gockel, L.J. "Two Year Report on BASE Method and Tool Deployment." In S. Przbylinski and P.J. Fowler, editors, *Transferring Software Engineering Tool Technology.* New York: IEEE Computer Society Press, 1988.

[42] Katz, R. "Toward a Unified Framework for Version Modeling in Engineering Databases." *ACM Computing Surveys.* Peter Peregrinus Ltd., 1990.

[43] Kellner, M.I., Feiler, P.H., Finkelstein, A., Katayama, T., Osterweil, L.J., Penedo, M.H., & Rombach, H.D. "ISPW-6 Software Process Example." *Proceedings of the First International Conference on the Software Process.* pp 176-186, Redondo Beach, California, October 1991.

[44] Klinger, C.D., Neviaser, M., Marmor-Squires, A.B., Lott, C.M., & Rombach, H.D. *A Process Programming Experiment: Initial Lessons Learned.* STARS Informal Technical Report, September 1991.

[45] Long, F.W. & Morris, E.J. *An Overview of PCTE: A Basis for a Portable Common Tool Environment.* Technical Report CMU/SEI-93-TR-1, ADA265202, Software Engineering Institute, Carnegie Mellon University, Pittsburgh, PA, March 1993.

[46] Marca, D. *SADT: Structured Analysis and Design Technique.* New York: McGraw-Hill, 1988.

[47] Masurka, V. "Requirements for a Practical Software Engineering Environment." *Proceedings of the 24th ACM/IEEE Design Automation Conference.* pp 67-73, June 1987.

[48] Mercurio, V.J., Meyers, B.F., Nisbet, A.M., & Radin, G. "AD/Cycle Strategy and Architecture." *IBM Systems Journal 29*(2), 1990.

[49] Morris, E., Smith, D., Martin, D., & Feiler, P. *Lessons Learned from Previous Environment Efforts.* Special Report, Software Engineering Institute, Carnegie Mellon University, Pittsburgh, PA, June 1992.

[50] Nejmeh, B. *Characteristics of Integrable Software Tools.* Technical Report INTEG_S/W_TOOLS-89036-N Version 1.0, Software Productivity Consortium, May 1989.

[51] *The Network Software Environment.* Sun Technical Report, Sun Microsystems Inc., Mountain View, CA, 1989.

[52] Oakes, K.S., Smith, D., & Morris, E. *Guide to CASE Adoption.* Technical Report CMU/SEI-92-TR-15, ADA258852, Software Engineering Institute, Carnegie Mellon University, Pittsburgh, PA, November 1992.

[53] Oliver, H. Private Communication, September 1991.

[54] Osterweil, L. "Software Processes Are Software Too." *Proceedings of the 9th International Conference on Software Engineering.* pp 3-12, IEEE Society Press, 1987.

[55] Parker, B. "Introducing EIA-CDIF: The CASE Data Interchange Format Standard." *Proceedings of the Second Symposium on the Assessment of Quality Software Development Tools.* New Orleans, LA, May 27-29, 1992, IEEE Computer Society Press, 1992.

[56] Paulk, M.C., Curtis, B., & Chrissis, M.B. *Capability Maturity Model for Software.* Technical Report CMU/SEI-91-TR-24, ADA240603, Software Engineering Institute, Carnegie Mellon University, Pittsburgh, PA, August 1991.

[57] Perry, D.E. & Kaiser, G.E. "Models of Software Development Environments." *Proceedings of the 10th International Conference on Software Engineering.* Singapore, April 11-15, 1988, pp 60-68, IEEE Society Press, 1988.

References

[58] Ploedereder, E. & Fergany, A. "The Data Model of the Configuration Management Assistant." *Proceedings of the 2nd International Workshop on Software Configuration Management.* ACM SIGSOFT, October 1989.

[59] *Portable Common Tool Environment (PCTE) Abstract Specification.* European Computer Manufacturers Association (ECMA), ECMA-149, 1990.

[60] *Proceedings of the 5th International Software Process Workshop.* IEEE Computer Society Press, 1989.

[61] Rader J.A., Morris, E.J., & Brown A.W. "An Investigation into the State of the Practice of CASE Tool Integration." *Proceedings of SEE'93.* IEEE Computer Society Press, July 1993.

[62] *A Reference Model for Frameworks of Software Engineering Environments (Version 3).* ECMA & NIST, August 1993, ECMA Report Number TR/55 Version 3, NIST Report Number SP 500-211.

[63] *A Reference Model for Project Support Environment Standards.* Version 2.0, SEI & NIST, November 1993, Technical Report CMU/SEI-TR-93-23, NIST Report Number SP 500-213, November 1993.

[64] Reiss, S.P. "Connecting Tools Using Message Passing in the FIELD Environment." *IEEE Software.* pp 57-99, June 1990.

[65] Reiss, S.P. "Interacting with the FIELD Environment." *Software Practice and Experience 20*, June 1990.

[66] *Report on the Progress of NGCR PSESWG.* Draft Version 1.0, U.S. Navy NGCR Program, Naval Air Warfare Center, Aircraft Division, Warminster, PA, September 1993

[67] Reps, T. & Teitelbaum, T. "The Synthesizer Generator." *SIGPLAN Notices (Proceedings of the ACM SIGSoft/SIGPlan Software Engineering Symposium on Practical Software Engineering Environments).* pp 42-48, May 1984.

[68] Slomer, H.M. & Christie, A.M. *Analysis of a Software Maintenance System: A Case Study.* Technical Report CMU/SEI-92-TR-31, ADA258459, Software Engineering Institute, Carnegie Mellon University, Pittsburgh, PA, November 1992.

[69] Strelich, T. "The Software Life-Cycle Support Environment (SLCSE): A Computer-Based Framework for Developing Software Systems." *Proceedings of ACM SIGSOFT/SIGPLAN Software Engineering Symposium on Practical Software Engineering Environments*. Boston, MA, 1988.

[70] Suchman, L.A. "Office Procedures as Practical Action: Models of Work and System Design." *ACM Transactions on Office Information Systems* *1*(4), pp 320-328, October 1983.

[71] *A Technical Overview of the Information Resource Dictionary System (Second Edition)*. The National Bureau of Standards, Gaithersburg, MD, January 1988, NBSIR 85-3164.

[72] Teitelman, W. & Masinter, L. "The Interlisp Programming Environment." *Tutorial: Software Development Environments*. pp 73-81, Computer Society Press, Los Alamitos, CA, 1981.

[73] Thomas, I. "Tool Integration in the PACT Environment." *Proceedings of the 11th International Conference on Software Engineering*. Pittsburgh, PA, May 16-18, 1989, IEEE Computer Society Press, 1989.

[74] Thomas, I. & Nejmeh, B. *Tool Integration in a Software Engineering Environment*. Technical Report SESD-91-11, Revision 1.1, Hewlett-Packard, 1991.

[75] Thomas, I. & Nejmeh, B. "Definitions of Tool Integration for Environments." *IEEE Software* *9*(3), pp 29-35, March 1992.

[76] Wallnau, K.C. & Feiler, P.H. *Tool Integration and Environment Architectures*. Technical Report CMU/SEI-91-TR-11, ADA237810, Software Engineering Institute, Carnegie Mellon University, Pittsburgh, PA, May 1991.

[77] Wasserman, A. "Tool Integration in Software Engineering Environments." In F. Long, editor, *Software Engineering Environments. Lecture Notes in Computer Science 467*, pp 138-150, Springer-Verlag, Berlin, Germany, 1990.

APPENDIX A
Sample Descriptions of CASE Integration Efforts

This appendix provides a short overview of four of the organizations interviewed in the second of the CASE environments studies described in Chapter 12, highlighting the major characteristics of their CASE tool integration efforts.

A.1   Organization A

Organization A is a large aerospace firm involved in the production of both commercial and DoD systems. The tool integration efforts of Organization A were an outgrowth of the organization's software process improvement program. This program identified improved documentation of systems (particularly DoD-STD-2167A documentation) as critical for improving the software process.

Initial efforts at providing automated documentation support (circa 1988) were primarily small-scale efforts aimed at generating portions of Mil-Std documentation for specific projects. These initial efforts integrated two COTS analysis and design tools with in-house documentation capabilities. Integrations consisted of scripts that extracted data flow and other information from analysis and design tool databases and inserted this information into documents. Consistency among documents and analysis and design tool databases was maintained by the periodic regeneration of design documents. These integrations operated in a proprietary operating system environment, required significant manual effort, and were difficult to maintain.

In spite of problems, both developer and customer reaction to the generated documentation was favorable. Internal regard for the integration effort was positive enough to encourage other projects to adopt and enhance the system. One early enhancement involved the introduction of a popular COTS documentation tool. Other early enhancements included expanding the range of documents generated, and migrating from the proprietary operating system to UNIX systems.

As successful projects using the capability were completed, project members experienced with the tools were much in demand for new projects. The integrated capability was applied to larger systems, now including a number in the 100-500K source lines of code (SLOC) range. Experience with the methods and toolset is now considered essential for technical leadership positions.

Approximately three person years of effort have gone into the system, divided up between a number of individuals working on independent projects. Currently, the toolset can automatically generate a full range of DoD-STD-2167A documents. Alternative versions of the integrated toolset have been produced, with substitutions for both documentation tools and analysis and design tools. The analysis and design/documentation tool integration consists of approximately 20K lines of tool scripts and C code.

Distinct versions of the toolset are used to support software written in Ada and C. Due to differences in the languages and methodologies, the versions are becoming increasingly divergent.

A multilevel CM library structure for documents and source code has been developed to support the integrated toolset. Tools have been developed to handle promotion of documents and source code within the structure, and to regenerate documentation at any level.

A number of problems have been identified, including:

- The redelivery of new versions of the integrated toolset when a new version of a tool is released is difficult, and has gotten worse as the complexity of the integration has increased.

- The tools used do not allow the level of interaction necessary for traceability.
- Integration with the organization's CM capabilities has been difficult.
- COTS tools appear to be written to be used independently, and not under the control of other tools.
- The management of in-line pictures and equations is difficult.
- Some resistance is commonly met during transition of the toolset.

A.2 Organization B

Organization B is a large aerospace firm involved in a variety of commercial and defense-oriented projects. In approximately 1988, managers at Organization B saw a demonstration of CASE tools. In addition, senior-level technical staff had experimented with CASE technology. Following this initial exposure, Organization B invited two well-known CASE vendors to demonstrate their tools. The tool vendors subsequently demonstrated their products and discussed integration of their tool with a documentation system to produce DoD-STD-2167A-compliant documentation. Based on the presentations and the company's other requirements, an analysis and design tool was chosen. In addition, it was determined that the linkage of the analysis and design tool and the documentation system would be exploited.

The integrated analysis and design/documentation capability delivered to Organization B allowed the user to define the structure of the Mil-Std documents using the analysis and design tool interface. While effort needed to accomplish this task was straightforward, the documentation produced was deficient in two ways:

- The data extracted from the analysis and design tool database were insufficient. In particular, additional descriptive text was necessary for diagrams, particularly around data flows. Also, documentation for requirements traceability was poorly addressed.
- The formatting of the resulting document was unacceptable. Font sizes used were inconsistent, and diagrams were poorly laid out on pages.

To improve the quality of the documentation produced, enhancements were made to the integration. C language code was developed by Organization B to access the analysis and design tool database, extract additional information, and generate the appropriate documentation tool markup language enhancements. Special information in the analysis and design tool database was identified by the use of hard-coded "markers." Code was also produced to extract and include Ada source files from source libraries. All told, approximately 2,500 lines of C code and 250 lines of operating system scripts were generated, requiring two person years of effort.

During the integration effort, a number of impediments to progress were identified. These include:

- The documentation tool's markup language was not sufficiently documented, making it difficult to determine required enhancements.
- Initial versions of the tools were not robust. Tools corrupted data and crashed frequently. Subsequent versions of the tools were more robust.
- The analysis and design tool text editing capability was not adequate.
- New tool versions sometimes required reworking of the C interface.

The results of the integration effort appear to be mixed. Among the major findings are:

- A moderate amount of manual effort is still required to generate acceptable documents. This effort includes fixing figure references in the text and tidying up complicated diagrams.
- The unfamiliarity of users with CASE tools and structured methods has been a significant cost factor in the project.
- Training on methods has been essential.
- The integrated toolset has been used on one major project, with unclear impact.
- Momentum for enhancements and adoption of the capability has been greatly affected by the availability of a strong CASE champion within the organization.

A.3   Organization C

Organization C is a large aerospace/defense firm that is acting as the prime contractor on a large defense procurement. Personnel from this large contract are assembling a set of integrated tools for use during the procurement. However, the potential target audience for the integrated capability is extremely large and includes the corporation as well as the defense department customer.

Organization C and contract personnel have a history of using individual CASE tools for analysis and design, document generation, and simulation and modeling. They have over the years developed extensive enhancements to the basic integration capabilities of a popular analysis and design tool/documentation tool combination. Some of those enhancements were given back to the CASE tool

A.3 Organization C

vendors and subsequently were incorporated in the tools and the integration capabilities.

To provide a more capable environment for the current defense procurement and for the company in general, Organization C is enhancing the existing tool integrations and incorporating new integrations into the environment. The scope of the resulting integrated toolset is anticipated to be much wider than for the other integration efforts we interviewed. At least seven commercial tools, including tools for system requirements analysis, software requirements analysis and design, documentation, database support, requirements management, configuration management, and simulation and modeling, will be incorporated. Separate but closely cooperating process and tool groups have been important in determining the scope and direction of the integration effort.

The approach taken by Organization C in assembling an integrated toolset is somewhat unique. Because of the large size of the contract and the organization, it has been moderately successful in encouraging CASE tool vendors to provide integrated capabilities conforming to requirements written by Organization C. When Organization C requires an integrated capability, it establishes the requirements and encourages COTS tool vendors to offer a solution. Organization C does not fund the vendor's integration activity, but rather suggests that a large number of future sales are dependent on the integration.

To the chagrin of some CASE vendors that considered themselves to be well established at Organization C, the provision of a specific tool or integration capability has proven to be highly competed by many vendors. A key to such competition appears to be the unified voice with which Organization C is speaking. However, in spite of the healthy competition and strong general position of Organization C, vendors have not always followed through on commitments in a timely manner.

The types of integration solutions provided by COTS vendors are variable, but frequently entail the extraction of tool data from one tool and the insertion of that data into a second tool. For example, data are extracted from a number of tools and incorporated into design documents and reports.

The integrated toolset is not yet completed. However, incremental capabilities are in use on a number of projects. One of those projects employs over 300 software engineers.

Organization C initially used vendor-provided training for its integrated toolset. However, most training is now done in-house to exert control over the content and timing of the training.

A.4 Organization D

Organization D is a large real-time engineering applications firm with a strong in-house software tool integration and environment activity. This activity pursues three major goals: to encourage the use of best practices and procedures, to integrate and support the best of class CASE tools, and to provide a conduit for training and support from vendors.

The initial tool integration efforts of organization D involved building point-to-point integrations of analysis and design, code manipulation, and CM tools. This initial integration effort was offered to internal customers as a monolithic (all or none) system. This approach met with very limited success.

Subsequent integration efforts have used a commercially available message passing framework as part of a more general solution. The resulting integrated toolset is offered to internal users as a set of unbundled products and services with phased availability. This approach appears to be much more successful. As the benefits of the integrated capability have become more apparent, specific projects have provided additional funding for the integration efforts.

Approximately 10-20 person years have already been spent on the effort, including time learning and integrating tools and transitioning the technology to individual projects. Support is also provided to train and encourage modern software engineering practices. In addition, each new tool introduced is a significant investment, requiring another full-time person.

Organization D has found that the integration of a project's process and tools is essential for success. In recognition of this need, introduction of the integrated toolset into a project is highly customized. An ongoing dialog between the producers and consumers of the integrated capability is necessary to match needs to individual tools, relate tools to process, and determine how best to introduce the capability.

Other major lessons include:

- Frameworks reduce the effort necessary to integrate tools. However, users are generally not willing to pay for framework products.
- Multi-user support is a major problem. Many tools do not support groups of users well.
- For integration efforts to be successful, users must be able to tailor and enhance their integrated toolsets. However, customer tailoring causes problems with maintenance when problems arise since it is sometimes difficult to determine the source of a bug.

- Licensing of integration technology and CASE tools to customers (even internal customers) can be a problem. The use of encryption technology and license servers can help in controlling access to integrated toolsets.

APPENDIX B
List of Figures

FIGURE 1	A Typical CASE Environment.	16
FIGURE 2	The Data Maintained by the Version Management Tool.	19
FIGURE 3	The Data Maintained by the Project Management Tool.	19
FIGURE 4	The Data Maintained by the Bug Tracking Tool.	20
FIGURE 5	The Data Maintained by the Combined Toolset.	23
FIGURE 6	Three Integration Dimensions.	31
FIGURE 7	Integration Relationships Between Environment Components.	33

FIGURE 8	The Evolution of CASE Environments.	38
FIGURE 9	Elements of the IPSE Concept.	40
FIGURE 10	Coalition Environments.	43
FIGURE 11	A Three-Level Conceptual Model of CASE Environment Integration.	49
FIGURE 12	An Example of a Federated Approach.	55
FIGURE 13	Relationships of Tools, Tasks, and Services.	63
FIGURE 14	Relationship Between Conceptual and Actual Worlds.	64
FIGURE 15	A Graphical Depiction of the Reference Model Service Groups.	65
FIGURE 16	Foreign Tool Encapsulation.	96
FIGURE 17	File-Level Integration.	97
FIGURE 18	Structured Integration.	98
FIGURE 19	Integration Through Message Passing.	110
FIGURE 20	CORBA Structure.	122
FIGURE 21	Life-Cycle Implications for Tool Integration.	143
FIGURE 22	Integration of Different Tools Within a Single Process Step.	145
FIGURE 23	Overlap Among CASE Tools Across Life-Cycle Steps.	146
FIGURE 24	Top-Level IDEF0 Diagram.	157
FIGURE 25	Second-Level IDEF0 Diagram.	158
FIGURE 26	Two-Level Configuration Management.	161
FIGURE 27	Process Controller User Interface.	166

List of Figures

FIGURE 28	Development Status Before Code Modification.	167
FIGURE 29	Development Status After Modification, Testing, and Analysis.	167
FIGURE 30	Tool and Framework Structure.	179
FIGURE 31	Message Service Interface Structure.	180
FIGURE 32	BMS and ToolTalk Message Delivery.	184
FIGURE 33	Profiling CM Systems by CM User Category.	198
FIGURE 34	Profiles Within the Developer CM User Category.	199
FIGURE 35	Deriver and Check Out/In.	203
FIGURE 36	CM-Managed Data Dictionary.	205
FIGURE 37	Private Data Dictionaries.	206
FIGURE 38	Shared Data Dictionaries — 1.	207
FIGURE 39	Shared Data Dictionaries — 2.	208
FIGURE 40	Shared Data Dictionaries — 3.	209
FIGURE 41	Multiple Nested Workspaces.	211

APPENDIX C
List of Tables

TABLE 1	Comparison of IPSE and CASE Approaches	39
TABLE 2	Comparison of Import/Export and Common Data Store	87
TABLE 3	Comparison of Commercial and Software Engineering Databases (derived from Brown [7])	93
TABLE 4	Five Levels of Message Passing	125

Index

A

ANSI 35, 101, 130
ANSI X3H6 99, 130
Apple Computer 131
architecture 37, 48, 63, 71, 110, 200, 240
Atherton Technology 99
ATIS 98
attribute 29, 95, 200

B

back-end CASE tool 14
BMS 116, 128, 154, 163, 170, 178, 183

C

Cadre Technologies 103
carrier integration 124
CASE 3, 12
CASE coalition 38, 42, 54
CASE Communique 129
CASE environment 3, 16, 27, 152, 194, 218
CASE Interoperability Alliance 130
CASE tool 3, 14, 140
CDIF 102
CMM 137, 140, 229
common data format 91, 102
common data store 86, 94, 98

common schema 22, 90, 100, 101
conceptual model 28, 48, 59, 124
configuration management 88, 127, 141, 160, 169, 193
control integration 29, 74, 77, 108, 154, 161
CORBA 121, 126
COSE 130, 180

D
data integration 29, 74, 77, 83, 104, 154, 161
DEC 99, 113, 121, 130, 187
development tool 14

E
ECMA 35, 67, 94
EIA 102
Emeraude 153
encapsulation 96, 99, 128, 161, 172
Encapsulator 116, 131, 161, 180
entity-relationship 18, 90, 92, 95, 100, 101, 234

F
federated environment 53, 170, 241
FIELD 113, 126
framework 62, 67, 152, 181, 225
front-end CASE tool 14
FUSE 113, 187

H
Hewlett-Packard 116, 121, 129, 130
horizontal CASE tool 14
hybrid CASE environment 154

I
IBM 101, 113, 121, 129, 130, 131

IBM Information Model 101
IDEF0 155, 157
IEEE 35, 62
import/export 21, 84, 101, 103, 160, 172, 203
information model 90
integration 4, 17, 27, 28, 46, 51, 54, 124, 153, 195, 242
interface 34, 48, 61, 69
IPSE 15, 37, 39, 217, 219
IRDS 100
ISO 35, 95, 101

L
lexical integration 124
life-cycle model 142
link 90, 95, 104, 207, 210

M
mechanism 48, 75, 77, 200, 243
message 78, 99, 110, 125, 177
message passing 110, 113, 178
message server 110, 185
method 78, 99
method integration 125
Microsoft 121, 131

N
NIST 67
NIST/ECMA reference model 67
NSE 144, 198, 199, 202

O
object 95, 99, 121
object management system 41, 86, 95
object-oriented 78, 90, 92, 99, 118, 121

Index

OLE 131
OMG 121
OpenDoc 131

P
PCTE 94, 154, 161, 169, 179, 211, 234
point-to-point integration 43, 105, 112, 225
presentation integration 29, 75, 78
PROCASE 202
process 45, 49, 53, 133, 164, 171, 196, 227, 244
process automation 139
process improvement 137
process integration 75, 134, 171
process support 45, 139, 171
ProNet 156
PSE reference model 61
PSESWG 60

R
reference model 59, 60, 61, 67
relationship 31, 49, 61, 74, 135, 136, 197
repository 20, 33, 86, 161, 195, 218, 224

S
schema 34, 90, 95, 162, 173
SDE 15
SEE 15, 78, 233
semantic integration 125
service 32, 44, 49, 61, 62, 194, 197, 224, 243
SLCSE 40, 140, 218, 233
SMARTSystem 144, 198, 199, 202
SoftBench 116, 126, 177
Stoneman report 37, 39, 217
Sun Microsystems 118, 121, 130, 179, 202
syntactic integration 125

T
task 62
Teamwork 103
three-level model 50, 134, 195, 240
tool 32, 62
ToolTalk 118, 126, 131, 183

U
UNIX 35, 128, 130, 163, 173, 207

V
vertical CASE tool 14

W
WorkBench/6000 113
workspace 195, 202, 210